T0368892

'An illuminating guide to the man and the science behind the Higgs boson . . . the tale of the conception and discovery of the Higgs boson, a tiny tremor in an energy field that pervades the whole universe, is one of the most important in modern physics. Close, a particle physicist who has served as head of communications and public education at CERN, is an excellent guide to the knotty science of that story'
Ananyo Bhattacharya, *Guardian*

'A five star book – it reaches parts other books on the Higgs have failed to reach' Brian Clegg, *Popular Science*

'Thorough and fascinating . . . Close spoke at length to Higgs and the result is a highly detailed and rich narrative . . . a piece of scientific history' Jay Elwes, *Spectator*

'Close is among today's best writers on the history of quantum mechanics . . . the account of the decades-long search for the boson is one of the best parts of *Elusive*. Close offers a pacey insider's story of the ups, downs and international politics of building cathedral-sized, cutting-edge scientific machines' *Economist*

'In *Elusive*, Mr. Higgs's friend and colleague Frank Close offers a sympathetic biography of the "shy, modest" man and famous particle'
Wall Street Journal

'A perfect marriage of subject and writer. With verve, insight, and rigor, Frank Close beautifully illuminates the life and times of one of physics' great, unheralded giants. *Elusive* is a triumph of a book, and one worthy of its subject's extraordinary contributions'
Jimmy Soni, bestselling author of *The Founders*

'A compelling account of the long search for the Higgs boson'
Economist, Books of the Year

'*Elusive* is both a deep, exciting intellectual history and an elegantly told portrait of a quiet man whose "one great idea" changed modern physics forever. Close marries the exotic details of contemporary particle physics theory with the very human aspects of how that theory came to be. An enlightening read from one of our very best writers and practitioners of physics' David N. Schwartz, author of
The Last Man Who Knew Everything

ABOUT THE AUTHOR

Frank Close is a Fellow of the Royal Society, Professor Emeritus of Theoretical Physics at Oxford University and Fellow Emeritus in Physics at Exeter College, Oxford. He is the author of *The Infinity Puzzle: Quantum Field Theory and the Hunt for an Orderly Universe* and most recently *Trinity: The Treachery and Pursuit of the Most Dangerous Spy in History*. He was formerly Head of the Theoretical Physics Division at the Rutherford Appleton Laboratory at Harwell, and vice president of the British Association for Advancement of Science and Head of Communications and Public Education at CERN. He was awarded the Kelvin Medal of the Institute of Physics for his 'outstanding contributions to the public understanding of physics' in 1996, an OBE for 'services to research and the public understanding of science' in 2000, and the Royal Society Michael Faraday Prize for communicating science in 2013.

FRANK CLOSE

Elusive

*How Peter Higgs Solved the
Mystery of Mass*

PENGUIN BOOKS

PENGUIN BOOKS

UK | USA | Canada | Ireland | Australia
India | New Zealand | South Africa

Penguin Books is part of the Penguin Random House group of companies
whose addresses can be found at global.penguinrandomhouse.com.

First published in the United States of America by Basic Books,
an imprint of Perseus Books, LLC 2022
First published in Great Britain by Allen Lane 2022
First published in Penguin Books 2023
002

Printed and bound in Great Britain by Clays Ltd, Elcograf S.p.A.

The authorized representative in the EEA is Penguin Random House Ireland,
Morrison Chambers, 32 Nassau Street, Dublin D02 YH68

A CIP catalogue record for this book is available from the British Library

ISBN: 978-0-141-99758-2

www.greenpenguin.co.uk

MIX
Paper | Supporting
responsible forestry
FSC® C018179

Penguin Random House is committed to a
sustainable future for our business, our readers
and our planet. This book is made from Forest
Stewardship Council® certified paper.

CONTENTS

PART 3

ELUSIVE

PREFACE

To MANY, THE Large Hadron Collider (LHC) at CERN in Geneva is synony-mous with Peter Higgs, the physicist after whom the particle accelerator's primary target—the Higgs boson—is named. But what is the Higgs boson, and why is it so singular to have been dubbed in media headlines the God Particle? And not least, who is Higgs?

This breakthrough goes back to 1964 when the thirty-five-year-old phys-icist seeded a theory about the nature of matter and the fundamental forces of nature that had remarkable consequences. This theory assumes that even if space were to be emptied completely of matter and all known sources of energy, it would still be filled by a ghostlike field that cannot be shut down. Immersed in this essence forever, we have nonetheless been unaware of it. The concept of an elusive elixir is so revolutionary, and so removed from our normal senses, that it took half a century to prove it, leading to Higgs' Nobel Prize in 2013.

I have known Peter Higgs for many years, as a colleague in the scientific community and as a friend. After publication in 2011 of my history of par-ticle physics in the late twentieth century, *The Infinity Puzzle*, Higgs agreed to join me in conversations at several science and literary festivals to help explain the universe and promote public understanding of his work. *Elusive* draws on those and other discussions, supplemented by a series of lengthy weekly phone conversations held during the COVID-19 lockdown, by let-ters, and by interviews of other leading actors in the decades-long quest for the Higgs boson. Memories of events that happened in the distant past are easily conflated, and wherever possible I have cross-checked the recollections of Higgs and other interviewees with documentary records, failing which, with one another's knowledge of the events. If anyone has archived information that would lead to corrections, please let me know.

Originally, I had envisaged a detailed biography of Higgs with some personal memories of reactions to his theory and the path to its experimental proof. All projects evolve, and this one did especially. The unforeseen arrival of the COVID pandemic prevented access not just to Higgs and his papers but also to libraries and other tools of the trade, which we have often taken for granted until they suddenly went out of reach. Thanks to the internet, much of the research I wanted to undertake remained possible, though not access to Higgs himself. Peter Higgs has managed to avoid much of the pace of modern life. In addition to having no television in his Edinburgh apartment, he does not use the internet and is not accessible by email— historically emails sent to him at Edinburgh University would be administered by departmental assistants. He has no public mobile phone contact. Other than personal visits, Higgs has been accessible only by me first leaving messages on a landline answerphone to agree on times for a conversation, or by sending letters through the post.

I am a trained physicist, not a psychologist or social scientist, but as well as describing how the effort to confirm Higgs' theory appeared to scientists at large for half a century, I wanted to explore the human side of science, not least to reveal the emotional roller coaster that Higgs experienced as the saga consumed his later years to such an extent that he told me it had "ruined my life".[1] The result is not so much a biography of the man but of the boson named after him, from conception through gestation to birth, and its creator's feelings during the half-century saga that culminated in its discovery in 2012.

As Thomas Edison famously said, "Genius is 1 percent inspiration, 99 percent perspiration". What drives an individual to invest that 99 percent without any guarantee that the inspiration will follow? Why was it to Higgs and not some other more star-spangled scientist that the discovery fell? Some, uncharitably, dismiss Higgs' singular success as luck. Without doubt fortune was involved here, as it is in many discoveries, but being in the right place at the right time is not enough; having the preparation to be able to act on serendipity is also important. Higgs' story is a scientific analogue of the wisdom expounded by golfer Gary Player. After he holed a remarkable putt to win a major tournament, someone remarked, "Gary—that was lucky!" Player supposedly replied: "And the more I practice, the luckier I become!"[2] Higgs' one visible triumph was the result of years of practice, in his case of intense scholarship as he deepened his understanding of a profound enigma in theoretical physics and persisted until perfection was achieved.

As a student, Higgs wrote a theoretical physics paper that excited molecular biologists, but apart from that, prediction of the Higgs boson was his one triumph. There was no previous work by him in particle physics that would have singled him out as midwife of a revolution. Having made the breakthrough, Higgs himself developed no further new pathways; it would be others who built on his creation and drove the quest associated with his name. A shy, modest person, Higgs was fated to be thrust into the limelight when from the late 1980s interest in the boson suddenly blossomed. As the world's media responded to the needs of particle physicists for a totem to promote their construction of the LHC, his life became public property. There are some who revel in fame and public adulation; Higgs is not one of them. On the morning when the Nobel Prize was to be announced, he disappeared, to avoid the media circus.

How did Peter Higgs feel to have been proven correct after waiting so long? Did he ever doubt his theory, or worry that he was wrong as thousands of scientists and engineers devoted years, decades even, of their careers to the pursuit of the boson? And when the eponymous particle was found, how did he react: with relief, or with trepidation that his life would be irrevocably changed? What does the discovery reveal about the cosmos and our place in the universe? These are the questions that I discussed with him over several years, as he lived through the dramatic days that moved a theory from speculation to lore, revealing for all time some of the most profound implications about the nature of the universe. His answers inspired this book.

Frank Close
Oxford, March 2022

PRELUDE

THE CASE OF THE DISAPPEARING PROFESSOR

IN THE WEEKS leading up to the day of the Nobel announcement in 2013, media excitement had grown intense in the expectation that this year the eighty-four-year-old scientist would win. The pressure on Peter Higgs had built over previous years, reporters even occasionally lurking uninvited outside the home of this intensely private man in Edinburgh's New Town. For Higgs, the potential euphoria of winning the Nobel threatened to be overwhelmed by the demands of the media. Worse, if after all the anticipation the award were to go elsewhere, interest would only be magnified. Whatever the result was going to be, Peter Higgs had spent twelve months preparing.

Higgs' apartment at the top of a three-storey Georgian tenement building is reached by a bare staircase of well-worn stone steps. As there are no lifts in the architecturally preserved townhouses of this UNESCO heritage site, Higgs has to climb eighty-four steps every time he returns home. In 2013, that meant one step for each year of his life. Such exercise has kept him fit into his ninth decade, well prepared for the sharp hills of Edinburgh's spectacular volcanic scenery. On that October morning, he planned a stroll of about a mile to Princes Street where he would take a bus to Leith, on the shore of the Firth of Forth. He wanted to be well out of reach when the Nobel Prize was announced.

The view through the two sash windows in Higgs' living room is historic and inspiring. Directly ahead stretch the cobbles of Darnaway Street, at the base of a canyon of sandstone townhouses which leads into Heriot Row and its pleasantly manicured gardens. Fifty metres away, on the left and opposite those gardens, is India Street, where at number 14 in 1831 was born the mathematician and architect of the theory of electromagnetism, James Clerk Maxwell. It was in Maxwell's work that Higgs, back in 1964, had found the key to solving a fundamental problem in physics, and had first made himself a candidate for the Nobel Prize. Between the rooftops of Heriot Row and India Street are visible the River Forth and, on a clear day, the shores of Fife by Kirkcaldy, some thirty miles away.

We can imagine the bespectacled, rosy-faced professor, with his domed bald head and strands of white hair, as he stood at the edge of the window, unseen by any lurking journalist. The coast seemed clear. His disinformation plan—that he was away in the Scottish Highlands—appeared to have worked, so any photographers were seeking their quarry elsewhere. The owners of the ground-floor and first-floor flats had been careful not to allow anyone masquerading as a visitor to pass through the secure outer door from the street to the stairwell, but even so Higgs checked the landing outside his flat before starting down to the main entrance.

The basement of the property is below street level, separated from the pavement by a sunken passage. A small bridge, which crosses the well and links the front door to the street, is adorned with ornamental cast-iron railings and a lamp. Now powered by electricity, the light's casing is the remnant of the gas lamp that illuminated the New Town in Georgian times. After a final glance to left and right he crossed the traverse, descended six steps to street level, and set off eastwards along Heriot Row.

It was a pleasant autumn morning, balmy for October in Scotland, with a gentle breeze from the south-west. Higgs was wearing a green-grey parka jacket, which would have been ideal camouflage had he indeed been in the

Scottish Highlands, but still helped him merge anonymously in the streets of Edinburgh. His destination, Leith, was about three miles away. With collar pulled up around his neck, the acclaimed professor made his getaway. It would be another hour before his absence was noticed.

Sixteen months earlier, in June 2012, I had introduced Peter Higgs to the audience at a book festival in Melrose, near Edinburgh. Two hundred people filled a large marquee in the gardens of a mansion adjacent to Melrose's ancient Abbey, at the height of summer. Peter Higgs was relaxed; it was his story, and he knew his lines. I was nervous. Although I have given talks about physics around the world for forty years, both to specialists and to the public, this was the first time I had taken the role of interlocutor to someone else's tale.

And what a tale. Nearly half a century before, in the space of a few months, Higgs and five other theorists had independently discovered the key to how beauty and order emerged from the chaotic debris of the Big Bang. Their breakthrough underpins modern understanding of why the universe consists of shapes and forms, rather than of massless particles rushing through space at the speed of light, without any possibility of being caught in atoms or molecules. It also explains why the sun barely stays alight, the force converting its hydrogen fuel into helium and liberating energy being so feeble that the sun, instead of burning its fuel fast and expiring almost immediately, has survived billions of years.

All atomic particles belong to one of two families: fermions or bosons. The names honour two scientists, Enrico Fermi and Satyendra Bose, who in the early days of quantum mechanics studied how particles behave when in large groups. Fermions are the basic seeds of matter, such as electrons or quarks, which in quantum mechanics are like cuckoos: two in the same nest are forbidden. Bosons are like penguins: large numbers cooperate as a colony. Bosons can accumulate into the lowest possible energy state—an effect known as Bose-Einstein condensation, after the two scientists whose work explains this phenomenon. This extremely low-energy state is manifested in weird phenomena, such as the superfluid ability of liquid helium to flow through narrow openings without friction; in superconductivity; and, if the six theorists were correct, Higgs bosons condense to produce a weird substance—today known as the Higgs field—that fills the universe.

Two millennia after Aristotle argued that the realisation of "nothing" is untenable, the Higgs field is in effect a physical confirmation of that philosophy. According to Higgs' theory, a truly empty vacuum devoid of all matter would be unstable. Add the Higgs field to this void, however, and it becomes stable. This may be counter-intuitive, but that is part of the theory's magic.

Physics students are taught how in the nineteenth century attempts to find a ubiquitous ether, by sensitive measurements on the behaviour of light-waves as they bounced off mirrors and mingled together, found no evidence for this hypothetical stuff. Moreover, the absence of this ether was presented as a foundation of Albert Einstein's celebrated special relativity theory on the nature of space and time. Yet in 1964 Higgs and those other theorists had found a loophole in the arguments that had dismissed the ether and, in effect, they resurrected it in the guise of what has become known as the Higgs field. At least, that was the theory; whether nature read their equations remained long unanswered.

At Melrose I began with a light-hearted provocation: "It is easier to be Shakespeare or Mendelssohn than a theoretical physicist." Being in Scotland, I suggested that changing a few words in *Macbeth*, or a few notes in Mendelssohn's *Hebrides Overture*, would still leave wonderful works of art; change a mere handful of symbols in Peter Higgs' equations, however, and they would not work. Higgs' theory was exciting conceptually, constructed from beautiful mathematical structures. Had this been a symphony or a work of literature, its value would have been recognised decades earlier. However, the ultimate value of a theory in physics is never decided by intrinsic elegance, let alone public opinion, but always by experimental test.

Of that sextet of theorists who had variously stumbled on the same idea—known by colleagues as the Gang of Six—Higgs alone had identified a means of testing the theory by direct experiment. To do so, he drew attention to an exceptionally ephemeral particle, now known as the Higgs boson, which the theory implies must exist. Find it, confirm that it behaves as the theory predicts, and you will have made a profound breakthrough in understanding nature.

On stage in Melrose, I explained that Higgs' scribbled equations on a sheet of paper half a century ago had inspired CERN—the particle physics laboratory in Geneva—to build a vast machine capable of simulating the conditions of extreme heat that occurred in the aftermath of the Big Bang itself. Some of the smartest brains on the planet—more than ten thousand scientists, engineers, and technicians from around the world—had combined their expertise to collaborate in the quest.

The machine—an engineering marvel—is as large as can be fitted into the stable geology surrounding CERN, between Lake Geneva and the Jura Mountains. It was also at the limit of what could be afforded—about €10 billion. Even then, the combined efforts of many nations, and of the CERN management focusing its resources on this single enterprise for several years, were needed to bring the LHC to fruition. The purpose of all this in the public perception was to find Higgs' boson. That was not wholly the case (as we shall see), but the amount of publicity which the gigantic venture excited had thrust him into the limelight.

If this huge weight of responsibility weighed on him, he did not show it. So, my first question at Melrose was this: "Peter, if tomorrow you found a mistake in your arithmetic, would you tell anybody?" It was a rhetorical question to help break the ice. There were no mistakes, of course. Over the decades many other mathematicians have checked and verified Higgs' algebra, its basic ideas used like pieces of Lego to build other theories that have been tested experimentally. Hints of the boson's existence had been seen and had given clues, like the footprints of some exotic creature in the snow might be used to puzzle out its identity. Forty-eight years previously, in 1964, no one could have foreseen the implications of the equations which Higgs had written on his sheet of paper in his office one July afternoon. One of his colleagues returned from summer vacation to find a note from Higgs on his desk: "This summer I had the only really original idea I've *ever* had."[1]

PART 1

PART 1

CHAPTER 1

A NAME ON THE BOARD

PETER WARE HIGGS was born on 29 May 1929, in Newcastle upon Tyne. When Higgs first came to public notice in the 1980s, his Edinburgh professorship caused some media to describe him as Scottish, or even "Scotch". He was in fact one-quarter Scottish. His parents came from Bristol, and his father's family, who were descended from Saxon peasants, had lived in the west of England for generations.[1]

Peter's grandfather, Albert Higgs, was in his late forties when he died suddenly, in 1911, after losing all his money. The cause of his death was probably suicide following ruin from gambling, but the truth remained a family secret. None of them would tell Peter the reason, and he clearly got the message: "Don't ask!" Albert's widow, Charlotte, now penniless and facing destitution, was left to care for Tom, their only child.

Charlotte and Tom joined forces with her widowed sister-in-law, Nelly, and her son, John, Tom's cousin; the two families lived communally in the Redland area of Bristol. Charlotte contributed to the finances by working as a shop assistant, while Nelly looked after the boys' welfare at home. Peter's father, Tom, then age thirteen, was a high-flying classics scholar at Bristol Grammar School and was offered a bursary to cover his fees. With his interest in classics and influenced at home by Aunt Nelly, who was "disgustingly pious", Tom expected to go into the church as a career. But World War I changed everything.[2]

In November 1916 Tom reached eighteen years of age and was conscripted. The first Battle of the Somme had been raging for four months. He was sent to fight in the trenches of northern France for what became two years of abomination and was "absolutely disgusted by the Church of England padres who exhorted the troops to go over the top and kill Germans". As a child he had been fed Christian dogma, whose representatives in the trenches acted hypocritically, and he had also been instructed to follow the Ten Commandments, whose interpretation appeared now to be negotiable. These experiences established in Tom a sceptical attitude to religion, while the relegation of his colleagues to mere cannon fodder at the whims of remote generals encouraged a hatred of war which his son later inherited.

In France Tom was befriended by a fellow Bristolian, Charles Coghill, who after demobilisation in 1919 introduced Tom to his sister Gertrude, Peter's mother. Gertrude had been born in 1895 in Shropshire close to the Welsh border, where her father was a physician. It was through her father's side that Scotland could claim its quarter of Peter Higgs' ancestry.

Her grandparents, Higgs' great-grandparents, John and Alexandrina Coghill, came from Thurso, the northernmost town on the British mainland. They had two sons. The elder, John George Sinclair Coghill, Peter Higgs' great-uncle, himself had scientific distinction, collaborating at the University of Edinburgh in 1869 with James Simpson on pioneering work in anaesthesia. Peter's grandfather was the younger brother, James Davidson McKay Coghill, who was born in Edinburgh in 1839.[3]

James also studied medicine, though at a less rarefied level than his brother. A general practitioner (GP) interested in tropical diseases, he spent twenty years in Ceylon (now known as Sri Lanka) until in 1891 he returned to the United Kingdom, divorced his wife, and took a post at the General Hospital in Birmingham. There he met and married a nurse—Peter Higgs' free-spirited maternal grandmother Emily Margaret, known to everyone as Maggie, who memorably spoke with a pronounced "Brummie" accent.

Maggie's background was a Victorian classic. She was one of nineteen children, few of whom survived childhood. Her mother had given birth to her first child at age nineteen, followed by one every year until she herself died, age thirty-eight, in childbirth.[4]

James and Maggie had three children: James, Charles, and their elder sister, Gertrude—Peter Higgs' mother. Their father appears to have been a typical remote Victorian patrician, leaving the children's upbringing to Maggie. He teased her about her Brummie accent, so much so that Gertrude feared lest any child of her own one day might speak that way, or indeed with anything other than good elocution. Two of Maggie's sisters lived in Bristol, so when her husband James died in 1906, she and the three children moved to that city to be near them.

A SOLITARY CHILD

Like many others who had experienced the horrors of the trenches, on demobilisation Tom Higgs returned home to Bristol deeply traumatised. His thoughts of the church gone, an interest in radio steered Tom towards electrical engineering. Born with natural curiosity and an enquiring mind, he was among the one in a hundred who entered university in those days. In his opinion, Oxford and Cambridge "were for the sons of the idle rich to waste their time and also that of their tutors", so he enrolled in his hometown at Bristol University. After graduation, in 1922 he joined the nascent BBC in Newcastle upon Tyne, as deputy chief engineer for the north-east region.

Tom and Gertrude married at Christ Church in the Clifton area of Bristol in 1924 and settled in Newcastle. Seriously depressed by the trauma of fighting on the Western Front, and convinced that humankind had no future, Tom didn't want to add to human misery by producing children. After five years of marriage, however, Gertrude managed to "sabotage their traditional method of contraception",[5] fortunately for Peter, who would be their only child.

A few months after Peter was born, the family moved to Birmingham, where they lived for the next decade. If the child is father of the man, then Peter Higgs' tendency to be a loner who would go his own way, never mind what other people think, was the product of his early years. Peter was a sickly boy. He was born with severe eczema, so bad that at night he wore cardboard tubes encasing his forearms to prevent him from scratching the rash in bed. After a time, the eczema disappeared only to be replaced with chronic asthma. As the asthma seemed to be brought on by vigorous exercise, his parents banned him from playing with other children. This quarantine carried on beyond his fifth birthday and prevented him starting primary school in September 1934.

His father was uncomfortable with children and left Peter's upbringing to his mother. Gertrude was now haunted by memories of her own maternal upbringing, and of her mother's distinct elocution. Because Peter's family had moved away from Newcastle while he was still a baby, he had escaped speaking like a Geordie—a native of that city—but only by the irony of the family ending up in Birmingham, the locus of Maggie's fear. Her son was now "at risk of speaking Brummie English!" She insisted that Peter have private schooling to ensure that he learned "received pronunciation".[6]

Because of Peter's fragile health, his formal education was delayed as he remained at home for a year. A school inspector came to their house to ask why they weren't sending the boy to school. As Higgs recalled, his mother had taught him "the three R's and the Lord's Prayer" and "convinced the guy she'd taught me as much as was reasonable for a five-year-old child to learn". More than reasonable, even, for by the time he started school in 1935, age six, he could already read and write fluently and was so far ahead of his contemporaries that he was put in a class of children two years older than himself. "My health problems gave me a head start", he said, adding: "I grew up a rather isolated child."[7]

This isolation helped determine his personality. On the one hand it amplified some of the disadvantages of being an only child: a tendency to be socially distant and ill at ease with strangers or in groups. It also developed a single-mindedness that would make it hard for him to compromise when circumstances were not, in his view, ideal. More positively, this early experience of learning on his own helped establish a lifelong love of scholarship and independent study. Gifted with an excellent memory, he accumulated a wealth of knowledge, with interests in politics, history, art, and food, all of which in his adult life made him a welcome companion for those with whom he felt at ease.

Within a year Higgs' belated schooling was interrupted when in 1936 he had bronchitis and then double pneumonia, which put him in bed for six weeks. This happened three times at intervals of two years—at age seven, then at nine, and finally in 1940 at age eleven. This was at a time before antibiotics. His father, as was common back then, was a heavy smoker. On the third occasion, the family doctor finally realised that this was part of the problem and warned, "If you want your son to live, don't go near him while you're smoking". Not surprisingly, Peter Higgs himself never smoked.

Higgs' mother came from a strict Episcopalian background, where she had received "a taste of Christianity enough to think she should do something about my religious upbringing". In addition to having taught him the Lord's Prayer, she read him Bible stories "to make sure I wouldn't go to Hell!" By age nine, however, he suddenly realised "I didn't know why I was doing this" and stopped listening. "Having survived the year without being struck by a thunderbolt I called myself atheist or agnostic."

The hardship which Tom Higgs had experienced during childhood, an era when the workhouse was ever present in the background, had taught Tom to live frugally and responsibly, as a role model for his younger cousin John, and had given him a rigid sense of right and wrong. Tom's experiences would fuse in his son and, together with Peter's isolation from other children in his early years, help to mould the scientist's character and life as a loner.[8]

Most children who have no siblings learn social politics from their interaction with playmates and school friends, but Higgs' early education in Birmingham had been as much from home as from school and, secluded from much wider merrymaking, he had to find ways of self-entertainment. His father's bookshelves contained several texts on engineering from his student days at Bristol University. Thanks to this home library, Peter taught himself basic trigonometry, algebra, and calculus "before anyone at a school I went to taught it to me". He attributes his dedication to mathematics as a direct result of his circumstances: "Physical health problems enabled me to forge ahead of my contemporaries, in maths especially."

THE COTHAM SCHOOL ALUMNUS

In 1940 Higgs gained a place at Halesowen Grammar School, just beyond the western fringe of Birmingham where the family was living. He found it a pleasure to be at a good state school—"and one for pupils of both sexes"— where he mixed with children from various social classes. He recalled, "Some of them spoke with Brummie-type accents, which I was no longer likely to acquire to any significant extent". Classes were frequently interrupted by spells in the air-raid shelter during the Battle of Britain.[9]

After only two terms at Halesowen, news arrived that the BBC were shifting his father to Bristol. The BBC had decided to move its headquarters from London, which it thought was going to be bombed to destruction in the next stage of the war, to somewhere safer, and judged that Bristol, 120 miles westwards, would be sufficiently far from German aircraft. But they were wrong. On Good Friday 1941, just hours before Tom—by now a senior engineer—and his wife prepared to return to the city of their childhood, its medieval centre was destroyed by Luftwaffe bombing.

They found a house much bigger than they would normally have been able to afford because the owner, who was scared by the bombing and had moved out into the countryside, was letting it at a very modest rent. The house was in Stoke Bishop, an affluent suburb on the way out to Avonmouth. While there the Higgs family had to move out for a couple of days and stay with friends because a German aircraft returning from an attack on the oil storage facilities at Avonmouth had jettisoned one of its bombs in woodland across the road from their house. The bomb disposal officer said the device was "ticking like a clock", but when he dealt with it, he discovered it was faulty. He thought it had been built in Czechoslovakia by workers who didn't want to help the Nazis and were sabotaging the ordnance.

A consequence of the blitz of Avonmouth and Bristol was that the BBC decided it had made a mistake to relocate there. By October 1941, Higgs' father had been moved away, along with lots of other staff, to Bedford, which is where they set up the new BBC headquarters, in the rural east of England. Although closer to Germany, and only fifty miles from London, it wasn't a military target.

Higgs and his mother continued to live in Bristol for the next five years, separated from his father because the accommodation available in Bedford was far too small to house families. They moved to a flat at 102 Coldharbour Road in the same Redland area of Bristol where Tom had grown up. The absence of his father in Bedford during the war—he visited the family at weekends whenever possible—helped quarantine Peter from tobacco smoke, and by age fourteen his respiratory problems were gone. His father eventually quit smoking after the war. In the postwar Labour government, Chancellor of the Exchequer Stafford Cripps imposed a huge tax on tobacco. Tom Higgs, whom Peter described as a staunch Tory, stated, "I'm not going to contribute to a load of socialists!" and never smoked again. "He was foul-tempered for about six months, and then came out of it."[10]

In Bristol, the intention was that Peter should attend Bristol Grammar School, where his father had been a pupil. However, his father took a dislike to the headmaster, so they settled for the most academic of the local state schools, then called Cotham Secondary School. During their decade in Birmingham, his mother had successfully ensured that he went to middle-class schools and spoke with "received pronunciation". Now at Cotham, he picked up the local intonations. The gentle Bristolian burr with its rhotic regal pronunciation of "off" as "orf" would remain with him thereafter.

Cotham School played a crucial role in Higgs' life. Each morning, pupils and staff assembled in a hall that doubled as a gymnasium. Children were in the body of the auditorium while the staff conducted the singing of "dreadful hymns" from a platform at the front. On his first day, standing at the back of the assembly hall, Higgs scanned the honours board that listed distinctions won by former pupils. One name, which appeared several times, attracted his attention: Paul Adrien Maurice Dirac. That made Higgs curious: "What had this boy done?"[11]

He soon discovered that Dirac was a Swiss national whose father, Charles, from the Valais in Switzerland, had become the principal teacher of French at the school. Paul's mother was a Bristolian; he and his father became British by naturalisation in 1919 when Paul was seventeen.[12] Higgs' discovery of Dirac's achievements came later with one of Higgs' own prizes: a book token with which he bought a popular work titled *Marvels and Mysteries of Science*. From that book he first learned of the "new-fangled quantum mechanics", which Dirac had pioneered. Higgs discovered too that his first physics teacher, Mr Willis, had thirty years earlier also taught Paul Dirac.

Paul Dirac was intensely shy, almost incapable of conversation, but hugely eloquent in the language of mathematics. Today he is perhaps best known for his prediction in 1928 of the existence of antimatter, a mirror world to our familiar material one. This revelation emerged from his equations like a rabbit from the magician's cloak when he combined the two great theories of twentieth-century physics into one with his marriage of quantum mechanics—which describes the behaviour of atoms and their basic particles—and Einstein's special relativity theory. Surpassing even this, Dirac created the quantum theory of electromagnetism: quantum electrodynamics (QED).

More than sixty years previously, in 1865, the Edinburgh scientist James Clerk Maxwell had posited his theory of the electromagnetic field that exerts a force on electrically charged objects. Maxwell's equations describe how a static-electric charge is surrounded by an electric field. Shaking the charge disrupts the electric field, and a burst of electromagnetic radiation spreads out at the speed of light. Something similar happens if a magnet is shaken and its magnetic field disturbed. In quantum theory, developed by Dirac, the resulting electromagnetic waves are staccato bursts of photons, massless particles of light. Furthermore, photons can appear and disappear. Strike a match or flick a light switch and vast numbers of photons will flash into existence. But photons are not forever. For example, those in sunlight are being absorbed by plants and their energy turned into life through the process known as photosynthesis; as you read this page, photons of light are entering your retina and vanishing, their energy triggering electrical signals in the optic nerve.

There is no place in Maxwell's classic theory where photons appear from nowhere and then disappear into oblivion. Dirac's quantum description of the electromagnetic field generalises Maxwell's laws and accommodates the creation or destruction of photons. Combining quantum mechanics, special relativity, and electromagnetic theory, Dirac's construction of quantum electrodynamics has for nearly a century been the paradigm for quantum theories of force fields. In 1933, Dirac became Cotham School's first Nobel laureate, and, by the 1940s, Peter Higgs' role model.

During Higgs' time at Cotham School, he won prizes for mathematics, languages, and chemistry, and for the best overall aggregate. But he found the school physics syllabus "very boring" and, appreciating the irony, admitted, "I never won a prize for physics at school". By 1944, his interest in the subject had come mainly from his own reading, including Max Born's classic text, *Atomic Physics*, which included information about Dirac's achievements. It had also become clear to him that he would not become an engineer (like his father) because of his lack of practical skills; instead, he would become a physicist. However, that same lack of practical skills, which made him incompetent in the laboratory, would prevent him from becoming an experimental physicist. Instead, theoretical physics would become his domain.[13]

A NUCLEAR AWAKENING

In 1945 Peter Higgs was in the science sixth form, at age sixteen. Politically, he was still very much following his parents' example. As the 1945 general election happened, the school staged a mock election and Higgs took the side of the Conservatives, which was the family tradition. Once the Attlee government was elected and he saw how it was transforming the country, he was very rapidly converted. "The NHS [National Health Service] was part of it but the whole programme was quite inspiring. It was clear that it would transform the country in a way I was sympathetic to", he explained. He went on to support socialist ideals for the rest of his life.

Higgs' teenage search for self-identity was settling around a love for physics inspired by Paul Dirac when suddenly news broke that atomic bombs had been dropped over Hiroshima and Nagasaki. He was distraught. His father's experiences in World War I had already imprinted a hatred of warfare, and now tens of thousands of Japanese civilians had been extinguished by the result of the physics which drew him. For a time, he even "contemplated a change of career".[14]

Within days of the announcement, Bristol City Museum hosted a small topical exhibit showing a rod of the metal uranium—the fuel for the bomb dropped on Hiroshima—and the natural ores from which it is obtained. These included pitchblende from Slovakia and Ontario, and torbernite from Cornwall. They were accompanied by a label giving the main principle of the atomic bomb.[15]

Bristol University physics professor Neville Mott spoke about the bomb at a Bristol Rotary lunch on 20 August, in a talk titled "The Bomb Which Might End Wars—or Civilisation". He told the audience, "The centre of the atomic bomb explosion is very like the core of the sun—hotter if anything." Mott warned that "the bomb dropped on Hiroshima was a Mark 1. In 10 years, these things will be bigger and better. We must improve the Charter of the United Nations to the point where there is only one armed-force in the world."[16]

Mott's remarks to this small gathering were reported in the press and piqued public interest. He and his physics colleague, Professor Cecil Powell, decided it was their duty to stage a public lecture and inform Bristolians of the background to the bombs, insofar as it was possible for them to do so. The US War Department had issued 250 pages of information about the weapon's development in the Smyth Report on 12 August, just three days after the bombing of Nagasaki, but many technical details of the project remained highly secret. The university was near to Cotham School but a long way from his home, so after school was ended for the afternoon, Higgs remained and then walked over to the university to listen.[17]

The event took place in early October. Powell gave an account of the basic nuclear physics involved, followed by Mott's assessment of the political and practical implications. Higgs recalled that the hall in the university was full, "the audience packed tightly on the benches".[18]

There is no surviving record of Powell's speech, but its context suggests that Powell would have explained how the basic physics of an atomic bomb begins with the fact that everything is made of atoms. An atom consists of electrons encircling a compact central nucleus. The atomic nucleus is positively charged, whereas electrons are negatively charged. An atom is then held together by the electrical attraction of opposite charges.

Chemical elements are distinguished by the complexity of their atoms. The simplest, hydrogen, normally consists of a single electron circling a single positively charged proton; the nucleus of helium has 2 protons, carbon has 6, and the atom of the heaviest naturally occurring element, uranium, has 92. In 1932, the neutron was discovered. The neutron is an electrically neutral twin of the proton. Along with the proton, the neutron is one of the two fundamental constituents of all atomic nuclei and plays an important role in their stability.

The rule of electric forces—like charges repel—means that the large numbers of positive protons in heavy nuclei mutually repel one another. This makes very large nuclei inherently unstable. That nuclei exist at all is because deep within these clusters of particles, a strong attractive force is at work in which the neutral neutrons play an important role. Even so, in the case of uranium with 92 positively charged protons, the electrical disruption is at the limit beyond which dense clusters of protons and neutrons no longer survive.

In atomic nuclei, the neutrons and protons adjust themselves to make the most stable configuration. This is an example of nature's golden rule: the most stable structure is the one that will survive the longest. Just as a pile of stones stabilises by collapsing to rubble, for an atomic nucleus to achieve stability the effects of the electrical forces disrupting the cluster of protons must be minimised. Atomic nuclei adjust naturally from configurations of higher to lower energy, emitting the excess energy in what we call radioactivity, until stability is reached. Radioactivity typically emits a million times more energy, atom for atom, than that liberated in a chemical reaction, and it was chemical reactions that formed all processes known from primitive times until the early twentieth century.

Powell continued by telling the audience what physicists had known since around the start of the war before secrecy took over atomic science. The breakthrough that led to the atomic bomb was the discovery in 1938 of nuclear fission, which releases nuclear energy on a scale previously unimagined. The key is a rare form of uranium known as U-235—where uranium's 92 protons are delicately stabilised by the presence of 143 neutrons, making a total of 235 constituents in the nucleus.

Nuclei of these atypical uranium atoms are so fragile that a mere touch by a slow neutron can be enough to split the pack. When the nucleus of a uranium atom splits this way, the total energy released is over one hundred times greater even than in radioactivity. Comparison to chemical reactions is stark: fission frees nearly a billion times the energy. This, the audience learned, was the first step towards the newly arrived atomic age. The discovery that opened the route to the atomic bomb had come early in 1939 when scientists found that the fission of a uranium nucleus also liberates neutrons. If these secondary neutrons hit other atoms within the lump of uranium and cause them to divide with the release of both energy and further neutrons, a self-sustaining nuclear chain reaction is possible. This causes an immense release of energy and in extremis a nuclear explosion.

Higgs now heard Powell explain that this was the basic idea behind the bomb that had been dropped over Hiroshima. The horror didn't end there as

Powell then announced that the newly released information revealed there was another way of making an atomic explosion, which was used at Nagasaki. Scientists had discovered that when neutrons hit uranium, it is possible to make an entirely new element, one not found naturally on Earth and existing beyond uranium in the periodic table: plutonium.

Mott's vision of the implications was depressing. No one yet knew for sure, because much was still highly secret, but he suspected—correctly— that nations would build arsenals of these new atomic weapons. He conjectured that a United Kingdom of big cities would be vulnerable to attack by atomic bombs, and he portrayed a dystopian society readjusting to a form of existence more familiar in the days of Henry V, when the population was scattered among many small towns. He also warned that if an atomic bomb exploded on the ground instead of in the air, the place where it fell "might remain radioactive for weeks or even years". Humans visiting the site would sustain internal burns which would develop later. "You would go and do rescue work on an atom-bomb site at your peril", he warned the audience. He added more optimistically that there was vast potential for atomic energy to be used for peaceful means such as power, though he tempered this vision with an observation about the vast cost: "At the moment it is not an economical alternative to coal petrol and other existing fuels."

The effect on the young Higgs was a lifelong abhorrence of nuclear weapons.

The experience convinced Powell that there was an audience for popular science lectures, so the following year, 1946, he gave a series of talks about his own research. These lectures, in which he described photographic emulsions and demonstrated their ability to reveal the passage of particles smaller than atoms, were Higgs' first exposure to the experimental side of a new field of science: particle physics.

Whereas the first public lecture in Bristol had presented Higgs with a hellish picture of nuclear physics, this time he learned there was a more optimistic vision of what it could offer in understanding the workings of nature. Powell's talk also implicitly pointed at a profound puzzle: the fact that atomic nuclei exist at all. The audience were familiar with the force of gravity, which controlled the motion of the planets, and the effects of electrical discharges and magnets, which were manifestations of the electromagnetic force. But if gravity and electromagnetic forces were everything, then atomic nuclei could not exist. The electrical disruption among electrically charged protons is huge and their mutual gravitational attraction trifling by comparison. That atomic nuclei manage to survive implies the existence of a strong attractive force between protons and neutrons, at least when they are in close proximity. One of the questions puzzling Powell and other scientists was the nature of this *strong force*. One means of finding out could be to see how easily nuclei could be disrupted by violent impacts, and what happens when they are.

The newly elected Labour government had set up a scientific committee to encourage nuclear research outside the immediate concerns of national defence—in other words, nuclear physics as a route to knowledge. There were two ways forwards; one was to develop accelerators of particles, and the other was to investigate ways of recording the passage of energetic subatomic particles using photographic emulsions. Powell told his audience that the latter was the route he planned to follow with the goal of understanding the atomic nucleus.

Although atoms are very small—typically 100,000 of them could span the width of a single human hair—they are nonetheless vast compared to the atomic nucleus. In relative size, the nucleus is like a fly in the atomic cathedral. The atomic nucleus may appear inaccessible, but Powell began with the exciting announcement that nature has gifted us a way of smashing it apart. He told his audience about cosmic rays.

Thousands of metres above the Earth's surface, the outer atmosphere experiences a continuous bombardment of atomic particles, known as cosmic radiation. The particles—which are mainly the nuclei of atoms—have been whisked to very high energy by magnetic fields deep in space. The Earth's own magnetic field reaches out for tens of thousands of miles and attracts some of these extraterrestrials. They smash into atoms in the upper atmosphere and break them up, their energy spawning showers of novel particles.

At ground level, the overlying atmosphere protects us from the full force of cosmic rays, so to study their full power Powell planned to send photographic emulsions to high altitude in balloons. Collisions between cosmic rays and nuclei of atoms in the emulsion would disrupt these nuclei, and the results would energise the emulsion, enabling their trails to be revealed once the images were returned to Earth and developed. He had great hopes for this new venture, not least as cosmic rays had already revealed hints of unusual varieties of stuff hitherto unknown on Earth. Bristol's greatest scientific product, Paul Dirac, had predicted the existence of antimatter, and this had been dramatically confirmed in 1932 with the discovery in cosmic rays of the positron, the positively charged antimatter counterpart to the negatively charged electron. In 1937, cosmic rays had revealed a heavy version of the electron, known today as the muon. Whereas the positron had been predicted and fitted into the emerging world view, the muon was a complete surprise. One scientist exclaimed "Who ordered that?", a question that remains only partly answered even today.[19]

Powell speculated that cosmic rays would reveal many surprises. Even as he spoke, this prediction was being fulfilled with the imminent discovery in cosmic rays of *strange* particles. Within a few years, earthly analogues of the collisions of cosmic rays in the form of experiments at particle accelerators would become feasible. As Higgs prepared to move on to university, in 1947, a new field of research—high-energy particle physics—was about to flower.

THE CITY OF LONDON

At the end of the war, the BBC had transferred Tom Higgs to their World Service headquarters at Bush House in London. Reuniting the family was now possible, and in 1946 they moved to a red-bricked Victorian flat at 29 Goldhurst Terrace, Swiss Cottage, a multilingual North London area full of refugees. Peter attended the City of London School for one year.[20]

The school was just two hundred metres south of St Paul's Cathedral in the heart of the city—or what remained of it after the wartime bombing. Most of Christopher Wren's churches had been destroyed or badly damaged. What remained of the office blocks were stumps about a metre high, leaving cavities in the landscape. Exposed to view were the remnants of the Roman Wall of ancient Londinium, which followed a roughly semicircular route from the Tower to the Watergate. The largest piece in the north-west corner, where the wall turned southwards, was the area known as Barbican, which is now host to 1970s brutalist architecture.

During lunch breaks as Higgs explored these sites, he developed an interest in archaeology. Meanwhile, he had joined the Mathematical Sixth Form stream, who received extra lessons that he found "quite novel. Maths that was fun!"

The school was training this select group of students in the hope they would be admitted to Cambridge for the Maths Tripos—the undergraduate course in pure and applied mathematics. Higgs' teachers were upset when he said that he didn't want to go to either Oxford or Cambridge University. He was influenced by his father and his prejudice that "Oxbridge was where the children of the idle rich went to waste their and their tutors' time". To add insult to injury, in the end-of-year exams he scored the highest mark and won the school's mathematics prize.[21]

Mathematics contains a logical scheme with explicit rules, such that a mathematical theorem once proved is good forever. Fresh axioms might produce extensions of the theorem, or reveal assumptions that when correctly accounted for lead to new implications. Higgs loved the machinery of mathematics—its algebraic codes, the differential geometries of shapes and maps, the strange symbols of integration and differential calculus. Some find joy in manipulating the equations, much as for some the technical performance of Vladimir Horowitz at the piano keyboard is a wonder in its own right; for Higgs, however, the music was the delight, the ability of mathematics to reveal the beauty hidden in nature. That is what crystallised his decision to become a theoretical physicist.

The question now was at which university he might pursue this goal. He "didn't like the sound of 'Imperial'" in London University's Imperial College of Science and Technology and instead applied to two other London schools, University College and King's College. He knew of King's by chance; in the other flat at Coldharbour Road in Bristol there had been a young man who was studying engineering at the college. University College's offhand response was that they would "get in touch eventually". Higgs regarded their admissions process as "very bureaucratic", whereas King's, which was just around the corner from the City of London School, was more engaged. So Higgs visited King's, where he was welcomed for a chat and received an offer while University College was still making up its mind. Most people enrolling in colleges and universities at that time were ex–service people, which made it hard for a school-leaver like Higgs to get in. He felt he couldn't be fussy.

Thus in the autumn of 1947 Higgs enrolled at King's College London as an undergraduate in physics. For the atheist student, King's was an ironic choice as the motivation, for its foundation in 1829 had been to have a college in London with a Christian ethos, unlike the "godless [University] College in Gower Street".[22] Here, in central London, in Georgian buildings between the Thames embankment and the Strand, Higgs was introduced to the mathematics of quantum theory and began to understand how to apply the creations of Cotham School's former pupil Paul Dirac.

Among Higgs' fellow students at King's was Michael Fisher. They met in Higgs' second year and became lifelong friends. Fisher's entry to King's mirrored Higgs' own experience. Fisher too had preferred the "godless" University College but, tired of waiting, accepted a place at King's. He lived at home in Finchley, North London, and Higgs grew to know the family very well. Higgs found the household vibrant, full of ideas, and always open to discussion, in contrast to his own parents who, in his perception, had "limited cultural horizons". "In a sense the Fishers were more influential on my development than my own parents."[23]

Fisher was two years younger than Higgs and started at King's the year after him. At school, Higgs had focused on succeeding, saying that "I had to be top dog". Fisher was the first contemporary of whom Higgs would say, "I could see he was smarter than me". After graduating in 1958, Fisher first took a PhD at King's and then continued to lecture there, eventually becoming professor in 1965. The two maintained regular contact, tutoring one another about developments in their respective fields—Higgs in particle physics and Fisher in the theory of materials, today known as "condensed matter". In 1966, Fisher joined the brain drain to the United States and joined Cornell University. Contact became more sporadic but continued throughout their lives. Whatever their relative merits they were both singular, destined to win the Wolf Prize in physics, and both entered the Nobel orbit. Fisher's expertise would influence Higgs' own.

CHAPTER 2

THE SINGLE HELIX

IN DECEMBER OF Higgs' third university year, 1949, before finals, the head of department interviewed potential research students. When Higgs said he wanted to do theoretical physics, he was referred to Professor Charles Coulson. Coulson was an applied mathematician who specialised in theoretical chemistry; unfortunately for Higgs, however, Coulson was not up to speed in Higgs' preferred speciality. When Higgs told him, "I want to do theoretical research in elementary particles", Coulson replied: "Well, it's a rather risky field to work in at the moment as it's in a mess. Quantum electrodynamics gives infinity as the answer. Solve that and you'll get a Nobel Prize; more likely is you'll end up with nothing."[1]

If the fundamental particles are the bricks of nature's construct, the natural forces are the cement that determines its form. One implication of quantum field theory is that these forces act by the exchange of particles. For example, in quantum electrodynamics (QED) an electron at one point may emit a photon that carries away energy and momentum. When this photon hits another charged particle, it sets that particle in motion. Newton's laws of motion tell us that a change in motion is the result of a force, and when this is the result of electrical attraction or repulsion, traditionally it is called the electromagnetic force. The electromagnetic force between two electrically charged particles thus arises by the transient exchange of one or more photons. In the jargon of physics, the photon is the carrier or "agent" of the electromagnetic force.

Since its appearance in 1927, Paul Dirac's formulation of QED had experienced two decades of mixed fortune. The problem was that when QED was applied other than in the simplest approximation it gave nonsense predictions that the probability of some processes occurring could be infinite, in some sense, more often than always. Infinity is beyond measure, and in the context of the questions that scientists were posing, it signified a failure of understanding rather than a real answer. There were serious worries that the theory was fundamentally flawed.

Nor was this flaw confined to some arcane piece of atomic science. The simple act of an electron absorbing or emitting a photon, the basic particle of light, underlies much of modern technology and many forms of life. Yet QED seemed unable to agree with even this most rudimentary of processes. If you can't calculate something as basic as the chance of a photon being absorbed by an electron, you haven't got a theory—it's as fundamental as that.

One of the most direct examples of this incapacity is the computation in QED of the magnitude of an electron's magnetism, which experiments could measure relative to some standard scale. All that is required is to solve the algebraic equation describing the act of an electron absorbing a single photon. If the electron were alone in the void, this would be a straightforward calculation and the result within one part in a thousand of the empirical value.

This appears to be a great success, until you realise that experiment can measure the value to a precision of better than one part in a trillion. The subtle difference between the measured value and that in the straightforward calculation arises because the electron in question is not alone in the void; according to quantum field theory, a vacuum is not empty but seethes with transient particles of matter and antimatter, such as electrons and positrons, which bubble in and out of existence. Although these will-o'-the-wisps are invisible to our normal senses, they disturb the photon and electron in the moment of their union and contribute to the number that the experiment measures.

QED contains the means of calculating the effect of each of these disturbances, one by one. There is an infinity of them, the contributions of all but a few being so trifling that they can be ignored—so long as you are prepared to accept some limit to the precision of what you are computing. The trick—known as "perturbation"—is to start with the most important, then add in the next, and then continue by including the effects of smaller and smaller contributions, the sum total approaching the "true" answer ever more accurately.

An infinite sum can have a finite answer (such as $1 + \frac{1}{2} + \frac{1}{4} + \frac{1}{8} + \cdots = 2$). Add together just the first four terms and your inaccuracy will be less than 10 percent. It is merely a pragmatic question of how precise an answer you need as to how many terms you use and how much work you have to do.

Or so physicists thought in their early explorations of QED. However, what they found was that the result, 2, was multiplied by an algebraic expression describing the way energy is shared between the electrically charged particles and the electromagnetic field. When this expression was computed, its magnitude was infinity. That was the reason that Coulson told Higgs that QED theory was in a mess.

Coulson, however, was not up to date, for in 1947 the solution to this "infinity puzzle" had been found and QED had a renaissance.[2] Reinterpretation of the basic mathematical structures managed to avoid the hazards of infinity and produce finite results. This restructuring is known as renormalisation.

The source of the problem was that Dirac's equation, which was a key component of the theory, assumed that an electron is no more than a piece of electric charge at a point in a spatial void. QED implied that as you attempt to resolve that elusive point, you become increasingly aware of an unseen swarm of ghostly spectators—the aforementioned virtual clouds of electrons and positrons, and the electromagnetic fields surrounding these charges. The physical electron is not the same as the ideal entity in Dirac's equation. Instead, what experimentalists interpret as the electron's mass is the result of Dirac's theoretical electron interacting with its own electromagnetic field and with the vacuum polarisation that fills the void. A "real" electron is a much more sophisticated thing than Dirac's equation describes.

The effect of these presences on what we measure as an electron's mass becomes obvious when we go back to basics and think carefully about how an electron behaves when it is near a magnet. At first sight this appears straightforward: the magnetic field sets the electron in motion and the ratio of the force to the acceleration defines its inertia or mass. However, the electron is itself the source of an electric field throughout the surrounding space. As the electron begins to move it drags this field along with it. Consequently, the resistance to acceleration involves not just its material mass but also the inertia in its electric field. The idea behind renormalisation is to make a pragmatic trade-off. Instead of trying to calculate the behaviour of both a material electron and its electric field, use the experimentally measured mass of an electron in your equations and forget about the associated electrical effects. The point is that the experimentally measured inertia already includes the effects of the electron interacting with its electric field—known as its self-energy.

At first sight this way of avoiding infinity, while physically intuitive, also threatens to undermine all practical ability to make useful predictions as there are so many disparate potential infinities associated with the complexity of the quantum vacuum. The breakthrough was the proof that whatever you calculate, the way that infinity emerges from the mathematics is often the same from one process to the next. For example, when physicists calculated one quantity, they found a morass of algebra whose value is infinite multiplied by, say, the number 1. Then they calculated some other quantity and found the very same algebraic formula, but this time multiplied by, let's suppose, 2. So this second quantity was predicted to be twice the size of the first. If an experiment had already measured the true (finite!) value for the first quantity, QED could then confidently predict the magnitude of the second as being twice as great, and experiment confirmed this to be true. So the specific piece of infinite algebra could be subsumed, hidden from view as if it didn't exist, leaving an apparently pristine theory on display.

The marvel in QED is that the measured values of an electron's electric charge and its mass are sufficient to provide benchmarks for anything else that we may wish to compute in the theory. Calculation of the electron's charge or the electrical contributions to its mass in QED would produce infinity—but we can use the theory to calculate everything else relative to these experimentally determined quantities. Instead of infinity the answers now turn out to be finite, and, even better, the values are correct. For example, after renormalisation, the agreement between calculation and measurement (of an electron's magnetic moment, for example) is better than one part in a trillion. That degree of accuracy is like measuring the width of the Atlantic to the precision of a hair's breadth.

QED is thus a finite theory with remarkable accuracy. This has remained the case for over seventy years. In 1949, however, Coulson, unaware of QED's renaissance and that its central problem was already solved, inadvertently steered Higgs away from it. It was this chance that diverted him into the application of theoretical physics to chemistry.

During that final year as an undergraduate, Higgs was president of the students' Maxwell Society. His Presidential Lecture to the society was Higgs' first ever public presentation, and he described himself as, simply, "scared". His friend Michael Fisher's artistic skills provided some posters to advertise the talk, which Higgs gave on the wonders of Fourier analysis—the mathematical technique of representing complicated algebraic functions as sums of simpler ones. This was a subject he had become fascinated by after hearing lectures on optics and microscopy from Professor Maurice Wilkins.

Wilkins, one of the pioneers of biophysics, was at this time beginning the research in X-ray diffraction that would reveal the double helix of deoxyribonucleic acid (DNA). When his colleagues heard Higgs' talk, they thought, "Ah, here's someone who will help us with our analysis of our data". Higgs' impression was that they were being held back because they didn't have anyone with a very mathematical understanding of their results. In 1950, after graduating BSc with first class honours, he steered clear of QED and instead stayed on at King's.[3]

MOLECULAR PHYSICS AND DNA

In 1946, Britain's Medical Research Council (MRC) initiated a project to encourage scientifically trained people who were returning from the war and interested in the future of biology into so-called biophysics units. The goal was to apply the principles and experimental methods of physics to understand the molecular structure and behaviour of biological systems. In part this was driven by the need at the dawn of the nuclear age to understand the effects of nuclear radiation on humans. Its primary inspiration, however, and ultimately its most far-reaching impact, grew out of advances in instrumentation—the emergence of electron and X-ray microscopy with great potential for biology. To that end the MRC set up a unit under Lawrence Bragg at Cambridge, and another under John Randall at King's. The initiative worked. Among its roll of successes in the subsequent decades, the most influential was the discovery of the double helix structure of DNA.

Maurice Wilkins, a physicist who had worked on the Manhattan Project and whose lectures on microscopy had fascinated Higgs, was one of Randall's team at King's. Like Higgs, he had been appalled by the use to which nuclear physics had been put. Wilkins turned eagerly to biophysics, and in 1951 he recruited Rosalind Franklin, a thirty-one-year-old postdoctoral assistant highly accomplished in X-ray crystallography.

By this stage, Wilkins' team was at base camp in an expedition whose summit would be the molecular structure of DNA. The molecular biologists were disappointed when Higgs chose to pursue theoretical physics rather than join them. Higgs recalled that there was a "great gulf" between those in the biophysics and molecular biology teams and the theoretical physics group. He knew what was going on in Wilkins' area, however, because he worked as a demonstrator in the undergraduate laboratories alongside a biophysicist who kept him up to date. Higgs' office was about four doors along the corridor from Franklin's laboratory. He was nine years her junior and remembered her as "very shy and retiring. She was an early feminist who had spent time in France and wasn't happy in the masculine environment at King's. She experienced sexist jokes and wasn't allowed to enter the all-male staff club."[4]

He also recalled some of the internal tensions from that time, which arose from two different perspectives on Franklin's status. According to Wilkins she was recruited to be part of his spectroscopy team, under his leadership. In Higgs' opinion, Randall was a lousy manager who could be somewhat ambiguous in what he told people, "to say the least". Franklin got the impression from what Randall told her that she would have total charge of her research, and not be subject to control by others, hence the upset when

Wilkins showed her photograph of DNA to Jim Watson, leading to the infamous dispute which Watson described in his autobiographical account, *The Double Helix*.[5]

In 1950, Higgs' first task as a new research student was to write a one-year MSc thesis on the electronic structure of crystalline organic molecules and how thermal vibrations smear their X-ray diffraction patterns. This inspired in him an interest in molecular vibrations and spectroscopy. It was during this period that Wilkins and Franklin's student, Ray Gosling, obtained the first clearly crystalline X-ray diffraction patterns from DNA fibres. Their colleague Alex Stokes interpreted these as indicating that DNA was helical in structure, heralding the subsequent decoding of the famous double helix.

Coulson, who had been supervising Higgs' research, left King's in 1952 to go to Oxford University. Higgs remained at King's rather than move with Coulson. His reasons were both scientific and personal. First, Coulson as head of theoretical physics saw political advantage in members of his department publishing large numbers of papers. Following Coulson's tradition, Higgs wrote a series of short papers on aspects of a single topic. He remarked, "I wrote too many [and] should have merged them into a larger paper". Higgs disliked this ethos of encouraging a production line of "lots of lightweight papers". When the hundredth paper from King's theoretical physics department was published, Coulson held a party. In Higgs' opinion, Coulson "should have been ashamed of himself". Perhaps in reaction to this, Higgs went to the other extreme for the rest of his career, publishing only sparingly and always as sole author.[6]

Nonetheless, had Coulson's successor been in a different field, Higgs would have had to move to Oxford to continue with his thesis. He still shared his father's dislike of "Oxbridge", so it was fortunate that by the time he had to make up his mind, he knew from the short list of candidates for Coulson's post that he could continue at King's.

Coulson was a Methodist lay preacher who tolerated nonbelievers, but even so Higgs had found the middle-aged professor to be "austere". His successor, Christopher Longuet-Higgins, was very different. He was only six years older than Higgs, and the pair immediately bonded.[7] They began by going out for a lunch, deciding which problems were interesting and then which ones each of them would investigate.[8]

They decided it would be interesting to study helical molecules because they knew that the American chemist Linus Pauling had a theory of proteins based on a helical structure. Together with Stokes' belief that DNA too was helical in structure, this meant that Higgs was taking his first steps in research at the same time as helical structures became the "in thing" at King's. Longuet-Higgins studied the electronic structure of molecules with helical symmetry, and Higgs wrote a paper on their vibrational spectra. Apart from his breakthrough of 1964, this was perhaps the most significant of his papers, and, as he recalled, was "pounced upon by Randall". It led to Higgs winning a prestigious Senior Studentship—the 1851 Exhibition Scholarship, among whose previous winners was Paul Dirac—which made him the "wealthiest Ph.D. student at King's College London". The scholarship was really intended for a postdoctoral holder, and as Higgs was still studying for his PhD and therefore logically had not completed his doctorate, he was in those days not taxed on it: "I had a year of unprecedented wealth!"[9]

EDINBURGH AND GAUGE INVARIANCE

Three years earlier when he had talked to Coulson about QED, Higgs had said the only person he knew of in that field in the United Kingdom was Dirac. Higgs explained that Dirac had been at the same high school as himself, but beyond that, he knew little of him. Coulson's advice about QED had been out of date, but he was a fount of knowledge about Dirac. Dirac was at Cambridge University, but "nobody gets to work with Dirac, he won't take on students. All the students who want to work with Dirac end up being supervised by Nicholas Kemmer, so you should go and work with Kemmer."[10]

It was now 1954. Higgs had spent three years working on molecular spectroscopy at King's College, had obtained his PhD, and still had one year of the scholarship remaining. He learned that Kemmer had moved from Cambridge to Edinburgh as Tait Professor of Mathematical Physics, and as he still hadn't given up hope of studying theoretical particle physics, Higgs wrote to the Studentship Commissioners. He cautiously asked if he could use the money he had been awarded to go to Edinburgh, to shift his field of research to that of elementary particles in Kemmer's department. Higgs took a train to Edinburgh, gave a seminar to justify them paying his train fare, and talked Kemmer into taking him on as a postdoc with his own money for one year. He moved to Edinburgh in the new year of 1955.

At this juncture, Higgs should have been called for two years of national service. He searched his conscience to decide whether he wanted to hold out for his pacifist beliefs, until he heard from a fellow student at King's, who had the same history of childhood asthma, that the service wouldn't take him anyway. His informant was right. Higgs was interviewed for call-up, rejected because of his asthma, and so happily went up to Edinburgh. When Coulson, in Oxford, heard the news that Higgs had quit working on molecular physics in favour of quantum field theory, he remarked to a colleague: "That's a pity. He's ruined his career!"[11]

Then forty-nine years old, Nicholas Kemmer had been born in Russia, grown up in Germany, and studied in Zurich. He had arrived in the UK as a migrant in 1938, settled at Trinity College, Cambridge, and worked on the nuclear physics of the atomic bomb. In 1940, Kemmer proposed the naming of the new elements—neptunium and plutonium—by analogy with the outer planets Neptune and Pluto beyond Uranus (uranium having previously been the limit of the known table of atomic elements). A polyglot wit, he spoke Russian, English, and German and was addicted to cryptic crossword puzzles. Yet for all his confidence, when Kemmer had been a student in Zurich, his supervisor, the irascible and sharp-tongued theoretical physicist Wolfgang Pauli, had given him such a tough problem that Kemmer had wrongly feared he was not good enough for research. The experience marked him, such that when he became a professor, he was reluctant to give students any problems to work on, fearing that he would subject them to damnation. Nonetheless, he passed on suggestions for potential topics to several brilliant Cambridge students before moving to Edinburgh and was very influential in theoretical physics in the early postwar years.

When Higgs arrived, Kemmer summoned him for a chat; said, "I no longer understand this stuff, but these are the important papers"; and presented him with a "colossal reading list". From the papers on the list Higgs learned of the huge advances made with QED in recent years, entirely contradicting the false impression that Coulson had given him. Having started in a vibrant molecular physics unit at King's College London, where great advances were taking place, Higgs transferred to particle physics in Edinburgh, which left him treading water. He worked largely on his own: "I went back to [Kemmer] occasionally for a bit of prompting on something but I spent a lot of my first year reading rather than trying to write papers because I didn't know enough about the subject."[12]

The proofs that QED can be renormalised are profound and technically difficult. This is true even today, when the whole edifice is much better understood than it was in the 1950s when Higgs first encountered the theory. For more than a decade after the original demonstration in 1947 of QED's viability, there was debate about the reliability of the proofs. It was unclear whether some of the algebraic manipulations were completely valid or whether errors of logic had occurred in the analysis of the reams of equations. There were also deep questions about the physical meaning of the renormalisation procedure, a debate that still remains active.

One key feature of the original proof was that QED has a property known as gauge invariance. The name may appear to be jargon, but its meaning is simple. For example, midday in New York is five p.m. in London; setting your watch to Greenwich Mean Time (GMT) or Eastern Standard Time (EST) is your choice of gauge. The number of hours it takes to fly the Atlantic is the same whether you're on GMT or EST—it is gauge invariant. For theories of the fundamental forces, gauge invariance broadly means that the strength of the fields must be independent of the definitions of the potential. For gravity, when an object falls from a table, the speed at which it hits the floor is the same whether that table is on the ground floor or in a room at the top of a high-rise building. It is the change in the gravitational potential—the height from the tabletop to the floor—that matters, not their individual absolute elevation. Similarly, for electric current to flow, you need a change in the voltage. Whether the difference is 240 and 0, or 1240 and 1000, your power plugs will work equally well.

In the example of flying the Atlantic it hardly matters which time gauge you use, though if you choose to set your watch to zero at the start of the journey, you can avoid a trivial extra piece of arithmetic. In QED, the quantum waves associated with all particles—such as electrons and positrons as well as photons—give added complexity to the algebraic structures, and the consequent level of difficulty in solving the equations may vary radically in different gauges. There is no magic gauge where the calculations are easiest—instead, gauge A may be easiest when calculating one process, and gauge B may be more transparent for some other case. In QED, whichever gauge you choose to use, if you make no errors the result will be the same, but the step-by-step procedures can be very different.

For example, the arguments and narrative in this book are the same whether you read it in English or Chinese or some other translation: it is *language invariant*. However, there is not a simple replacement word by word. Concepts in Chinese differ from those in English, the nuances are not the same, and some analogies may be easier in one language than in another. In the case of quantum field theory and gauge invariance, instead of English or Chinese, think the *Coulomb gauge* or *radiation gauge*, two common accounting schemes in electromagnetic theory. Some feel more at home with the equations' patterns in radiation gauge; others, such as Higgs, found Coulomb gauge more to their taste. The result must be identical, whichever scheme you use to do the calculation, but along the way, some aspects are easier to follow in one gauge, others in another. If you want artistic beauty, then Chinese symbols have much to offer, but if you are composing text at a typewriter keyboard, the alphabet is easier.

Gauge invariance is profound and can place severe restrictions on what is possible. One example follows from the fact that all electrons in the universe have the same sign and magnitude of electric charge. The response of an electron to some stimulus, such as a magnetic field, follows the laws of electromagnetism and cannot depend on whether the experiment is done in Europe, in America, or on the moon. If the quantum equations are set up independently in these locations in different gauges, the dynamics of my electron and that in another continent or on the moon must be consistently accounted for; the results must be independent of the local choice of gauge. In 1947, in his pioneering work on renormalizing QED, American theorist Julian Schwinger proved that for this gauge invariance to occur there must be some connection linking the various electrons and allowing us to compare the situation at the different locations. In quantum field theory, this connection consists of particles. The maths implied that the connection cares about direction—it is a vector—and the associated particle acts like a boson because of bosons' ability to act cooperatively, in this case by building up the vector field connecting the electrically charged particles. So was born the concept of the *gauge boson*, which in the case of electromagnetism is the familiar photon.

The connection must be able to act over very large distances, and in quantum field theory this equates to the gauge boson having no mass. In summary, Schwinger had proved that gauge invariance implies that an electromagnetic force necessarily occurs between electrically charged bodies, and that this force is carried by a photon of zero mass. That a photon has no mass and travels through the void at nature's speed limit is fundamental to Einstein's special relativity theory. However, according to QED the vacuum is not empty because the photon is immersed in a sea of virtual electrons and positrons, which ensnare it, interrupting its flight. As QED implies that an electron at rest gains an infinite energy—or mass—because of these interactions, how does a photon manage to avoid a similar fate?

By carefully examining the formulae in QED theory, Schwinger concluded that gauge invariance in QED underpins this phenomenon of the massless photon. This link between gauge invariance, the existence of a force, the vanishing mass of a photon, and the ability to make QED viable thanks to renormalisation was a profound result, which in the course of time would have far-reaching implications.

LONDON AND GENERAL RELATIVITY

Settled in Edinburgh in January 1955, Higgs found Kemmer's reading list on QED quite intimidating. He spent his time learning how quantum field theory works and puzzling out how the correct mathematical description of correlations between different events—known as *Green functions*—emerge from the fundamental theory. This led to a single paper with the daunting title "Vacuum Expectation Values as Sums over Histories", which was all but ignored.[13] In 1956 his fellowship money expired, and the university provided financial support for a second year. He competed for a vacant lectureship, but it went to another candidate. He applied for a lectureship in Birmingham, but this involved teaching a particular postgraduate course in which he wasn't experienced. Finally, he landed a fellowship at Imperial College in London and in 1957 moved south.

He wrote his next paper while based at Imperial, even though he spent some of his time back at King's learning about classical general relativity from Hermann Bondi, one of the world's leading cosmologists. Higgs went to a Bondi public lecture on models of the universe, which he found very entertaining. He already knew about the subject because at Edinburgh Kemmer had assigned him the task of giving the final-year undergraduate course on general relativity and he had found doing so a great learning experience.

Whereas today the evidence shows that the universe erupted out of nothing in what has become known as the Big Bang nearly fourteen billion years ago, back in 1956 there were two possible explanations, each of which was mind-bending. One was that the universe has existed forever, in a *steady state*, where matter is perpetually being created and destroyed. The other—which unlike the steady state theory has survived decades of experiments—avoided the conundrum of an infinite regression of yesterdays by positing the Big Bang. This of course has puzzles of its own, such as what was happening—and where—on the day before the Big Bang (or, as was once asked after a popular lecture, "Why didn't the Big Bang happen sooner?").

The idea of a first day is common to many origin myths and is a favourite of religions that posit that some deity provided the spark. Bondi, who had no interest in religion, favoured the steady state theory, and this set the agenda for his lecture. Recalling that King's was a college dominated by the doctrines of the Church of England, for which Genesis asserted that God made the universe in seven days, Bondi said, "The oldest cosmological model is a Big Bang theory proposed by a religious believer, so I shall talk about the steady state theory".[14]

During this period in London Higgs regularly attended the King's College relativity seminars and became interested in the problem of how to construct a quantum theory of gravity. Its many technical challenges include profound questions on how to incorporate the constraints of gauge invariance in a mathematically consistent theory. Dirac, among others, was wrestling with this problem. Higgs wrote a short paper on the subject, which was published in the journal *Physical Review Letters*.[15] While these papers made little impact in the grand flow of physics, they began to give him recognition in the arcane specialism of mathematical physicists interested in quantum gravity.

In 1958, now twenty-nine years old, Higgs moved from Imperial to a temporary lectureship at University College London (UCL), where he produced what he deemed a "weird paper" that had nothing to do with physics and was all mathematical tricks. The background was that he had attended a seminar at Imperial by a mathematician who had spotted a peculiar feature of a class of gravitational theories that differed from Einstein's general relativity but couldn't explain why. After the seminar Higgs spent all night trying to understand this peculiarity and finally succeeded. By four a.m. he was ready to write his paper having discovered a mathematical manoeuvre that resolved the puzzle.[16]

CONSULTANT FOR THE CAMPAIGN FOR NUCLEAR DISARMAMENT

Higgs' political awakening, which had been inspired by the Labour Party's creation of the welfare state around 1947, was further transformed by his experiences in Edinburgh and London during the 1950s. At Edinburgh he met students from the former British colonies who, in Higgs' words, "had been on the receiving end of the British Empire". When he returned to London, two events further radicalised him. First was the British-French-Israeli attempt to take over the Suez Canal in October 1956. This was contemporaneous with the Soviet invasion of Hungary, where Higgs was disillusioned by the way that American-funded broadcasts gave the impression that the West would come to the aid of the Hungarian uprising, "without revealing that they couldn't afford the risk of giving the rebels any support".[17]

For the first time in his life, he attended a "Law Not War" rally in Trafalgar Square on 4 November 1956, where he heard an impassioned speech by the inspirational Labour Party politician Aneurin Bevan. Higgs' scientific awakening as a child had coincided with the horror of the atomic bomb explosions over Japan. Now the world was awash with atomic weapons, as nations of the Eastern and Western blocs engaged in the fragile standoff of the cold war. One miscalculation could realise the nightmare vision of the mushroom cloud and lead to the deaths of millions. The Campaign for Nuclear Disarmament (CND) was a popular movement in the United Kingdom, one of its bêtes noires being the Atomic Weapons Research Establishment at Aldermaston, about fifty miles west of London. Nick Kemmer, who had been involved in protest marches from London to

Aldermaston, knew that Higgs was sympathetic, so he contacted the secretary of the CND science committee in London and suggested they invite Higgs to join. In 1958, Antoinette Pirie, a biochemist and ophthalmologist from the University of Oxford and a leading member of CND's scientific committee, was preparing to go on sabbatical leave to the United States the following year, so the committee needed a stand-in. As Higgs recalled, a biologist from East Anglia looked at him and said, "What about you doing it?" "I took a gulp and said, OK."[18]

The year 1958 was a special time in the activities of CND because a moratorium on nuclear bomb tests had begun. When bombs are tested in the atmosphere, as had been the case for nearly a decade, they emit radioactive elements into the stratosphere that decay. The subsequent fallout is hazardous and also gives opponents clues about the nature and design of the weapon. One way that testing might continue in secret, in violation of the moratorium, would be to conduct tests underground. Scientists within CND therefore set out to assess whether it was possible to distinguish seismic waves caused by underground explosions from those due to natural phenomena such as earthquakes.

During 1959, Higgs became acting secretary of that group. In collaboration with Eric Burhop of UCL, he produced a report on the possibility of detecting underground nuclear testing. A committed communist on whom MI5 kept a file, Burhop was an experimentalist who investigated the sensitivity of seismic detectors, while Higgs the theorist studied the mathematical formulae of how different kinds of waves propagate through the Earth's strata. He rapidly concluded that information about the difference between a shear wave from an earthquake and a compression wave from an explosion was preserved as they passed through the Earth's interior. However, the information would be so scrambled that you couldn't decode it locally. A global network and backup computer system would be necessary to unscramble the signal, and he and Burhop wrote a report to that effect for CND. President Dwight Eisenhower's administration had already claimed that detecting underground tests was impossible. However, Higgs and Burhop's report for CND helped bring the truth into the public domain, and the Eisenhower administration admitted that detection was possible. The CND paper recognised that it was going to require a huge investment to build up the network required to detect underground tests and anticipated many of the ideas subsequently used to monitor nuclear tests.[19]

Higgs consulted for CND during the last two years of his time in London. Then in 1960 he landed a job as lecturer in mathematical physics at Edinburgh University and moved back, taking with him Antoinette Pirie's address book of scientists sympathetic to nuclear disarmament. So when he arrived in Edinburgh he already had a network of contacts all over the university, mainly in the science departments. Kemmer also immediately dumped on him all the things he himself was being asked to do for CND.

CHAPTER 3

THE PARTICLE EXPLOSION

IN HIGGS' SCHOOLDAYS, matter had appeared to be built from only three basic particles: electrons, protons, and neutrons. By 1960, however, a new menagerie of particles had been discovered. Members of this diverse collection ranged from the fleeting forms of strange extraterrestrial particles that had been discovered in cosmic rays to particles that lived no longer than the time light takes to cross an atomic nucleus, produced and identified in experiments at bespoke particle accelerators built during the 1950s.

Quantum field theory's prediction that the electromagnetic force acts by the exchange of particles—photons—inspired theorists to suspect that a similar story holds for the strong nuclear force that binds protons and neutrons to one another, forming the compact nuclei of atoms. In 1935 Hideki Yukawa, a Japanese theorist, had proposed that this was so and predicted the existence of a particle—the pion—as the carrier of that force. Shake a proton and the radiation which emerges from it consists not just of photons of electromagnetic radiation but mainly of pions, which are set forth when the nuclear force field is disturbed. Pions are much lighter than neutrons and protons and form an evanescent web between the nuclear constituents, binding them together. Only when nuclear particles collide at high energy can we see the pions liberated. When cosmic rays hit nuclei of atoms, vast numbers of pions—charged positive, negative, or neutral—are produced. In 1947, Cecil Powell, whose talk in Bristol the previous year had inspired Higgs, discovered trails of the electrically charged pions produced when cosmic rays hit atoms in photographic emulsions that he had prepared in an experiment atop the Pic du Midi, a mountain in the French Pyrenees.

Optimism that the forces of nature and the seeds of matter had been identified was short lived, however. Instead, Powell had started a revolution, for pions were just one variety in a veritable explosion of particles. The discovery of more strange beasts during the 1950s heralded a new field— particle physics—and inspired new lines of research.

There were too many of these particles for them all to be fundamental pieces of the natural world. A popular strategy at that time was to identify common features—*symmetries*—among groups of particles that would hopefully lead to a mathematical theory and eventual explanation for their existence. Out of this myriad, a small piece of order appeared, thanks to an insight from Nick Kemmer, the peripatetic nuclear theorist later to be Higgs' departmental head in Edinburgh. Soon after the pion had been postulated, Kemmer predicted that there should be three varieties, distinguished by their electrical charges. In 1949, two years after Powell's discovery of the positively and negatively charged pions, Kemmer was proved right when a third variety—the neutral pion—was identified in experiments at the Berkeley particle accelerator in California. Beyond that, little progress was made in understanding the zoo of particles for a decade. This was the state of knowledge, or rather of ignorance, about the strong interactions when Higgs took up his lectureship under Kemmer at Edinburgh in 1960.

1960: A MISSED OPPORTUNITY

Meanwhile in London, Higgs had been studying general relativity and trying to develop a quantum theory of gravity. Always modest, he later said that he had "not really done anything worthwhile in terms of particle physics" during this period.[1]

Just before Higgs started his lectureship in Edinburgh, he was told they were organising a summer school, and that he should come along to the first in what today has become a long series of Scottish Universities Summer Schools. The bulk of the funding came from the North Atlantic Treaty Organization (NATO) as part of an educational programme that Higgs described as "NATO's fig leaf".[2] The budget included money to cover the travel expenses of the speakers. However, one of the lecturers from the United States had separately obtained a travel grant from the National Science Foundation to cross the Atlantic, so a few hundred pounds were freed up in the school budget. The organisers decided to use it to buy wine for dinners during the school session, although NATO's funding rules banned grants from being used that way. Some judicious restructuring of the budget accounts enabled NATO's funds to be assigned to the specific items it allowed, while money from some Scottish Universities, with no such constraints, was assigned to the provision of food and drink. Higgs was given a job on the committee as a steward, with the responsibility to purchase the wine, deliver it to the tables at dinner, and look after it for the duration of the school session. He also had to be up early each morning to ensure that all was in order for breakfast, and in the lecture hall.

The school was held at Newbattle Abbey College, outside Edinburgh near Dalkeith. The abbey had a crypt dating from the thirteenth century, on which the present house was built several hundred years ago. An informal common room was established in the crypt where people had discussions late into the night. Among the students were Martinus ("Tini") Veltman, a solidly built, ebullient Dutchman, and Sheldon Glashow, a young American postdoc, full of chutzpah. Veltman and Glashow were unusual in sharing a grounding in quantum field theory, which by 1960 had fallen out of fashion. Within a decade, however, their work would become prominent in its renaissance. At the time of the Newbattle Abbey summer school, Glashow was in the process of writing a paper uniting the electromagnetic force with the weak nuclear force—the force responsible for *beta radioactivity*, in which an electron or positron is emitted during transmutation of a neutron into a proton, or vice versa.

The electromagnetic force can act over a long distance and emits radiation in the form of photons into the world around us; contrast this with the weak force, which acts only over a very short range, no bigger than the size of the atomic nucleus. To examine the weak force in action would require penetrating deep into the nucleus with forensic precision, and this was far beyond technical capability in 1960. All that could be detected were the trails of radioactivity's products, the particles—electrons or positrons—that emerge into the macroworld. By studying these patterns, physicists hoped to deduce the dynamics of their creation.

In 1957, Glashow had been a student of Julian Schwinger and become inspired by his mentor's ideas about the weak interaction. There may seem to be little similarity between the colours of a rainbow and radioactivity, but Schwinger suspected that they are in fact different manifestations of a single fundamental mechanism. First, they are both the result of radiation. Electromagnetic radiation had been recognised since Maxwell produced his equations in 1865, and radioactivity's very name testifies to its radiant nature. Closer examination of data on radioactivity led Schwinger to notice further similarities between the two. He was like the wily fox who noticed that while several trails of its prey entered a cave, none came out, and reasoned that the cave contained a bear. Schwinger compared the metaphorical trails of particles produced in the form of radioactivity known as beta decay—in which a neutron in an atomic nucleus converts into a proton, for example—with those of electromagnetic phenomena. From this he deduced what must be going on within the cave—the hidden depths of the atomic nucleus—when the weak force was at work. He knew that the electromagnetic force is transmitted by photons, and from the trails in radioactivity he inferred that the weak force too is transmitted by some unseen species of particle—the hidden bear. Schwinger chose the first letter of *weak force*—W—as the name for this analogue of the photon.

The nature of the trails showed that the W must be electrically charged, either positive or negative, equal in magnitude to the electric charges of a proton or electron. In the traditional notation of particle physics where electric charges are given as superscripts, these are referred to as W^+ and W^-, or generically simply as *W bosons* when the sign of the electric charge is irrelevant.

Schwinger was a small, heavy dapper wunderkind from Manhattan, born in 1918. At just fourteen he heard a lecture by Dirac, which inspired his interest in quantum field theory, and by fifteen he was writing research papers on the subject with professors at Columbia University in New York. By 1937, at only nineteen years old, he had published seven research papers. He was in his late twenties when in 1947 he produced his seminal work in which he scaled the mighty peak of establishing renormalisation in QED—in effect, demonstrating it to be a viable quantum theory of the electromagnetic field.[3]

From the beginning of his work on QED, Schwinger had been impressed with the remarkable consequences of gauge invariance, namely that an electromagnetic force necessarily occurs between electrically charged bodies, and that this force is carried by a massless particle, the photon. Furthermore, gauge invariance's implication that the photon is massless appeared to be key to QED's practical renormalisation.

In November 1956, Schwinger gave a series of lectures at Harvard University inspired by such ideas. In QED, an electron can change its momentum while remaining an electron by emitting or absorbing a photon. The equation describing this fundamental process contains a number, which in effect represents the number of coulombs of electric charge carried by the electron. Schwinger realised that matrices—rectangular arrays of numbers—provide a natural means for keeping the quantum field theory accounts when an electric charge transfers from one particle to another, such as from a neutron to a proton in beta decay (or from an electron to the electrically neutral neutrino). He conjectured that it might be possible to derive the existence of the weak force, responsible for beta radioactivity, as well as its properties by using arguments like those that had proved so useful for QED. Indeed he went further, suggesting that weak and electromagnetic forces might be two manifestations of a unique underlying theory where for the weak force the hitherto unknown particles—the electrically charged W bosons—play an analogous role to the electrically neutral photon of QED. As the photon transmits the electromagnetic force, so does the W boson carry the weak force of radioactivity.

To his delight, he found that the mathematics led to a beautifully symmetric parallel between weak and electromagnetic forces; to his despair, he also realised immediately that nature failed to act this way. First, exact symmetry between the electromagnetic and weak interactions would have implied that the W bosons are massless, like a photon. However, this is not how nature works. If electrically charged W bosons were massless, they would be as easy to produce and as straightforward to detect as photons, yet none has ever been seen. As Schwinger realised back in 1947, there are no massless electrically charged particles of any sort.

Empirically it is obvious also that there is no symmetry between the two forces as their strengths differ; the very name *weak* indicates the perceived feebleness of this force relative to the strength of the electromagnetic force. Schwinger's insight, which would later come to life after Higgs' breakthrough, was that this lack of symmetry might be an illusion. Its source: mass.

Massless photons can travel across interstellar space such that we perceive them as starlight, and they transmit the electromagnetic force over vast distances. A massive particle, such as the W, on the other hand, cannot do this. According to quantum field theory, it can transmit a force for only a very short distance. If it were very heavy—say, more than forty times the mass of a hydrogen atom—the range of the force would barely cross even an atomic nucleus. So, when we observe the effects of the weak force, we are like people who are looking at the cave from the outside but have never been inside to see the bear at work. Schwinger insisted that deep inside the cave, at the source—in the heart of the atomic nucleus—electromagnetic and weak forces could have the same strength.

The price was that the W boson must have a mass and, what's more, a mass much larger than any particle then known. Schwinger was fully aware that the mass of the W, in contrast to the massless photon, spoiled not only the symmetry of a perfect union but also the gauge symmetry that had inspired his construction in the first place. So he carefully avoided the word *unity*, instead describing the weak force as a "partner" of the electromagnetic.

In the month after Schwinger first outlined these ideas came an experimental discovery about the weak interaction that seems to have killed his interest. Physical processes controlled by electromagnetic and strong forces make no distinction between left and right; a sequence of events viewed in a mirror could equally take place in the real world. In the mathematics of quantum theory this is known as the *conservation of parity* or *mirror symmetry*. This was thought to be a fundamental symmetry, true in general, until the discovery in December 1956 that in beta radioactivity the chance of a particle interaction differed from that for its mirror image. In other words, the weak interaction violates mirror symmetry. In the jargon of particle physics, in our material world the weak interaction is *left-handed*, and in a world consisting of antimatter, the weak interaction is *right-handed*.

This radical phenomenological difference between weak and electromagnetic interactions seemingly spoiled any hope of partnership. What nature had cast asunder Schwinger stopped trying to bring together. However, he did not give up on his pet project entirely and suggested it to a new research student: Sheldon Glashow. Years later, after Glashow had won a Nobel Prize for what came out of this, he recalled: "Schwinger told me to think about [uniting the weak and electromagnetic forces]. So, I did. For two years—I thought about it."[4]

Glashow decided to ignore the showstopper that gauge invariance predicts the mass of W bosons to be zero. Instead, he modified the equations to take account of the fact that the W has a mass. By doing so, of course, he had done away with the fundamental principle of gauge invariance that had originally inspired the theory, but with the confidence of youth he airily dismissed this as a "stumbling block we must overlook". Where Glashow made his real breakthrough was in how he dealt with the newly discovered phenomenon of parity violation.

Glashow imposed parity violation on his equations for beta radioactivity involving W^+ and W^- to agree with the data, but in so doing he met an immediate problem: phenomena involving their neutral partner will also violate parity. This of course is quite unlike the electromagnetic interaction, transmitted by the neutral photon, where parity is conserved. This had led Schwinger to abandon his attempt to marry the two forces, but what he had perceived as a threat, Glashow saw as opportunity. He concluded—bravely, rashly, but ultimately correctly—that the electrically neutral partner of the charged W bosons is not the photon. He proposed that inside the metaphorical cave there lived another bear—an electrically massive neutral sibling to the charged Ws. This particle carried zero charge, so he named it Z, and like his native city New York, New York—so good they named it twice—he appended the traditional superscript 0 as well, making it Z^0. By introducing the Z^0—which became whimsically known as the particle of "heavy light"—Glashow had stumbled onto his ticket to immortality.

His mathematics implied the Z^0 must exist, but no one had ever seen any trails associated with it. For many that lack of evidence would have dimmed their enthusiasm, even convinced them they were wrong. Glashow, however, had nerve, had nothing to lose, and was young. He boldly predicted that a new form of radioactivity must exist and said that if people looked very carefully, they would find some clues to the presence of a hidden Z bear too.

Today, this *electroweak synthesis*—the linkage of electromagnetic and weak interactions—is recognized as the founding piece of the Core Theory of particles and forces, known prosaically as the *Standard Model*.[5] Back in 1960, however, his construct was far ahead of its time and, beset by some seemingly unsurmountable problems, appeared stillborn. First, to explain the perceived relative weakness of the force, his Z and W inventions had to be massive—thirty times or possibly even a hundred times heavier than a hydrogen atom. In 1960, there were relatively massive *strange* particles to be sure, but nothing even reached twice the mass of a proton. Factors of thirty, let alone one hundred, were off the scale for known fundamental particles and more akin to complex atoms, such as calcium, iron, or krypton. Glashow's postulate, requiring that such huge masses could be concentrated in a single fundamental particle of vanishingly small size, appeared more the mathematical fancy of a fevered theorist than a sensible goal for an experimentalist.

There was no way to produce such bulky particles with the technology of the time, nor did the experimentalists receive much encouragement from their theoretical colleagues to make long-term plans to produce these hypothetical entities. Additionally, most theorists were unaware of Glashow's model while the few who had looked at his paper rapidly dismissed it because of a fundamental flaw in its construction. They noticed that calculations in his model beyond the simplest approximation gave nonsense. With a sense of déjà vu, theorists saw the infinity plague that had almost wrecked QED resurrected.

For Dirac's quantum field theory of the electromagnetic force—QED—renormalisation had successfully purged the infinity nonsense. Why then should Glashow's arranged union with the weak force founder? Could not a marriage counsellor prescribe the same remedy that had worked for QED in its bachelor days?

Put bluntly, the answer is no. The mathematical proof that QED is a viable theory relies on the fact that the theory is gauge invariant and its consequence: that the agent of the electromagnetic force—the photon—has no mass. Had the analogous carriers of the weak force—the W and Z particles—been massless too, Glashow's union might have been viable. Unfortunately, though, his construction necessarily required them to have large masses, in which case the proof fails, leaving an insuperable infinity puzzle. Glashow's cavalier attitude to the disappearance of gauge invariance in his construct had become less a "stumbling block we must overlook" than a mountain range to be conquered.

Today, thanks to Higgs, Veltman, and others, we know the trails that can take us over and beyond those peaks. Glashow's cookery was fine, but his recipe was incomplete. Add a further ingredient, which when suitably prepared creates a dish known as a Higgs boson, and a gourmet banquet celebrating the Core Theory of particles and forces emerges.

ENCOUNTER IN THE STAFF CLUB

At Newbattle Abbey in 1960, however, no one foresaw these developments. Higgs' breakthrough was still four years in the future. A supreme irony is that while Veltman and Glashow discussed physics into the small hours and then stayed in bed during the first lecture each morning, Higgs' role as the newest member of the committee required him to be on call first thing every day, so he had early nights. Not only was Higgs therefore unaware of their seminal discussions, but he only learned later that the conversations had been lubricated by raids on his wine store.

Some of the lecturers had brought their families, including children. A group of wily students had noted which tables at dinner contained children or teetotallers, and hence left wine unused. These spies then smuggled any untouched bottles out and hid them in a large grandfather clock in the crypt for drinking after dark. Higgs described these gatherings in the crypt as "the informal part of the summer school where people educated themselves about problems in electromagnetic and weak interactions in 1960." His absence from those late-night informal brainstorms on what would mature into the electroweak interaction—to which others would later apply Higgs' mathematical insights—would be the first in a sequence of missed opportunities.

After the school ended, Higgs prepared for his new career at Edinburgh, where he would have "to teach things I had never really learned properly myself". He had written two papers on general relativity in London but now shed that subject as the Edinburgh lectureship was in theoretical particle physics, Higgs' longtime goal. He also had his strong moral commitment to combat development of nuclear weapons. Kemmer had helped focus this by pointing Higgs towards CND when he moved to London back in 1957; now Higgs had returned to Edinburgh, armed with Antoinette Pirie's list of contacts. This would be the first piece of chance that would determine Higgs' future personal life. Through that list he met his future wife, Jody Williamson, in the University Staff Club in Chambers Street, where people went to relax with their friends after work.[6]

Jody was American, a twenty-four-year-old graduate of the University of Illinois, where she had earned a degree in speech therapy. In Illinois, she had met someone on leave from Edinburgh who said, "Why don't you apply to join Edinburgh University; it has an excellent phonetics department and is a great city to live in." Jody duly came to Edinburgh in 1958 to pursue a diploma course in phonetics.

That evening in 1960, she was one of a group of friends who had been in the staff club before Higgs arrived. Initially unaware of the "glamorous American blond girl", Higgs was interacting with the people who were on the CND members list which he had brought from his days as the temporary secretary of the scientists' group. Then, as the evening progressed, he found himself chatting with the short, long-haired "typical college girl of the time". Theirs was no love at first sight, more a gradually deepening friendship that "took a year or two to warm up".

When they decided to marry, Higgs didn't call it getting engaged—"I didn't see what getting engaged was about. As far as I could make out it was an ancient custom that involved handing over an engagement ring to say to other males, 'keep your hands off my bird'." Reaction to the news in Illinois was more traditional. Higgs received a congratulatory letter from Dave Jackson, a physicist from Urbana whom he had met at the Scottish Universities Summer School in 1960. By chance Jackson's house backed onto that of Jody's parents. His letter included a clipping from the Urbana newspaper which, to Higgs' surprise, announced that "JoAnne Williamson was getting engaged to a physicist named Peter Higgs from Edinburgh".[7]

Her midwestern Presbyterian parents had counted it as an engagement. The marriage was arranged for September 1963, though they visited Dubrovnik, Croatia, for their "honeymoon" earlier that summer. Jody's parents at first said they weren't coming to the wedding because it was going to be in a registry office. She wrote them an "extremely angry letter" and they relented. Later Higgs learned that it was her aged grandmother—a "real tyrant"—who, upon learning where the couple planned to marry, said, "Registry offices are for white trash." Jody's mother stood up to the bullying and eventually her parents agreed to come. The event was celebrated at the University Staff Club.[8]

During those two years going out with Jody Williamson, Higgs had settled into life as a new member of the physics department. In addition to supervising a new research student, Jack Smith, Higgs was given charge of the university's theoretical physics research library, housed in the austere stone terraced buildings of the Tait Institute in Roxburgh Street.[9] This involved receiving journals and preprints—advance reports on research papers prior to their formal publication—then sorting them and putting them on display for other people to look at. "I got the first look at them", he recalled. That was how, in 1961, Higgs saw a paper by Japanese American theorist Yoichiro Nambu and launched the series of events that would inspire his own success.

CHAPTER 4

THE SUPER CONDUCTOR

THE EPISODE THAT led to Higgs' breakthrough effectively began one day in 1956 in a seminar room at the University of Chicago. Robert Schrieffer, a twenty-five-year-old graduate student, was talking about superconductivity.

Let us step back. In 1911 the Dutch physicist Heike Kamerlingh Onnes had discovered that when cooled to −269°C, solid mercury suddenly lost all resistance to the flow of electric current. This phenomenon—superconductivity—was later found in other materials at ultracold temperatures, such as tin and metal alloys. In a loop of wire made of superconducting material, electric currents can flow for years without needing any voltage to be applied. This remarkable phenomenon defied explanation for decades. A breakthrough in understanding superconductivity occurred in 1950, in what was then the Soviet Union. Two leading Soviet theorists, Vitaly Ginzburg and Lev Landau, made a successful description of the phenomenon, but it was the time of the cold war and no one in the West seems to have noticed the paper, written in Russian and published behind the Iron Curtain.

Electrical conductors are materials that let electric currents pass through them easily. Electric current is the flow of electrons, and in conductors such as copper, steel, or mercury the current arises from electrons that have been freed from atoms in the host material. Having liberated these negatively charged electrons, the parent atoms of the metal lattice remain with a positive charge. These electrically charged atoms are known as ions.

When electrons move through the lattice, they are attracted electrically by the positive ions. The electrical force on an electron is equal in size and opposite in direction to that on a charged ion. However, the resulting acceleration of the puny electron is much larger than the trifling disturbance on the massive atomic ions of the metallic lattice. Electrons are kicked out of the smooth current, and this obstruction is the source of a conductor's electrical resistance; the jostling of electric charges emits low-frequency electromagnetic radiation and makes small vibrations of the lattice, which we experience as heat. These are the microscopic dynamics causing electrical phenomena with which we are all familiar. Less familiar is what happens to some conductors in deep freeze, where below some critical temperature all electrical resistance suddenly vanishes, and the material becomes a superconductor.

In their attempt to describe the phenomenon, Ginzburg and Landau simply assumed that the probability that the metal contains superconducting stuff is either zero or some unknown positive amount. In their equations they assumed that its magnitude depends on temperature because superconductivity occurs only at temperatures below some critical amount T_c. However, they had no idea what this unusual state of superconducting matter actually consisted of. Which brings us to Schrieffer in Chicago.

Schrieffer and two more senior colleagues, Leon Cooper and John Bardeen, had found an explanation of the phenomenon and identified the nature of the superconducting medium. That day in Chicago was the first that many had heard of what became known as the *BCS theory of superconductivity*. The three theorists—Bardeen, Cooper, and Schrieffer—have been immortalised by a three-letter acronym.

Cooper was the first to unravel the dynamics of how superconductivity happens. Although the interaction between the electron and an ion mostly disturbs the electron, there is nonetheless a small reaction by the ion. This slight distortion of the ionic lattice may persist for a short while after the electron has moved away. Cooper's insight was that if a second electron comes by and if the timing, speed, and magnetic orientation of the electron are all right, the interactions with the lattice of the first and the second electron cause them to attract one another magnetically. These two electrons may be far apart in space but will act cooperatively like a single particle. In Cooper's mathematical analysis of this sequence of events, he concluded that this attraction arises when the individual magnetism of the pair of electrons has cancelled out. These are known as *Cooper pairs*.

The magnetic correlation between the two electrons enables them to flow through the lattice undisturbed. An electrical pull on one is matched by a push on the other and vice versa. The result is that these Cooper pairs stream through the superconductor without any resistance.

In the audience listening to Schrieffer's talk that day was the theorist Yoichiro Nambu, a visionary whose thinking has been described as "ten years ahead of everyone else". Nambu was born in Tokyo in 1921, and his brilliance was quickly recognised. At the young age of twenty-nine he was appointed professor of theoretical physics at Osaka University, and within two years he was recruited to the United States where, as professor at the University of Chicago, he spent the rest of his career. Although Nambu lived for decades in the United States, he never lost the politeness of his Japanese origins, such as a reluctance to express negativity directly. If Nambu agreed with someone's suggestion, he would quickly reply "Yes!"; a significant pause followed by a mezzopiano "yes", delivered with an intonation as if he were still considering the question, however, registered as "no". A slightly built man of medium height, with a long face topped by neatly combed short black hair, he had no strong physical presence, but his mind was so sharp that in company Nambu was always the centre of intellectual attention. His special talent was not just in understanding physics at a much deeper level than most, but in then exposing the weakest link in an argument and persisting until he broke through to new vistas. The BCS theory of superconductivity was a case in point.

Impressed by the boldness of the BCS theory, Nambu was nonetheless disturbed that it appeared to contradict the fundamental gauge symmetry requirement of QED. In this he was not alone. Many others who had tried to make theories of superconductivity and failed, or had developed their own theory, dismissed BCS because of this contradiction. On the other hand, those who came to the subject afresh and saw the achievements of the theory in describing the phenomenon were almost universally in favour. Nambu, with his background in particle physics and who had been drawn in by the gauge problem, was one such person. It took him two years to solve the enigma by finding a flaw in perceptions of the way in which symmetry governs natural phenomena. In his two years of rumination from 1957 to 1959, Nambu discovered that superconductivity is an example of symmetry being *spontaneously broken* and becoming *hidden*, an important phenomenon which had previously escaped attention. With this insight, he sparked the revolution whose implications are still being worked out.

HIDDEN SYMMETRY

We are all aware of symmetry when we see it, even if we are not mathematicians. To an aesthete, symmetry equates to beauty; to a mathematician, symmetry has an unromantic definition but one with powerful consequences. An arid definition of symmetry in mathematics is a situation where change produces no change. For example, a circle is symmetric under rotation: if change is the rotation of one's perspective, a circle remains a circle—there is no change. Symmetry is mathematically important because it limits what can happen. A partial view of something that you know to be mirror symmetric, for example, enables you to determine the full picture; knowing that a figure on a flat sheet of paper is rotationally symmetric constrains it immediately to be one or more concentric circles, or a point, which is a vanishingly small circle.

We have seen that the aspect of superconductivity that had inspired Nambu's investigation is the property of QED known as gauge invariance. In quantum theory, particles have a wavelike character. The regular repetition of the wave from peak to trough and back to the peak inspired an accounting scheme that measures the phase—that is, the distance within the wave cycle. The gauge is how one sets the zero for the phase, for example whether you choose it to be at a peak, or at a trough, or at some other point anywhere between (figure 4.1).

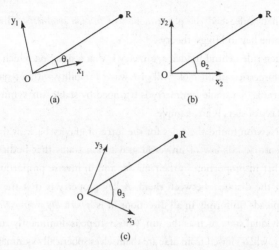

Figure 4.1: **Phase.** The line *OR* is the same in all examples. The "gauge" is the orientation of the horizontal and vertical axes, identified by *x* and *y* in each case. The choice of gauge is arbitrary; all that is required is that *x* and *y* are orthogonal—at 90° to one another. The angles θ_1, θ_2, and θ_3 are the phase angles relative to the reference axes in the different gauges.

Gauge symmetry in the theory of QED implies that if you change the phases of electrons' quantum waves at different places in space and time, the implications of the equations for the electrons' behaviours will remain unchanged. This gauge invariance is maintained from one location to another thanks to the presence of the massless photon—the gauge boson of QED. In Cooper's theory of superconductivity, pairs of electrons cooperate over large distances and time frames, forming more stable configurations than when each electron moves independently. The equations were complex, and Nambu worked through the algebra carefully. As he began to understand their message more deeply, he realised that the quantum waves of the two electrons in a Cooper pair are always in tune. This requirement of unison is not gauge invariant. However, the basic equations of electrodynamics *are* gauge invariant. In making the transition from uncorrelated electrons in a normal conductor to the correlated troupe in a superconductor, the fundamental property of gauge invariance appeared to have been lost.

This is what disturbed Nambu for two years, until he understood how the correlated electron pairs are not gauge invariant even while the underlying foundations of the BCS theory of superconductivity, rooted in QED, are.

Nambu had unleashed the phenomenon of *hidden symmetry*. This would later become key to Higgs' theory.

A golden rule behind hidden symmetry is that a situation which is at the outset symmetric but unstable will give way to stability without symmetry. The mantra is "Unstable symmetry is trumped by stable 'un'-symmetry." A spiral galaxy of stars is an example.

Isaac Newton found the rules for the force of gravity back in the seventeenth century. His law of universal gravitation states that bodies attract one another in proportion to their masses and in inverse proportion to the square of the distance between them. A key property is that the force of gravity spreads uniformly in all directions: it is *spherically symmetric*. Therefore, individual stars such as the sun, whose shape is dominantly controlled by gravity, when viewed from afar are themselves spherically symmetric. The force of gravity binds galaxies of stars, and for this reason many of them are spherical, but not all. Our Milky Way is far from spherical and more like a flat plate. As stars mutually attract one another over the eons, the flat plate is more stable than the illusory perfection of a sphere. The fundamental spherical symmetry of the force of gravity has become broken by the spontaneous transition to stability; it is hidden by the spiral galaxy having complicated structures in two dimensions, but little in the third.

The key is that by seeking better stability and reaching a state of lower potential energy, nature has sacrificed symmetry. Nambu realised this was at work in the case of the Cooper pairs. The pair of electrons has lower energy than two uncorrelated, gauge invariant electrons; in reaching this more stable state, gauge invariance has been sacrificed. To destroy the Cooper pairs requires the input of energy to make up this energy gap. This understanding gave Nambu a wonderful idea about the proton and neutron.

MASS FROM NOWHERE

Nambu's insight about the role of hidden symmetry in superconductivity revealed something unexpected. The equations describing the dynamics of an electron when in a Cooper pair, and those governing the electron when liberated, had an intriguing structure, exhibiting what is known as an *energy gap*. Nambu's analysis of these *gap equations* revealed that the electrons in the superconductor appear to gain mass. That set him wondering whether the fabric of the universe was like a superconductor, which by analogy could generate the mass of the proton and neutron.

Like all experts in quantum field theory, Nambu understood that the void can never be truly empty. The vacuum contains a ferment of transient *virtual* particles of matter and antimatter flitting in and out of existence. Nambu mused that if this quantum vacuum acts on neutrons and protons like a real superconductor does on electrons, the mass of these basic nuclear particles could arise spontaneously by analogy to the way electrons can gain mass in a superconductor. When he investigated this idea mathematically, he found the remarkable result that the algebra not only confirmed it but also gave a bonus; it implied existence of a massless particle looking very similar to the pion, carrier of the strong nuclear force. Nambu's theory for the origin of the neutron's and proton's mass had led naturally to an explanation of their powerful attraction through its agent: the lightweight pion.

His theory thus explained the existence of atomic nuclei. Had Nambu come up with this breakthrough fifteen years earlier he might have been credited with having solved all nuclear physics. Since then, however, a myriad of other particles which respond to the strong nuclear force had been discovered. During the 1950s attempts to understand the strong force and these strange particles were as inventive as they were unsuccessful. Theorists produced half-baked papers full of speculative ideas in the hope of staking a claim were someone later to make the breakthrough. If the idea was wrong, of course, it would soon be forgotten, and little reputational damage done. Yet from these wild oysters came the occasional pearl. Nambu's theory, emerging from ideas rooted in superconductivity, was destined to be especially lustrous.

Not everyone took note, however, as few immediately appreciated the significance of what he had done. It is easy to be wise once all is understood, but by 1960 confusion ruled. Nambu had explained one piece of physics, which was indeed a profound breakthrough, but his theory said nothing about the multitudes of other strongly interacting particles, nor did it offer any insight into the nature of the weak nuclear force responsible for radioactivity. The Austrian American theorist Victor Weisskopf, shortly to become director-general of CERN, bemoaned the state of particle theory in a lecture at Cornell University around that time. Presumably in reference to Nambu, he said that some theorists were so desperate they were even trying ideas borrowed from other areas of theoretical physics, such as *solid state physics*—a field that one well-known theorist arrogantly dismissed as "squalid state". In Weisskopf's lecture audience that day was Robert Brout, an American theorist who worked in "squalid state" physics. He immediately pricked up his ears and thought, "This is what I know all about; can I solve problems facing particle physicists?"[1]

Higgs had not been at Weisskopf's lecture and had missed Nambu's first paper in *Physical Review* in 1960, in which he outlined the subtle ways that gauge invariance applies in superconductivity. However, Higgs did spot his subsequent paper, written with Italian colleague Giovanni Jona-Lasinio, with its explanation of the pion, when its preprint arrived at the Tait library in 1961: "I did react to that."[2]

Meanwhile, Higgs' student Jack Smith was in his first year of a potential PhD but as preliminary had to write an MSc dissertation. Higgs had proposed that Smith read everything he could find about gauge invariance and summarise it. Back when he had been working through Kemmer's reading list of literature on QED, Higgs had become very puzzled about the way gauge invariance was formulated in the theory—"I thought it very fishy"— and decided that getting a new research student to read about it in parallel with him was a good way to proceed. Higgs was thus well prepared when he saw Nambu's paper, which was driven by the strange ability of gauge invariance to be hidden in a superconductor.

Higgs' interest was further piqued by Nambu having built on those insights to create models of nuclear particles, in which the pion appeared spontaneously from some mathematical legerdemain. Higgs found this empirically successful explanation of the pion remarkable. Even so, in his opinion the calculations were "a bit iffy". Nambu assumed that his initially massless protons and neutrons interacted at a point. Such a situation cannot be generally true for it would lead to infinities which, unlike the logically consistent case in QED, cannot be brushed under the rug. To keep the answers finite, Nambu had included cutoffs—in effect, he had stopped the computation at a chosen moment. It was messy. Nonetheless, it produced masses for his *nucleons*—the proton-neutron doublet—and successfully produced a particle that looked like a pion. However, the calculation predicted that this pion is massless, and although it is empirically much lighter than the nucleons, the real pion is not truly massless. There, Nambu was stuck. Higgs found the model so implausible that he could not figure out what the point of it really was.

GOLDSTONE'S BOSON

The answer to Higgs' puzzlement came in 1961 when Cambridge University theorist Jeffrey Goldstone discovered the fundamental reason for Nambu's breakthrough. Goldstone, who is from Manchester and has a penetrating mind, wrote a paper illustrating how in quantum field theory the spontaneous transition from unstable symmetry to stable asymmetry, thereby hiding the original symmetry, always causes the existence of a massless particle, such as the pion in Nambu's theory.[3] Goldstone's insight helped put Nambu's theory on solid foundations. Theoretical physicists began to educate themselves on the concept of spontaneously broken symmetry in hope of finding further applications—and were almost immediately frustrated.

Goldstone's observation was destined to be the fulcrum on which theoretical physics balanced in the early 1960s. On the one hand it explained in general terms why the pion had magically emerged from Nambu's theory. On the other, it seemed to dash hopes of applying spontaneously broken symmetry more widely in quantum field theory, due to a more general empirical absence of massless electrically charged particles. To understand why and set the context of Higgs' breakthrough merits a brief outline of how Goldstone came to his insight.

Goldstone initially didn't have a formal proof of his hypothesis but illustrated it by means of examples. The ideas behind his insight are best illustrated with the case of a small spherical ball atop the hump of a Mexican hat—figure 4.2. This picture—a bulge at the centre, which is surrounded by a circular valley forming the base, with the turned-up brim forming the far side of the valley—has become a paradigm for mathematical descriptions of spontaneous breaking of symmetry and was the starting point of Higgs' second paper in 1964, page 260. Viewed from above there is complete rotational symmetry; the view from all points of the compass is the same. Nature seeks to minimise potential energy—water runs downhill, its kinetic energy increasing as its gravitational potential energy falls. In the case of

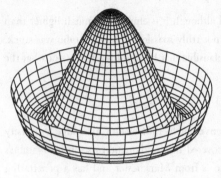

Figure 4.2: **The Mexican Hat or Wine Bottle model of Unstable Symmetry and Stable Asymmetry.** An unstable ball resting at the top of the hill minimises its potential energy by rolling into the valley to a stable position, which can occur at any angle around the base. Oscillations around this base give the *Goldstone boson*. Oscillations can also occur radially up and down the walls at the side of the valley—*Higgs bosons*. See also figure 5.2.

the ball and the hat, the slightest disturbance will dislodge the ball, which will minimize its gravitational potential energy by rolling downhill. Once stationary on the valley floor, its potential energy is at the minimum; we say that it has reached the *ground state*. However, there are infinite numbers of possible ground states corresponding to the different points around the circle at which the ball could settle.

Where previously we had rotational symmetry, we now have asymmetry—a ball at the southernmost point, maybe. The original symmetry remains, however, even if it is now hidden. Perform the experiment thousands of times and keep a record of where the ball falls. After a few trials you will have a wagon wheel with spokes pointing in some directions more than others. After more repeats, the entire circle will gradually fill. After lots of these experiments, balls will be distributed all around the circular valley, testifying to the rotational symmetry of the initial situation. Any individual test will spontaneously break the symmetry, causing the original symmetry to be hidden. This is key to a casino winning at roulette; on any individual trial the landing point of the ball is effectively unpredictable, whereas over a long period all possibilities will occur, including the zero, which goes to the house.

Goldstone's observation was that wherever the ball ends up around this circle, it will have the same potential energy because every point on the rim is the same vertical height below the original peak. It costs no energy to go from one of these stable states to another—after all, the ball being at the southernmost point in the valley, say, rather than in the east or in any other direction around the rim, is nothing more than a rotation of your perspective. In quantum field theory, energy is transmitted by particles, and as it costs nothing in energy to connect the different points of the compass, the associated particle has no mass. This became known later as the massless *Goldstone boson* and is the consequence of the original symmetry being spontaneously broken. In Nambu's specific theory of the neutron and proton, this is the pion.

Steven Weinberg, an American theorist who in 1962 helped elevate Goldstone's insight to a formal theorem, also developed a phenomenologically successful theory of pions and the nuclear force based on the hypothesis that pions in Nambu's theory are indeed examples of Goldstone bosons. Everything looked good. Nambu's success inspired hope that hidden symmetry might be the key to explaining all particles and forces.

However, hopes that this idea might apply more generally were soon dashed. The theory seemed to imply that there should be massless electrically charged particles associated with superconductivity or the weak interaction of radioactivity. As Schwinger had discovered in a different context in 1947, the prediction of massless electrically charged particles is the death of a theory; such particles would have been easy to see—for example, they would be radiated by a lightbulb—yet there was no sign of them. So, by the early 1960s Nambu's beautiful idea of hidden symmetry, while successful in the case of nuclear particles and the pion, appeared to be useless for the wider hopes of theoretical physicists.

Nambu's insight would eventually turn out to be far-reaching, but its real value was not immediately recognised. Nambu himself even seems to have given up on his idea, at least initially, as he made no further development of his theory. There was also a tantalising conundrum: empirically there is no Goldstone boson in superconductivity, the very phenomenon that had inspired Nambu and Goldstone to identify this strangely absent entity. Something was badly amiss. The scene was now set for Peter Higgs' seminal intervention.

CHAPTER 5

HIGGS' EPIPHANY

IN 1961, WHEN Higgs read Goldstone's paper showing that hidden symmetry in quantum field theory induces the existence of a massless particle, he began to understand both the success of Nambu's model and the source of its problems. Goldstone had been present the previous year at CERN when Nambu announced what he was doing and was thus in at the beginning. Goldstone realised intuitively that the BCS theory of superconductivity was akin to an artistic masterpiece whose perfection concealed its basic construction.[1]

Nambu had introduced mathematical sleights of hand to avoid having his calculations give nonsensical values of infinity in their output. Goldstone's paper showed that even so, the underlying scaffold—Nambu's insight about hidden symmetry—was robust. Goldstone duly demonstrated that a massless particle would appear whenever symmetry is spontaneously broken in quantum field theory, and the Nambu pion was a particular example. The Goldstone paper, with its theorem explaining the consequential massless particle, gave Higgs a feeling for what was going on.

Yet while Goldstone's theorem underpinned Nambu's successful explanation of the pion, it simultaneously exposed a fundamental problem with the inspiration for his breakthrough: the BCS theory of superconductivity. Two steps brought Goldstone to a paradox. First, there is no massless particle in the BCS theory. Second, the BCS theory relies on spontaneously broken symmetry. Their combination reveals the conundrum: according to Goldstone's theorem, spontaneous symmetry breaking—the second step—implies existence of a massless particle, in contradiction to the first step.

This incongruity was a mathematical puzzle for nearly five years. It also gave theorists the hope that the empirical absence of massless particles more generally might therefore not necessarily prevent further applications of spontaneous symmetry breaking in quantum field theory. However, there could be no progress until first the paradox itself was resolved. Higgs told me how his own contribution to the saga then came about. "What it took me a long time to appreciate—and by luck I got there before other people spotted what was going on—was that the Nambu model and Goldstone's theorem had overlooked something."[2]

Higgs' journey to this insight had begun with his worries about the physical significance and mathematical robustness of gauge invariance in QED. That in turn had led him to ask Jack Smith, his first graduate student, to review the subject. Smith graduated in 1963, so Higgs' breakthrough in July 1964 occurred during the apprenticeship of a new research student, Lewis Ryder. Ryder, who later became professor of theoretical physics at the University of Kent in Canterbury, was also a musician, sufficiently accomplished that he played the organ in Canterbury Cathedral. Upon returning to Edinburgh from vacation in August 1964, he found a note on his desk from Higgs: "This summer I had the only really original idea I've *ever* had."[3]

Higgs' enlightenment was the result of three years following dead-end trails. Then, in July 1964, he saw what nobody else had seen, or if they had, had failed to realise its importance: in Goldstone's mathematics there was no mention of the electromagnetic field. Goldstone ignored it because it wasn't in Nambu's analysis, and its absence there was because electromagnetic fields had no role in Nambu's theory of the strong nuclear force. Higgs explained to me how his insight flowed from his friendship with Michael Fisher. As we have seen, since their time together as students at King's College, their paths had diverged—both literally, as in 1966 Fisher had moved to Cornell University in the United States, and in physics.

Fisher's speciality was the theoretical physics of the solid state—what is nowadays called condensed matter—and their discussions had made Higgs bilingual: in addition to his mainstream interest in particle physics, Higgs was aware of work in Fisher's speciality and of superconductivity. As a result, Higgs was aware of an unusual property of superconductors: the ability of a superconducting metal to expel all magnetic fields from its interior. This property was discovered in 1933 by Walther Meissner and has been named the *Meissner effect* ever since. It is key to the modern technology of magnetic levitation as used in transport systems. When a magnet is brought near a normal metal, or a superconductor above the critical temperature, its magnetic field penetrates the metal freely. When a magnet is placed above the superconductor at the critical temperature, however, the superconductor pushes away the magnetic field. This causes the magnet to float a small distance above the superconductor, which is the basis of magnetic levitation for maglev transport systems.

The Meissner effect implies that a magnetic field can only penetrate a small distance inside the superconductor. Were our experiences those of living inside a superconductor, we would perceive magnetic fields, and by extension electromagnetic forces, to be short range. In quantum field theory the particles that transmit short-range forces are massive. So, within the confines of a superconductor, the photon—the quantum of the electromagnetic field—in effect becomes massive. So Higgs knew that the way superconductivity works, especially the Meissner effect, is very tied up with what happens to the electromagnetic field in the superconductor. To leave the electromagnetic field out of the analysis of hidden symmetry was to ignore an absolutely critical element. "That's what it's really all about", he told me.[4]

What Higgs did not know in 1964 was that back in 1950 Ginzburg and Landau had already taken account of this omission and all but anticipated what Higgs was about to complete. The pair had made what is known as a *phenomenological model* of superconductivity. Their formulae correctly described the phenomenon and how it occurs only below some critical temperature, but they gave no theory for the origin and dynamics of their superconducting material. When they married their formulae with Maxwell's equations of electromagnetism, they discovered that their model also explained the Meissner effect. The implication of Ginzburg and Landau's work, therefore, is that interaction of the electromagnetic field with the energy density of the superconducting stuff effectively gives a mass to the photon within the confines of the superconductor.

So in 1950 Ginzburg and Landau had produced a phenomenological model of superconductivity that agreed with the data. They had assumed the presence of superconducting material with an energy density that depends on temperature. Below the critical T_c where superconductivity occurs, this density is described mathematically by a formula that graphically looks like a Mexican hat. Thus, their model included features of spontaneously broken symmetry a decade before Nambu highlighted the importance of this phenomenon in nature. However, no one, including the two Russians, realised the full significance of this until years later. That here was also a mechanism for giving mass to the photon seems not to have captured anyone's attention. In the inspirational papers by Nambu, Goldstone, and soon by Higgs and others, there is no mention of Ginzburg and Landau's foresight. (The mathematical foundation of their model is in appendix 4.1.)

ANDERSON SHOWS THE WAY

With the benefit of hindsight, we can see that but for a series of missed opportunities Higgs' involvement in these developments would have been much reduced or even absent. Goldstone had looked at the effect of including an electromagnetic field in his model and found that it generated a mass for the photon. He was a young postdoctoral research fellow at Harvard at the time and tried to explain his finding to Schwinger at the group's weekly lunch. Years later, Goldstone told me Schwinger's comment was "something like 'of course a photon can have mass'".[5]

Goldstone appears to have taken the great physicist's reaction to mean he had found merely a piece of trivia. In any event, he thought there was no point publishing this aspect of his work, so he didn't. Goldstone has a high threshold for what he regards to be worth making public, with the result that over a long career he has issued only a handful of papers, each in its own way profound. He published his paper on hidden symmetry and the massless Goldstone boson only after being encouraged by Glashow. Goldstone was aware that he had no proof in 1960 even though he strongly believed his theorem to be true; Glashow said, "Publish it anyway." Goldstone did so but held back on his inclusion of the electromagnetic field.[6]

Goldstone's misfortune was to have raised this point with Schwinger while the maestro was undergoing a change of heart: Schwinger had concluded that his 1949 mathematical demonstration that gauge invariance in QED necessarily implies the photon to be massless was flawed. His proof had relied on perturbation theory—a mathematical technique valid when the electromagnetic interactions of electrons and photons are feeble. As that is in practice true, the conclusion had become dogma that no one had seriously questioned. Schwinger, meanwhile, had for some time tried to make a general proof without this assumption but had failed. By 1961 he had concluded there was no such proof and that gauge invariance might after all coexist with a massive carrier of the force. He wrote a paper to this effect in the summer of 1961, which was published in January 1962.[7]

Nonetheless, it is still a leap to go from Schwinger's published statement in his paper that gauge invariance does not necessarily imply zero mass to Goldstone's memory that Schwinger so positively had said "of course" it can be massive. It is possible that Schwinger, with his history of interest in gauge invariance, had taken special note that the photon acquires a mass in the BCS and Ginzburg-Landau theories of superconductivity. In any event, whatever Schwinger said seems to have been strong enough to have persuaded Goldstone that this mass mechanism for the photon—and in modern perception, of any gauge boson—was so obvious as to be unworthy of comment. Goldstone therefore restricted his paper to what developed into his famous theorem—the inexorable birth of a massless boson when symmetry is hidden.[8]

At the end of 1962, American theoretical physicist Philip Anderson published a paper about the mysterious absence of a Goldstone boson in the BCS theory of superconductivity. What Anderson drew attention to, and what everyone else—perhaps apart from Schwinger—seemed either to have been unaware of or to have forgotten, was that in the process of the superconducting medium hiding the gauge symmetry, something else had taken place: the superconductor expels magnetic fields, such that in effect the photon of the electromagnetic field acquires a mass. Anderson conjectured that the two massless entities—the massless photon of QED and the massless Goldstone boson of hidden symmetry—"seem capable of 'cancelling each other out' and leaving finite mass bosons only".[9] He gave no proof to back this up, however. It is ironic, therefore, that Goldstone had probably already found the proof in relativistic quantum field theory and not published it.

To back up his conjecture, Anderson produced an example in a pedagogic paper about the behaviour of electromagnetic fields in the presence of plasma. This direct example showed several fundamental things. It illustrated how in a plasma the massless Goldstone boson vanishes and the photon can acquire mass. Anderson's example did not satisfy Einstein's theory of relativity, however. Nonetheless, it had the basic ingredients of what Higgs and others would later demonstrate in relativistic quantum field theory. Indeed, some of the basic ideas are so similar that Anderson would subsequently claim credit, asserting that the phenomenon "was, in fact, discovered in [BCS] theory by me and applied to particle physics in 1963, a year before Higgs". In Anderson's opinion, Higgs was "a rather minor player".[10]

Plasma is sometimes called the fourth state of matter, after solid, liquid, and gas. Plasma consists of negatively charged electrons and positive ions acting like independent electrically charged fluids. There is an example more than one hundred kilometres above our heads—the ionosphere, which is formed by solar radiation hitting the upper atmosphere and splitting the atoms of the electrically neutral air into negative and positive ions. One of the most famous properties of the ionosphere is the way it affects the propagation of electromagnetic radiation, notably radio waves.

As electromagnetic waves travel through space, they interact with whatever lies in their path. If they meet plasma, what happens next depends sensitively on the frequency of the wave. When low-frequency radio waves hit the lower edge of the ionosphere, for example, they are reflected like light from a mirror. Having been turned back towards the ground, they bounce upwards from the surface of the Earth only to be reflected by the ionosphere again. This to-and-fro motion can enable the radio wave to skip across many thousands of miles, a phenomenon that years ago used to delight amateur radio enthusiasts in Europe when they detected transatlantic signals from North

America.[11] This is an example of the phenomenon in which low-frequency electromagnetic radiation cannot penetrate plasma. Nevertheless, the stars can be seen shining through the ionosphere; the ionospheric plasma is transparent to visible light—electromagnetic rays of higher frequency than radio waves—but opaque to low-frequency radiation.

An electromagnetic wave consists of intertwined electric and magnetic fields which jostle electrically charged particles such as electrons and ions in the plasma. The arrival of these electrical forces kicks lightweight electrons a lot, whereas the heavy ionised atoms are hardly disturbed. If all the negatively charged electrons in the plasma are displaced by a small amount relative to the massive positive ions, the attraction of opposite charges will pull the electrons back towards their original positions. Their inertia, however, will make them overshoot their starting point before being pulled back again. The result is that electrons in the plasma yo-yo back and forth around their positions of equilibrium. This makes a wave in the plasma itself, which oscillates at a rate known as the *plasma frequency*.

If the frequency of an incoming electromagnetic wave is higher than the plasma frequency, the wave will travel into and through the plasma, though modified in intensity and other ways. However, if the frequency of the incoming wave is lower than the plasma frequency, the electrical forces inside the plasma destroy it; the wave is unable to penetrate the plasma.

This property—that only waves of high frequency can pass through while those below the plasma frequency are cut off—gave Anderson his insight about the ways that photons of light can sometimes act like massive particles. To see how, imagine our experience if we lived inside plasma; we would only ever be aware of electromagnetic radiation whose frequency was higher than the plasma frequency. In quantum mechanics, the energy of each photon in an electromagnetic wave is proportional to the oscillation frequency of that wave. Thus, a nonzero minimum frequency corresponds to a nonzero minimum energy for the photon.

A massless photon can have any energy, the minimum in principle being zero. A massive object, on the other hand, can have any amount of *kinetic* energy, the amount getting smaller as the body slows towards rest. At this point the particle has its minimum energy, the amount of which, E, would correspond to a mass m given by Einstein's famous equation $E = mc^2$. A nonzero minimum energy is characteristic of a particle with mass. The conclusion is that the presence of plasma in effect gives mass to the photon.

But that is only half of the story, as Anderson now demonstrated the profound way that gauge invariance survives even with the massive photon. For light travelling in empty space, electric and magnetic fields vary only in the two dimensions perpendicular to the direction of the wave's travel, not in all three. As a result, these waves in free space are known as *transverse waves*. The failure to use all three available dimensions is intimately connected to the gauge invariance of the theory and the fact that photons have no mass. Had the photon been massive, the waves would have vibrated in all three dimensions, both transverse and parallel to the direction of travel (figure 5.1). A wave that oscillates along its path is called a *longitudinal* or *compression wave*. An example of a compression wave is a seismic wave which propagates through rocks after an earthquake—a phenomenon that Higgs had studied during his time consulting for CND. It is somewhat ironic that this experience would in a different context become crucial to his life's work later. Anderson now demonstrated how within plasma the electromagnetic wave recovers this missing longitudinal component.

When an electromagnetic wave arrives, electrons in the plasma displaced by the electromagnetic fields mutually interact with one another. This

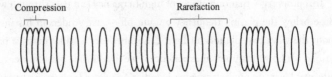

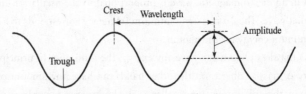

Figure 5.1: **Transverse and longitudinal waves.** In the lower figure, the transverse wave occurs at any angle relative to the page. The upper figure shows a longitudinal wave whose density oscillates along its path.

produces a compression wave of greater or lesser density in the direction that the electromagnetic wave is travelling. Within plasma, a photon has all the characteristics of a massive particle. So the final point of Anderson's example is this: if we had lived inside plasma our experiences of electromagnetic waves would have led us to a gauge invariant theory where photons have mass. This is but one example, but one is sufficient to prove the thesis: it is possible to have both a gauge invariant theory and a massive *gauge boson*—in this case, QED with a massive photon.

By invoking the presence of an additional medium or field—in this case the electrical forces within the plasma—Anderson had identified the metaphorical Rosetta Stone and eliminated the Goldstone boson. Even so, he had not actually found any fault with Goldstone's argument. Also, there was an important difference between what Anderson was doing and what the particle physics community was interested in. Goldstone had studied theories consistent with special relativity, which the BCS theory is not. This was not a failing of the BCS theory of superconductivity, because the conditions were not relativistic; the superconductor or plasma is in a particular frame of reference and the mathematics was set up in the frame where the superconductor is at rest. The fact that superconductivity has no massless Goldstone boson had no obvious relevance for the interests of the high-energy particle physicists; from their perspective the main challenge was to find a way around Goldstone's theorem in a completely relativistic theory. The BCS theory and Anderson's example of the plasma were nonrelativistic; particle physicists took little notice. For them, the problem remained. Anderson had provided the right destination, but the route map had yet to be found.

FROM ANDERSON TO HIGGS

Ben Lee was a Korean American theoretical physicist destined to play a lead role in interpreting the work on hidden symmetry and its revolutionary consequences. If not for his untimely death in a road accident in 1977 at age forty-two, his name would today probably be known more widely alongside that of Higgs and other central actors in the saga. His first entry into the debate led to the bridge linking Anderson's conjecture about the failure of Goldstone's theorem in the nonrelativistic situation of a superconductor with Higgs' eventual solution for a fully relativistic field theory.

In March 1964, Lee and his research supervisor, Abraham Klein, at the University of Pennsylvania in Philadelphia, published a paper questioning whether hidden symmetry necessarily implies massless Goldstone bosons. They showed that the mathematical argument on which the theorem relied included some technical assumptions that do not occur in a nonrelativistic situation, such as the BCS theory of superconductivity. Having identified the key feature that bypassed the Goldstone theorem in the nonrelativistic case, they speculated that a relativistic theory might exist with this feature. However, they did not have any example of such a theory. Peter Higgs read their paper but "could not see how to construct such a model".[12]

Looking back, decades later, Higgs said he was "amazed at the number of things I did that year [1964]".[13] During the autumn, department head Nick Kemmer was away on sabbatical and Higgs stood in for him on a university committee planning a new science area—which includes the present-day James Clerk Maxwell Building, home of the physics and astronomy departments, away from the centre of Edinburgh. The year had started badly, as from February and through the spring Higgs was incapacitated with hepatitis A. At first, he continued teaching but developed a "hell of a headache" and had to have a "long enforced rest".[14] He wasn't completely out of action, as he continued as the science representative on a university bursary committee. He was at home in bed, and on one occasion the other committee members had to come to his house. He gradually recovered. The timing proved fortuitous, as shortly after this the key paper appeared that would stimulate his flash of inspiration.

The link between Klein and Lee's insight and Higgs' breakthrough was a paper published by Walter Gilbert on 22 June 1964. Gilbert was an American theoretical physicist from Harvard who was about to transfer his research efforts to molecular biology, in which he later won a Nobel Prize. In what would be his final paper in theoretical physics, he translated Klein and Lee's analysis of the nonrelativistic situation into a more visual form. This reconfiguration would be the nexus of the saga and contain the key to its resolution.[15]

In the absence of relativity, the mathematical analysis of the laws of motion depends on your frame of reference—whether you are at rest relative to the experiment or in motion. In the case of the superconductor, it is natural to examine the circumstances in its rest frame. You could choose to make the analysis in some other frame, but the algebra will be more complicated. Gilbert effectively reconstructed Klein and Lee's equations adroitly to keep track of which frame of reference was being used. This he achieved by introducing a vector, which we can call **n**, to record how the maths of a nonrelativistic three-dimensional theory is embedded in the space-time mathematics of special relativity. Gilbert showed that in their nonrelativistic analysis of Goldstone's theorem, one of the equations—known as a *commutator*—depended on the vector **n**. Gilbert highlighted that the proof of Goldstone's theorem in the relativistic theory had relied on the *absence* of that vector, and the theorem does not apply in nonrelativistic situations because in that case the vector **n** is present.

This left the key challenge unresolved, however: can one circumvent Goldstone's theorem in the presence of relativity? Gilbert's paper implied that the theorem would fail if there was a vector of the form **n**, but he then killed that possibility by arguing that no such vector can occur in a relativistic field theory.

It is ironic that Gilbert's career path from theoretical particle physics to molecular biology mirrored that of Higgs—who had done his PhD thesis in molecular physics before transferring to particle theory—because it was Gilbert's intervention that now gave Higgs his inspiration. Thanks to the papers that Higgs had been reading during the previous years, he *did* know of a relativistic example containing the critical vector.

The idea of a "Eureka!" moment is cliché, but in this instance it could be near the truth. Half a century later, Higgs remembered "going home on Friday 17 July. And by Monday I had it".[16] He had completed the whole creative process in less than a week. Gilbert's paper appeared in *Physical Review Letters*, which is published in the United States. Having crossed the Atlantic, the edition containing his paper arrived at Edinburgh on Thursday 16 July. Higgs read it that day or the next, recognised the error, and then over the weekend reformulated the algebra, solved the equations, and realised their profound significance. Then he wrote a paper and mailed it on 24 July to a European journal, *Physics Letters*. The editor, based in Geneva, Switzerland, found it in his Monday morning mail on 27 July. As Higgs himself recalled: "What struck me within a day or two of reading Gilbert's letter was that I did indeed know an example of a fully relativistic field theory with a quite harmless dependence on a special [vector of the required type **n**]—quantum electrodynamics in Coulomb gauge." Higgs had found the way to evade Goldstone's theorem while keeping faith with relativity.[17]

HIGGS' FIRST PAPER DECODED

Higgs' short paper was titled "Broken Symmetries, Massless Particles and Gauge Fields", scientifically precise but hardly likely to attract the attention of busy theorists as they scanned through the contents of the latest journals. For those who looked beyond the title, there were few equations and little guidance on how to get from one step to the next. This was certainly not a pedagogic text. To understand its logic required familiarity with mathematical tools such as commutators, Fourier transforms, and the relationship between symmetry and conservation of charges. If you were expert in manipulating these tools you could verify the steps from one equation to the next, though only after some careful work. The paper is reproduced on page 256. Its content may look as unfamiliar as Mayan hieroglyphics, but we can attempt to decipher its meaning and establish its historical context. (A longer discussion appears in appendix 5.1, "Higgs' First Paper Decoded".) In summary, in the paper through to the end of the paragraph containing equation 4, Higgs reviews Gilbert's demonstration that the vector $\mathbf{n}_m$ is key to Goldstone's theorem. That paragraph ends with Gilbert's observation that the absence of a vector $\mathbf{n}_m$ in a relativistic theory "appears to rule out the possibility [of evading Goldstone's theorem]".[18]

The bulk of Higgs' paper is thus a summary of what Gilbert had developed, but having run most of the marathon in the lead, the Harvard physicist had taken a wrong turn at the end. The key observation that Gilbert had drawn the wrong conclusion occurs when Higgs remarks that in gauge theories (such as QED in Coulomb gauge) such a vector appears. He uses Maxwell's equations for the electromagnetic field and the fact that electric charge is conserved (equation 5) to prove that the key contribution of the vector $\mathbf{n}_m$ survives Gilbert's analysis (Higgs' equation 4). Gilbert's conjecture that there is no such term in a relativistic theory is therefore wrong, and Goldstone's theorem is not applicable if an electromagnetic field (or a similar gauge field) is present. Higgs explains this in the lead-up to equation

5 and makes the key conclusion: "We have thus exorcised . . . Goldstone's zero-mass boson."

So Higgs had shown a way around Goldstone's theorem. The impasse associated with the unwanted massless Goldstone boson could be circumvented in the presence of electromagnetic forces. Anderson had already anticipated this with his example of the plasma, but that was nonrelativistic; Higgs had generalised this to the broad canvas of relativistic field theory. This was a correct if rather dry conclusion, and there was little hint that here was a glimpse into a new way of perceiving the universe. As to the consequences and how they come about, he says nothing but promises to do so in a second paper.

Years later, Higgs confirmed the sudden nature of his insight: "The portion of my life for which I am known is rather small—three weeks in the summer of 1964."[19] The production and completion of his second paper (shown in appendix 5.2, on page 260) accounts for the "three weeks".

HIGGS' SECOND PAPER DECODED

In the eighteenth century, the French-Italian mathematician Joseph-Louis Lagrange showed that by writing a formula for the difference between an arrangement's kinetic and potential energies, it is possible to solve its dynamics much more rapidly than by using methods that went back to Isaac Newton. The resulting expression is called the *Lagrangian*. Today, the first step in solving quantum field theory is to write down the Lagrangian for the system. That is what Higgs does, at equation 1, the first of just four equations in a paper of fewer than a thousand words. (A more detailed discussion is in appendix 5.2.)

He introduces the same scalar field as used by Goldstone, and originally by Ginzburg and Landau, and like them uses the symbol φ—phi—to describe it in his algebra. The first line in this first equation represents the kinetic energy of this field; the quantity V on the second line refers to its potential energy. The key feature of V is that it has the shape like a Mexican hat which Goldstone and the Russians had used. If Higgs had stopped there and solved the dynamics implied by the Lagrangian, he would have reproduced Goldstone's result with its unavoidable unwanted massless boson. But Higgs' goal was to include also the electromagnetic field in his framework, and this he did by introducing the field denoted A which in quantum theory represents a photon.

A suitably expert reader could then use Lagrange's techniques to work out the equations of the dynamics for both the scalar phi-field and the electromagnetic field. This is standard fare in physics, so Higgs did not show the details, only the results. These are encapsulated in three equations, which are listed at the top of the right-hand column: 2a, 2b, and 2c. If there were no coupling between the phi-fields and the electromagnetic field, the translation of equation 2a would be "there is a massless boson associated with angular oscillations along the bottom of the valley": this is the infamous Goldstone boson associated with the ground states in the rim of the Mexican hat. Then equation 2c would say "the photon is massless", as in normal experience.

Where Higgs moved understanding of physics forwards was by solving these equations when an electromagnetic field interacts with the phi-field. Everything then changes dramatically. Where previously Goldstone's analysis led to a massless particle, Higgs' results implied that this massless particle vanishes from the stage. The way to bypass Goldstone's theorem in a relativistic field theory had been found.

That was itself an exciting discovery, but merely the threshold to a new vision of the physical universe. The first step was when Higgs saw through the mathematical manipulations and understood where the massless Goldstone particle had gone. Equation 3 implies that in effect it had been absorbed by the formerly massless photon, A, to make the massive photon, denoted by B. Higgs realised that this now recast photon, B, would have utterly different properties to what usually occurs. For example, whereas the effects of electricity and magnetism can normally be felt over large distances—the Earth's magnetic field, for example, extends far into outer space—having been modified by Goldstone's particle, the range of electromagnetic forces is drastically cut off. That is what the equations imply and is exactly what happens in superconductivity's Meissner effect: magnetic fields are unable to penetrate far into a superconductor. Recall that in the language of quantum field theory, which is what Higgs was using, this corresponds to the photon becoming massive within the superconductor. Goldstone's massless particle has not so much disappeared as been transfigured in giving mass to the photon.

This is the main implication of Higgs' paper: it is possible for photons to acquire mass by absorbing the unwanted Goldstone particle. This discovery was so startling that it seems to have diverted attention from what would in time become the most celebrated result implicit in the paper, namely equation 2b. The photon gained mass when the unwanted Goldstone boson disappeared, but, like the smile of the Cheshire Cat, the Goldstone field is still present; this equation describes its dynamics. Higgs states, "Equation 2b describes waves whose quanta have . . . mass." Translated, it says, "there is a massive scalar boson associated with radial

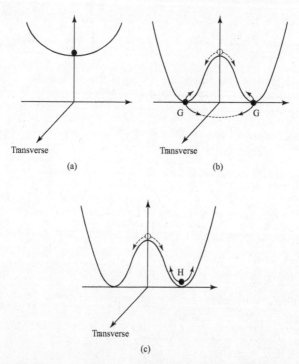

Figure 5.2: **Goldstone and Higgs: rotary and radial motion.** A ball rolling in the shell shown in (a) will end up at the bottom, where it has the lowest energy. If the shell has the shape shown in (b) or (c), the original point of stability will have higher energy than the valley floor. The ball will roll into the valley at some random point around the base. Oscillations around the valley floor—mode G in (b)—cost no energy, but those up and down the valley walls do—mode H in (c). Mode G is analogous to the massless Goldstone boson; mode H is analogous to the massive Higgs boson.

oscillations up and down the walls on either side of the valley floor." (This is illustrated in figure 5.2.) It is a property of the phi-field alone and occurs whether electromagnetic fields are present or not. This massive boson is a manifestation of the phi-field's reality and has become known as the Higgs boson—although this equation was already in Goldstone's 1961 paper! Higgs himself gave no indication that he had yet appreciated the massive boson's deep significance, for he made little of it. In 1964, it received but this passing mention in his paper. Half a century later, finding this entity would become the holy grail of particle physics.

CHAPTER 6

NOW WE ARE SIX

HIGGS MADE HIS breakthrough in July 1964. Within a few weeks, however, he found he was not alone. Five other theoretical physicists had independently discovered how to eliminate Goldstone's boson in relativistic quantum field theory and give mass to the photon. Among them was Robert Brout, who had been alerted by hearing Weisskopf's lament back in 1960. By 1964 Brout had moved from the United States to Brussels, and there he and François Englert completed work that led them to the same breakthrough as Higgs. Higgs might not have yet appreciated the significance of the massive boson, but at least he had written an equation and introduced it. Fortunately for him, no one else had mentioned this boson.

Robert Brout, born in New York in 1928, was a professor at Cornell when he heard Weisskopf's talk in 1960. His research assistant was a twenty-eight-year-old Belgian visiting scientist named François Englert. Brout was specialising in theoretical condensed-matter physics. He was especially interested in how collections of items—magnetic atoms or electrons—organise into different configurations or *phases* (such as liquid and solid in the macroscopic world).

A change from one configuration to another is known as a *phase transition*. Englert had trained as an aeronautical engineer, and Brout as a chemist. Each had made a metaphorical phase transition to condensed matter physics, and at the start of the 1960s they were about to complete their odysseys by a transition into particle physics.

Brout had pricked up his ears during Weisskopf's talk because the concept of a massless particle—the output of Nambu's theory and the lead player in Goldstone's theorem—was familiar to him thanks to his studies of magnetism. A simple model of magnetism gave him a ready picture of the massless particle that Goldstone insisted must be there. However, Brout was troubled because a small modification of the model seemed to avoid Goldstone's theorem. In other words, there appeared to be some fine print that enabled nature to bypass this apparent axiom. Brout and Englert set out to understand this.

Brout's model of magnetism involved the humble electron. In quantum theory the electron has a bipolar property known as *spin*. An electron can spin in one of two orientations: with the axis of spin parallel or opposite to the direction of a magnetic field. The direction of its spin then determines whether the electron is attracted or repelled by the magnetic force—in effect, in which direction it moves. Magnetism occurs in a material if its electrons, or atoms, all spin in the same direction.

The theorist can imagine configurations that could exist in principle but are hard or even impossible to achieve in practice. This can be a good technique when trying to understand the physical principles underlying more realistic situations. In this vein, Brout was intrigued by a mathematical model where atomic ions that are spinning and acting like magnets are placed uniform distances apart along a straight line. Adjacent ions mutually attract by magnetic forces if they are spinning in the same direction and repel if their spins are aligned opposite to one another. The total energy of the collection depends on the relative orientations of the entire assembly. The energy will be a minimum if all are spinning the same way. Their model is illustrated in figure 6.1.

Imagine this in a world with no gravity, where there is no meaning to *up* or *down* but there's a matrix of distant stars against which their orientation can be measured. The entire set of spinning ions can be rotated uniformly, and the new configuration will have the same energy as before. This is no different from you having rotated your perspective slightly. This means there is an infinite number of states with the same energy.

Brout's strength was in mental imagery; Englert's was in mathematical formalism. Brout realised that this simple model gave an intuitive under-standing of Goldstone's theorem. With Englert, he then developed the idea into a set of formulae capable of describing an imagined situation: an in-finitely long collection of spinners where each member can interact magnet-ically with the immediate neighbour to either side. They then investigated mathematically how the system would behave. The result was remarkable.

First, imagine that you somehow rotate one spin slightly. The magnetic force will pull its neighbours into the new alignment. In turn these reori-ented electrons will act on their neighbours, and so on down the line. Once you have initiated the process, these interactions will pull the spins into alignment along the full extent of the chain. With an infinitely long chain you can ignore the initial tweak that set it off infinitely far away and focus solely on the wave of readjustments that propagates along the line. If the as-sembly is infinitely large, then as the wavelength of the reorienting spinners itself becomes infinite, all will have rotated into the new configuration.

This new configuration is one of that infinity of rotated states with the same energy as the original. This means no energy has been transported by the infinitely long wave of spin rotations along the line. Recall the mantra: in quantum field theory the energy of a wave is carried by a particle, and by Ein-stein's equivalence between energy and mass, a particle that carries no energy has no mass.[1] In this model, this corresponds to Goldstone's massless particle.

Goldstone had proved that in situations of symmetry, where nature chooses one out of a host of identical configurations (in this case, rotate your perspective to experience the rotational symmetry of the situation), a mass-less particle is unavoidable. With this model, Brout and Englert could visu-alise Goldstone's theorem at work. What troubled them, however, was that with a small change to the model they could remove the massless particle, in contradiction to his theorem. This is how.

In their model, the only interaction was between immediate neighbours. If they allowed interactions to range further—to include the next-to-nearest neighbours, for example—the conclusions were the same. This was no surprise: extending the range of the interaction a finite amount was trifling relative to an infinitely long line. However, if they allowed the range of interaction itself to become truly long range, so that a spinner could interact with one infinitely far away, energy was unavoidably transferred and the massless Goldstone particle in their model disappeared.

They had understood this much by the end of 1961, at which time Englert's scholarship at Cornell ended and he returned to Brussels. Brout then arranged to visit Brussels. Segregation was still rife in the United States, and the civil rights movement was beginning. Brout, a socialist, found the prospect of life in Europe more amenable than in America and eventually settled in Brussels permanently. He and Englert resumed their investigations.

They were unsettled by their discovery that in their model the Goldstone boson disappeared when they allowed interactions to have infinite extent. Infinite-range forces in infinitely long chains of particles are beyond visualisation. Results that emerge from the mathematics might be artefacts. How

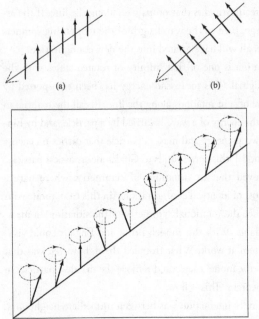

Figure 6.1: **Line of spinning atomic magnets.** (a) Aligned in a ground state. (b) Aligned at a different orientation but otherwise identical energy. The two examples are simply related by a rotation of perspective. Rotating from one to another is analogous to mode G in figure 5.2. (c) A spin wave with energy is analogous to the radial motion mode H in figure 5.2.

many have been plagued by their children who insist that infinity plus one must be larger than infinity? Infinity is a concept in mathematics, but introducing infinity into physics can be fraught with pitfalls. Goldstone's theorem seemed to say there had to be a massless particle, no *if*s or *but*s, and Brout and Englert held off on publishing their work, convinced there was something wrong with their analysis.[2]

By the spring of 1964, unable to find any error, they decided to put their reputations on the line and publish their findings. Like Goldstone earlier, and like Ginzburg and Landau before him, they supposed there is some field acting on particles. Unlike those previous authors, however, they made no hypothesis about its specific form except for the common assumption that the vacuum is more stable when the field is present than when it is absent. They investigated what happens when a photon interacts with such a field and confirmed both that the photon acquires mass and that gauge invariance survives—in effect, becomes hidden. In so doing, Brout and Englert were the first to demonstrate the *mass mechanism* in relativistic quantum field theory.

They wrote a paper of about a thousand words and twelve equations and submitted it for publication to *Physical Review Letters* in New York. It arrived in the editorial office on 26 June 1964. At this stage Higgs had yet to see the paper by Gilbert that inspired his own epiphany, and his first paper on the topic was still a month away.

There was a postal strike in the United Kingdom, so even had Brout and Englert sent out advance manuscripts and included particle physicists on their mailing list, the news would not have reached Higgs. In the meantime, the editor of *Physical Review Letters* sent Brout and Englert's paper in confidence to Nambu for evaluation. Nambu was impressed and recommended publication, and their paper duly appeared in the issue of 31 August 1964.[3]

FATE AND HIGGS' SECOND PAPER

Higgs' first paper, which the editor of the European journal *Physics Letters* had received on 27 July, had been accepted for publication and appeared on 15 September. Meanwhile, his second paper had arrived at the offices of *Physical Review Letters* coincidentally on the same day that the paper by Brout and Englert was published. That Higgs' paper ended up there by a circuitous route, and a full month after he had completed his draft, illustrates the general lack of interest in quantum field theory among the wider community of physicists and their low-key reaction to what Higgs had done.

His first paper had demonstrated a mathematical loophole in the proof of Goldstone's theorem. This was, of course, profoundly significant as it released a blockage in the application of spontaneous symmetry breaking to relativistic quantum field theories. However, put starkly, that was all it did. Higgs had demonstrated that the theorem fell once gauge invariant field theory, such as QED, was included, but he didn't expand on how the evasion works, nor did he illustrate its implications for QED. By Friday 24 July, not only had Higgs mailed off his first paper to the editor, but he had also understood the nature of the evasion and its effects on the photon of QED. This was the stimulus for his second paper.

When you spend a long time trying to solve a difficult problem in a highly competitive field such as theoretical physics, and finally succeed, often what has seemed impenetrable to you for ages suddenly appears blindingly obvious. A natural reaction is then to wonder if others have already discovered this, unknown to you, or even whether the answer has been in the literature all along, unnoticed. Higgs now set about this nerve-racking quest and "spent a few days searching the literature to check whether it had been done before".

He thought that if anyone already knew of this mathematical device, it was most likely to have been Julian Schwinger. Higgs checked Schwinger's work carefully and satisfied himself that Schwinger had not noticed that hiding gauge symmetry this way could generate a photon mass. He checked the papers of other experts to see if any had developed new lines of research after reading Schwinger's 1962 paper in which he had raised the question about gauge invariance and the photon mass.[4]

By the end of July, Higgs was satisfied he had discovered something truly novel and sent his follow-up manuscript to the editor of *Physics Letters*. The editor was based at CERN, in the theoretical physics group, and consulted members there about Higgs' new paper. None of them could see the point of what Higgs had done, and the editor rejected the manuscript.

His first paper had been essentially mathematical, showing that a previously accepted theorem could be bypassed. That argument was clearly correct and publishable. The subsequent paper gave a physical example to illustrate the point made in his first paper. The European particle theory scene at that time was focused on trying to build theories of the strong nuclear force and particles with techniques known as *S-matrix theory*, *Regge theory*, and *bootstraps*. The perspective of many, typified by those at CERN, was that although the mathematical proof of Higgs' first paper was interesting, it related to a field of theoretical physics that seemed to have little to offer to the phenomenology of the strong nuclear interaction, and his new paper contained nothing that was not already implicit in his first paper. Quantum field theory had fallen out of fashion in Europe.

Higgs knew that theorists in the United States were more tuned in to quantum field theory and that the American journal *Physical Review Letters* still published papers in that field. He decided that his original draft had been "short on sales talk", and so he added two extra paragraphs with comments about application of spontaneously broken symmetry to the emerging families of strongly interacting particles. Today we can see that these two paragraphs, which appear to be little more than giving a nod to the strong interaction caucus, are a sideshow to the essence of his paper, which is all in the original version that ended at the close of the paragraph after equation 4. Fatefully, the revised version included equation 2b describing the massive boson, although he did not draw any special attention to this.

The "three weeks" of his life "for which [Higgs] is known" would have been even less had he not added those "practical consequences of the theory. That took [a] week and included the [Higgs] boson". On the other hand, it was the initial rejection of his second paper that led Higgs to include the feature that helped set him apart from the pack. From conception to birth, Higgs' inclusion of the boson had come in the interregnum between his first paper and the revision of his second one. He recalled, "The amount of labour was rather small, and I am staggered by the consequences."[5]

The editor of *Physical Review Letters* sent the paper to be refereed by Nambu, who recommended that it be published but invited Higgs to add a comment to the paper by Brout and Englert. Apart from the journal's editor, Nambu at that time was the only scientist to have seen their paper. Higgs eventually received a copy of it late in September.

Brout, Englert, and Higgs had independently found the way to eliminate unwanted massless Goldstone bosons and in the process generate mass for the photon. When Higgs visited Imperial College to talk about his work in October, he discovered that three more people had also come to similar conclusions.

GURALNIK, HAGEN, AND KIBBLE

In 1964 Gerald Guralnik was a twenty-eight-year-old theoretical physics postdoctoral assistant who had studied under Walter Gilbert. Guralnik and his fellow American colleague Carl Hagen were at London's Imperial College, working with faculty professor Tom Kibble. Kibble had broad interests and was an expert in quantum field theory, which was an exciting subject for him; he saw its problems as challenges to be solved, not avoided. According to Wikipedia the trio "co-discovered the Higgs mechanism and Higgs boson" and were "controversially" not included in the Nobel Prize. While it is widely accepted that they independently discovered the mechanism, they published nothing until two months after Higgs had made his breakthrough and more than three months after Brout and Englert had completed their own paper. This makes their omission from the Nobel Prize, which in any event can be awarded to a maximum of three individuals, hardly "controversial". As for the massive Higgs boson, there is no mention of it in their paper.[6]

Although they lost the race, Guralnik at least seems to have started the course quite early on. His journey suggests that all roads lead to Harvard, Goldstone, and Schwinger. The story begins back in 1962 when he was a student of Gilbert at Harvard, where Schwinger was the guru of field theory. It was around this time that Schwinger published his paper about gauge invariance and the possibility of a photon acquiring mass. This was also around the time when Goldstone, who was on a visiting fellowship at Harvard, talked about this very topic to Schwinger. The idea must have been in the air at Harvard, as Gilbert began to investigate a theory where a photon interacted with a spinless boson. He discovered that the photon could gain mass, and he talked to his student Guralnik about this.

The following year, 1963, Guralnik moved to Imperial College, where he had long discussions with Kibble about the failure of Goldstone's theorem in superconductivity—the same observation that had inspired Anderson's proposal, though they were unaware of Anderson's work at that time. Sometime in 1963, Guralnik realised that if an electromagnetic field was included in Goldstone's model, the unwanted Goldstone boson would disappear, and the photon could become massive. There is no certain record of how distinct this was from what Gilbert had already understood, but in any event Guralnik felt that his own analysis was not watertight, and it was not until 1964—when Hagen joined him at Imperial—that their discussions with Kibble finally bore fruit.

Even so, by the summer of 1964, when Higgs suddenly had his insight and within days produced his papers, it seems that the Imperial trio were still in the dark. Guralnik visited his mentor Walter Gilbert, who was at a summer school in Italy. This was within weeks of Gilbert having made his intervention on avoiding Goldstone's theorem that had triggered Higgs' success. That Gilbert did not react excitedly to Guralnik at this time suggests that the Imperial team were not as advanced as some memories decades later believed. After all, once one saw the signpost, the journey was not long— Higgs completed his proof "within forty-eight hours". Had Guralnik been anywhere near completing the course, Gilbert likely would have urged him on to the finishing line. There is little doubt that when Higgs produced his seminal papers at the end of July, the Imperial College team were still unable to see a way through the labyrinth.

The British postal strike—which had delayed Higgs' knowledge of Brout and Englert and enabled him to make his own independent discovery—now dealt the Imperial trio a cruel blow. The strike stopped at the end of July, leaving mountains of mail to be delivered. Sometime later that summer, Kibble discovered in the backlog that eventually reached the Imperial College's theoretical physics department "three papers, one by Robert Brout and François Englert, and two by Peter Higgs", who had all discovered how a gauge boson could become massive.[7]

The Imperial team's mathematical arguments, in their opinion at least, were more rigorous than those in the two papers that had scooped them. Guralnik later claimed that, partly because of this, "we did not take these papers seriously when Kibble found them". They wrote up a summary of their own ideas and mailed the paper to *Physical Review Letters*, where the editor in New York received it on 12 October. It is not clear whether this submission took place before or after the date when Higgs first learned of their work, which was 5 October, the day when he visited Imperial College to give a seminar about his own breakthrough.[8]

While the claim that Guralnik, Hagen, and Kibble independently discovered the *Higgs mechanism*—the means of purging Goldstone's massless boson whereby the gauge field photon acquires mass—has merit, there is no mention of the massive *Higgs boson* in their work. Like Brout and Englert, and indeed Higgs too, their goal was to remove the unwanted massless Goldstone boson. Although their mathematical analysis was in some ways more rigorous than that of their competitors, it had a deficiency in one respect: they removed some unnecessary ingredients. This helped them achieve their goal but had an unintended consequence: the significance of what would have been the Higgs boson was obscured.

The paper by Guralnik, Hagen, and Kibble includes an equation that might have led them to the Higgs boson, but the mathematical route they had chosen unwittingly closed off this destination. The result of their modification meant their equation revealed a mere shadow of the real thing: their boson appears to be massless. Nature has no place for *any* massless scalar boson, and the trio dismissed this particle as "merely a passive spectator, which decouples from the rest"—in effect, as a quirk of the mathematics that has no significance for the physics. Any claim to have co-discovered the Higgs boson went there and then.

A DEAFENING SILENCE

Initially few took notice. There was no hint that these papers, by Brout and Englert and by Higgs, or the echo by Guralnik, Hagen, and Kibble, heralded the start of a revolution that would unearth the origin of structure in the material world of atoms and molecules and explain the long timescales of evolution thanks to the slow-burning sun, let alone that half a century would pass before the full implications were revealed.

The breakthrough had been inspired by the phenomenon of superconductivity, but the sextet of theorists all realized that the mechanism for generating mass could have a wide range of applications. What was good for superconductivity would work for any medium where symmetry and asymmetry are delicately balanced. So was born the idea of an all-pervading field, today known as the *Higgs field*, in which particles such as photons can gain mass. In 1964 this field was just a theoretical possibility—after all, the photon in practice is massless. Or at least it is massless in much of our experience, but not always, as superconductivity and its behaviour in plasma had demonstrated.

Suppose that we, and everything, are immersed in some omnipresent ether which is transparent to the photons of light but opaque to all other basic particles and tips the scales from unstable symmetry to more stable asymmetry. Being transparent to photons is why these bundles of light remain massless in normal experience, and why attempts in the nineteenth century to detect an ether using beams of light failed. Other fundamental particles are influenced by the field as they flow through it, however, which gives them the property that we call mass.[9]

This was a seductive mathematical theory, but that is all it was: a theory. Among the six, Higgs alone would draw attention to an experimentally testable consequence: existence of a massive particle—the Higgs boson—which can be used to establish the reality of this omnipresent field. That insight put Higgs at centre stage.

The idea leading to the Higgs boson is like something quite familiar: the nature of light as an electromagnetic wave. A compass needle will point towards the north magnetic pole as it senses the presence of the Earth's magnetic field. Add energy to that field in the form of, say, heat, and it can stimulate an electromagnetic wave—a radio wave, or a sunbeam—that consists of bundles of photons: massless particles of light. A similar idea applies to the Higgs field: add energy, and Higgs bosons—the analogues of the photons—will emerge.

The Higgs field is everywhere. Unlike a light, you cannot switch it off. As an analogy, imagine space as an infinitely deep placid lake, whose surface is so smooth that we are unaware of it in everyday affairs. Supply energy, however, and waves form. In the real universe, these ripples, which herald the Higgs boson, are the telltale signs of that profound, all-pervading stuff: the Higgs field.

Reaction to the breakthrough by the Gang of Six was slow and muted. Higgs recalled: "I talked about my 1964 work twice in Cambridge. The first was only a few months later, in autumn 1964 or the beginning of 1965, and they didn't believe in that sort of 'nonsense' so didn't take any notice." By 1966, however, the Cambridge group realised that Higgs was on to something, and "they invited me back to tell them the same story again". Higgs was slightly embarrassed during the first Cambridge seminar when he realised that the person who had come in slightly late and was settled in at the back of the lecture room, rather isolated from the rest of the group, was Jeffrey Goldstone. Higgs said to the organisers, "I don't know why you people have invited *me* to give this talk; Jeffrey Goldstone knows a lot of these things much better than I do and he's already in Cambridge."[10]

An irony is that it was never really Higgs' boson. Recall the model of unstable symmetry that Ginzburg and Landau, then Goldstone, and now Higgs had used. This supposed that there is some field of influence whose potential energy varied like the shape of a Mexican hat or the base of a wine bottle—a central peak surrounded by a circular valley. Jeffrey Goldstone had used this picture back in 1961 and, if one imagines this as a real construct as in a physical wine bottle, identified two ways a ball might roll after falling from the unstable equilibrium atop the central peak. One possible outcome was that the ball rolls around the base of the valley, the other that it oscillates radially up and down the valley's walls. When translated back into the language of quantum field theory, the first of these corresponds to the existence of a massless boson—the so-called Goldstone boson—and the second to a massive particle, which I shall refer to as Goldstone's other boson. This other boson is the one that today is named after Higgs—recall figure 5.2 on page 79.

Everyone's attention had focused on the first of these, Goldstone's massless boson, which the maths required but which nature seemed to disavow. This massless particle was seemingly the unwanted consequence of this model of spontaneous symmetry breaking, at least until Higgs and the rest of the Gang of Six showed that in the presence of a long-range field like the electromagnetic field this mode is transformed. They also found the profound consequence of this remodelling: the carrier of the long-range field—the photon—gains mass.

Without doubt they had found the way to resolve the paradox of Goldstone's massless boson, and in so doing found a wonderful mechanism for generating mass. In this mathematical process, Goldstone's second boson—the one with mass—had played no direct role. Higgs alone showed how it could be key to establishing the physical reality of the whole enterprise.

An axiom in science is that however elegant a mathematical theory may be, its value is limited if nature does not read it. The question that Higgs effectively addressed was: Is this just a clever piece of mathematics or does nature really work this way? That electromagnetic fields exist was not in doubt, but is there really some other energy field whose presence stabilises the vacuum? Higgs understood that if there really is such a field, then the massive boson is its herald.

Higgs now prepared a third paper, whose purpose would be to establish the mathematical consistency of his theory.[11] It would be in this paper that Higgs fortuitously showed how to establish the presence of what he called the "massive spinless boson" and to verify that the mass mechanism is indeed a natural phenomenon, not a mere mathematical curiosity.

CHAPTER 7

BIRTH OF A BOSON

LIVING IN LONDON in the 1950s, Higgs had become interested in general relativity and attempts to build a consistent quantum theory of gravity. It was a highly specialised, arcane activity, and to some degree it still is, where progress has been at a snail's pace compared to advances in the rest of particle physics. Previously, he had written three papers on quantum field theory, which had been all but ignored; one of them was cited on three occasions, one paper was cited once, and the other was cited not at all.[1] In 1958, he turned to general relativity and produced two papers which created some interest in this highly specialised and still relatively small field. The main consequence of this for Higgs' development as a theoretical physicist was that it introduced him to subtle issues of gauge symmetry in general relativity. This helped sharpen his interest and intuition in gauge symmetry and in symmetries more generally.

One of the foremost in the field of quantum gravity research at that time was Bryce de Witt, a tall, slim American theorist who had adopted his mother's name of de Witt instead of the patronymic Seligman after experiencing anti-Semitism in Europe. In 1957 he became professor at the University of North Carolina at Chapel Hill (UNC) and head of the grandly named Institute of Field Physics.

Higgs, meanwhile, had been refereeing papers on general relativity, which brought him to de Witt's attention as a kindred spirit. De Witt had taken note of one of Higgs' papers on constraints that must be satisfied when building quantum theories of gravity. Paul Dirac had produced two fundamental papers on this topic, and Higgs had come up with an alternative approach. Higgs regarded this arcane piece of mathematics as insubstantial, but as de Witt kindly remarked, "Even trivial things have to be said for the first time."[2] In 1963, de Witt invited Higgs to visit Chapel Hill the following academic year, from September 1964 to summer 1965. This invitation was extended before Higgs made his breakthrough. At that time he was deep into reading about gauge invariance, and the possibility of discussing this with people at de Witt's institute attracted him. However, Higgs had many commitments at Edinburgh which he couldn't shed easily at short notice. Fortunately, de Witt was happy for Higgs to take up the offer a year later, starting on Monday 7 September 1965.

By the beginning of that year, Higgs had written his two short papers on the mass mechanism. His description of the physics community's reaction as a deafening silence is not quite accurate, for there was some response: outright scepticism. "My brief notes which I published in 1964 were greeted with disbelief. In particular I had a letter from Walter Gilbert who was the author of one of the papers that purported to shut the door on spontaneous symmetry breaking in particle physics, telling me I'd made a mistake somewhere."[3]

Higgs checked his work, found a flaw in Gilbert's letter, and breathed a sigh of relief. A few weeks later, the Imperial College trio—Tom Kibble, Gerry Guralnik, and Carl Hagen—independently reproduced Higgs' mechanism for generating mass. They also exposed a minor misstep in Higgs' work, where he had mistakenly assumed that a certain quantity was independent of time. Fortunately, Higgs' discussion of Goldstone's theorem did not depend on that assumption. Even so, not everyone was convinced that his model was consistent with all the requirements of gauge invariance and Lorentz covariance—in other words, that its implications are the same for all observers, independent of their relative motion. The proof that it is consistent would be technically demanding, but Higgs found the tools he needed in a paper by Italian theorist Bruno Zumino that his student Jack Smith had read during his dissertation on gauge invariance back in 1961.[4] Higgs was sure he could extend Zumino's arguments and thereby establish the theoretical validity of his model.

Higgs decided to develop this logic and, if successful, present the proofs in a larger paper. He didn't do it right away because he was teaching a lot during the first half of 1965. By the time he and Jody set off for America in August that year, Higgs had a draft ready in his head, but he didn't start writing until he had settled in North Carolina. "De Witt thought I was going to work on quantum gravity. In fact, I wasn't. [By 1965] I had something which was to be far more important."[5]

1966: NORTH CAROLINA

Having married at age thirty-four in September 1963 and then suffered hepatitis during the spring of 1964, Peter Higgs hoped to start a family and had planned for their first child to be born "on the NHS" in Scotland before they flew to the United States.[6] "Unfortunately, we were naïve, and it didn't happen when it should." Their son Christopher was conceived a month too late and was expected to be born at the start of October. Higgs, meanwhile, was due to be in Chapel Hill by the first Monday in September—which ironically in American parlance is Labor Day. In those days, airline policy was not to carry pregnant women less than six weeks before the predicted date of birth. In Jody's case this meant she would have to travel before the middle of August, nearly a month before they were due in North Carolina.

She and Peter flew the Atlantic to New York on the last possible day. They spent a couple of nights there, to relax and acclimatise, though for a heavily pregnant woman at the height of a hot and humid East Coast summer it wasn't very pleasant. From New York they flew to Chicago's O'Hare airport, where they were met by Jody's parents, and drove to the family home in Urbana, Illinois, about 150 miles south of Chicago.

This was Higgs' first time in the United States. It was also his introduction to Jody's extended family. His in-laws were strongly religious, which created some delicate problems for the atheist Higgs. Come Sunday, all the

Williamson clan prepared for church. As Peter was on display, Jody's father explained that it would be hard for him if Peter was not present; Higgs decided to forgo his principles for the sake of family harmony.

By chance, the Williamson family home was almost back-to-back with physicist Dave Jackson's house in the next street. Jackson, who knew Higgs from the Scottish Universities Summer School in 1960, threw a party in his and Jody's honour one evening. Among the throng was John Bardeen, the B in the BCS trio who had come up with the explanation of superconductivity that had inspired Nambu and in turn Higgs. On this occasion Higgs and Bardeen had only passing party chat at most. Meanwhile, Higgs' father-in-law was anxious to introduce him to people in the university and asked if anyone was there whose work was in any way related to what he'd been doing. Higgs recalled, "I rashly said, the theory I've been doing in particle physics derives ultimately from the model on theory of superconductivity by Bardeen et al. So, he promptly got in touch with his golfing partner who was the dean of science and arranged a lunch at which I met John Bardeen at length. It was a bit intimidating for me as I was quite in awe of the great man."[7]

At the start of September Higgs had to be in North Carolina, so he left his heavily pregnant wife with her parents and set off by car for Chapel Hill, eight hundred miles away. The journey of two days showed him a cross-section of America. The first half of the trip was through the relatively flat industrialised states of Indiana and Ohio before climbing above 1,000 metres as he passed through West Virginia, a beautiful, rustic state contained completely within the Appalachian Mountains.

This trip also exposed Higgs to the vast inequalities between the living conditions of well-to-do whites and poor Black labourers in the United States. In the United Kingdom of 1965, people were aware of segregation and political tensions in the United States, the assassination of President Kennedy being still fresh in their memory and the civil rights movement prominent in the news. Nonetheless there remained a popular perception, fed by Hollywood and the can-do spirit of the National Aeronautics and Space Administration (NASA), that the United States was a nation of milk and honey, certainly by comparison with Britain. In reality, of course, there was much poverty in the United States, and with no analogue of Britain's

NHS, America's poor were cut off from specialist medical facilities that the more well-to-do took for granted. While travelling through West Virginia, Higgs had his first sight of the living conditions of an underclass. His year in North Carolina would deepen these experiences and reinforce his political perspective.

Having arrived in New York and spent two weeks in Illinois and two days driving across the industrial Midwest, upon reaching Chapel Hill Higgs felt he was "in the forests of North Carolina". Chapel Hill is named for a chapel that had been built soon after the American Revolution by a crossroads on a hill at the centre of a small settlement. In 1789 the university was founded—it was the first state university in the United States.[8] Two centuries later, elegant Georgian buildings of red brick and wooden houses retain a memory of that time.

Higgs found an apartment on East Rosemary Street, parallel to the main street, Franklin Street. It was a typical American wooden two-storey family house, converted into apartments, one on each level. The Higgs family occupied the ground floor with access to the surrounding garden; in the upper half of the house were some students.

An abiding memory for him was the climate when he arrived: "About 89°F and 89 percent humidity. It was not pleasant for somebody used to Edinburgh." Air conditioning—in those days almost unknown back home— made daytime life tolerable. The relative cool of the evenings was idyllic, and Higgs, an inveterate walker, explored the surroundings. The configuration of Chapel Hill remained simple, the university area and downtown consisting of two parallel avenues—Franklin and East Rosemary—with a few connecting cross streets. He soon discovered that walking in Chapel Hill, at least in 1965, was an "un-American activity". He had gone for a stroll along Franklin Street and headed west. At the edge of the town Higgs came across some impressive mansions. As he went past them a police car pulled over to ask why he was walking in the neighbourhood. As Higgs recalled, "when they heard my English accent, they seemed to decide I was a crazy foreigner" and let him continue. Half a mile farther along the road he had left behind the properties with manicured gardens and found himself in a different world, one with lots of single-room run-down shacks housing Black Americans.

On 24 September he was working in the physics department library when he received a phone call. Their son Christopher had arrived a week early, born in the same clinic as Jody, twenty-nine years afterwards. Peter set off on another two-day drive back to Illinois. As soon as Jody was in a state to travel, he drove them all to North Carolina, this time via the Cumberland Gap.

Higgs' commuting between the Midwest and North Carolina had by now accumulated three thousand miles. As soon as the family had settled in Chapel Hill, he set to work writing his long paper. His goal was to complete it by Christmas. He worked on it during the day in the university and at home in the evenings.

Autumn was spectacular as the trees in the surrounding forests began to change colour. In Edinburgh at this time of the year, trees turned yellow with hints of brown; in the eastern United States their leaves consumed the rainbow from its median green into all shades of golden orange, red, and deep maroon. The Higgses made expeditions out to the western part of the state towards the Smoky Mountains and marvelled at the slopes of rust-coloured foliage.

Social life was further flung than just the physics department in Chapel Hill. The Higgses' liberal socialist ethos brought them into contact with some of the people who in the previous year had desegregated the local cafés and restaurants. They began to appreciate the racial and political tensions beneath the surface of American life in the 1960s. At UNC, anyone who had pleaded the Fifth Amendment during the McCarthy era was banned from speaking on campus. After the end of the Civil War, North Carolina had grown a very large Black middle class, which was unusual for a southern state. This progress among Black Americans triggered a reaction among the white southern working class. Higgs discovered that the mysterious "gun clubs" he saw around the countryside were cover for the white supremacist Ku Klux Klan, and that North Carolina had the largest number of Ku Klux Klan organisations of any state in the union. As Higgs remarked, "When you took the lid off [in 1965], it wasn't a pleasant place."

DNA OF A BOSON

The paper was harder to complete than he had anticipated.[9] Part of the mathematical complexity was due to problems of gauge invariance—in effect, the mathematical language in which the calculations were made. He decided to do these calculations in the Coulomb gauge, which he knew would be safe.[10] However, it created a challenge, as he had to present the arguments in a way that would satisfy readers for whom the Coulomb gauge was not their primary tongue.

Thanks to gauge invariance his results would be true in any language, but to complete the calculation in Coulomb gauge would be tough. He had good reasons for choosing this particular approach: "I wanted to do this because I hadn't totally understood the workings of all the different gauges. I was still learning. It was lucky because while doing that I produced the predictions of how the 'missing particle' [the Higgs boson] would interact with various other elementary particles in proportion to their masses. It was an unplanned benefit which really paid off."

Higgs here is referring to the unique feature of his paper that set his work apart from the others and led to the sobriquet *Higgs boson*. He had made a bizarre hypothesis: a vacuum devoid of all matter has more energy than if it contains a field. The idea that adding something (the field) to nothing (the vacuum) reduces the total energy sounds incredible, but it led to a range of tantalising implications. He made no hypothesis of what this field consists of, or where it originates. All that was necessary for his theory was that the field affects particles. It can give mass to the photon, as Higgs and also Brout and Englert had pointed out in 1964. The equations in his 1966 paper revealed that this field can also give mass to the basic constituents of matter, such as the electron, and (in modern understanding) to the quarks that are the fundamental units of neutrons and protons.

Most far-reaching in his big paper was his demonstration that the mathematics implied something about the field itself. Under suitable conditions the field can bubble into radiant particles analogous to the photons of an electromagnetic field. These are what we now call Higgs bosons.

A big difference between a photon and the Higgs boson is that it is easy to create a particle of light as it has no mass—a torch (flashlight) battery is sufficient. Contrast the Higgs boson, which—as we now know—is very massive, weighing in at more than an atom of iron. To produce this beast out of the vacuum requires a huge concentration of energy, greater than has existed since the first moments of the Big Bang. This technological challenge was beyond reach for at least forty years after the theory was formulated, but the ideas underlying the Higgs boson increasingly interested the physics community: find evidence for Higgs' boson and you can prove the whole concept.

This inspires two key questions: how might you produce a Higgs boson, and, having done so, how can you be sure that you have identified the real thing and not an imposter? Higgs said nothing about how to produce the boson. What he did—uniquely among the six theorists who had constructed the mass mechanism—was to predict that the boson exists and provide a means to identify it, which is why the boson was later given his name. His hugely significant new finding was that the equations revealed that the relative chance that a Higgs boson decays into disparate varieties of particles depends, among other things, on the magnitude of their masses squared.[11] This is counter to normal experience in quantum physics of particles and of nuclear radioactivity, and in atomic physics. Higgs had in effect found the key diagnostic of the massive boson and thereby a unique way of identifying it and confirming the entire theory.

The irony is that this is not what Higgs had set out to do and, having fortuitously done so, he failed to realise the fact. This is what happened.

His goal had been to establish the mathematical consistency of his theory. This he did by using tools developed by Bruno Zumino, who in Higgs' opinion "deserved a Nobel Prize because he really sorted out [gauge invariance] and I benefited from what he'd done".[12] The resulting "sophisticated" mathematical proof is the culmination of Higgs' paper. He prefaced it, however, with an illustration of the model's consistency by, in his words, "the somewhat unsophisticated device of performing a few [simple] calculations".[13] These included determining how the massive boson interacts with other particles, and even with itself. It would decay into known particles lighter than itself, and Higgs calculated the chance for it to produce a pair of *vector bosons*—massive analogues of the photon like the (still hypothetical) W and Z bosons. The result was the first indication that decays of the Higgs boson should have an unusual dependence on the mass of the produced particles.

With this calculation, Higgs had elevated a piece of mathematics from theoretical possibility to one that could be tested by experiment. Remarkably, he failed to realise its significance. What's more, he remained ignorant of its import for nearly half a century until he heard it remarked upon in a colloquium:

"It was only shortly after the discovery of the Higgs boson [in 2012] that I came to understand that I had actually given them the way to look for it by saying that the amplitude for its decay mode is proportional to the mass of the particle that's going to be produced. I was completely naïve about that."[14]

Naïve but fortunate, for by including that "unsophisticated device" of a few calculations, Higgs had shown the way. The production of large numbers of Higgs bosons and confirmation of their DNA by a statistical survey of their progeny would define the course of Higgs' life and of thousands of scientists and engineers around the world.

Higgs completed his paper just before Christmas and sent it to the editor of *Physical Review* in New York, where it arrived on 27 December. The process of the paper being examined by a referee, getting editorial approval, and then being published meant that it did not appear to general view until the end of May 1966. In the meantime, as was traditional in those days, old-fashioned preprints—mimeographed copies of a typewritten manuscript with handwritten equations—were sent out by authors in advance of formal publication to people on the institute's circulation list. Bryce de Witt's impressively named Institute of Field Physics at UNC was just a modest group occupying a single corridor in the physics building. So Higgs' opus went out along with other preprints of the time to people who were on de Witt's mailing list. They were people who de Witt thought were interested in gravity. Among them was Freeman Dyson at the Institute for Advanced Study in Princeton, New Jersey.

Dyson was an iconoclastic English mathematician who in 1947 had played a key role in establishing the viability of QED as the description of the electromagnetic field and its interactions with matter. By the time of Higgs' work, Dyson had been on the institute's faculty already for two decades and eventually would spend the rest of his life there until his death in 2020 at age ninety-six. During his career, Dyson built a reputation not only as a leading thinker but also as an exceptional writer about science. In his seventy years in physics at Princeton, there was hardly a single theoretical physicist of note whom Dyson did not meet and influence. His judgement on what was good science was widely respected, so when Higgs received a letter from Dyson in the new year saying he had enjoyed reading the paper, which had "helped him understand some things he had been very puzzled about for a long time", Higgs had the first confirmation that his work had real significance.[15]

Dyson's letter included an invitation for Higgs to visit Princeton and talk about his paper. Higgs agreed to come in the spring, as he didn't want to travel up the East Coast on an extended trip with his wife and young baby in the winter. As events turned out, this was a wise decision, as the winter of 1966 was to become infamous.

There were no expectations of what was to come in the ambient conditions of North Carolina, where winter was usually pleasant—"like a good Edinburgh summer". The typical winter temperature was 70°F, but 1966 turned out to be an exception where an Edinburgh winter in comparison might have been preferable. Early in the new year Higgs joined his colleague Heinz Pagels, with whom he had become friendly, and flew to New York for the meeting of the American Physical Society, held annually in January. Higgs saw some of the leading American physicists for the first time, but the most memorable thing about the visit was that a blizzard hit the eastern United States. From 29 to 31 January, more than two metres of snow blanketed upstate New York, with winds over 60 miles per hour.

In New York City conditions were less extreme but airports were closed. Higgs and Pagels were stranded. Pagels' mother lived in a suburb of Philadelphia, about a hundred miles south of New York. As this was on their way home, they took a train to the city. When they alighted, the platforms that extended beyond the canopy of the station were waist deep in snow. They took a local train to the suburbs and stayed with Pagels' mother for two nights. A thaw arrived, which allowed them to take a train to Washington, DC, and then fly to Raleigh, about thirty miles west of Chapel Hill.

The blizzard of 1966 reached as far south as Georgia. It killed large numbers of Black Americans living in wooden shanties, which were unsuitable for that sort of storm. In the unusual conditions, their desperate attempts to keep warm by burning wood and anything combustible set many of the wooden shacks alight, killing the inhabitants.

"YOU'VE DEFINITELY GOT SOMETHING WRONG"

Higgs had accepted Dyson's invitation, agreeing to come up to Princeton, about fifty miles from New York City, as soon as the worst of the winter weather was over. His talk was scheduled for the afternoon of Monday 14 March, so he drove up north over the weekend with Jody and Christopher. He also had an invitation to give a talk at Harvard, in Boston, a further half day's drive north from Princeton.

For a theoretical physicist, being asked to present your work to an audience at the Institute for Advanced Study is like a pianist being invited to perform a concerto at Carnegie Hall. The address—1 Einstein Drive—reflects its standing in the world of intellectual enquiry. The institute was founded in 1930; its mission is the "pursuit of knowledge for its own sake". With no students to teach or supervise, researchers are left to pursue their own goals. For nearly a century this ultimate research institute has attracted the world's leading thinkers; its alumni include Albert Einstein, the mathematician Kurt Gödel, and polymath John von Neumann. Hardly a single leader in the fields of theoretical physics, mathematics, and philosophy has not worked or performed at the institute at some time in their career. In 1966, the director was the former leader of the Manhattan Project, the physicist J. Robert Oppenheimer.

By the time of Higgs' visit, Oppenheimer was gravely ill and so was absent, but Higgs was prepared to face a formidable examination nonetheless. Like any debutante, he was nervous. For Higgs it was a "legendary place because of its associations with Einstein. When I saw the sign for Princeton on the freeway, I had to pull onto the side of the road because I was trembling."[16]

His presentation was scheduled for the late afternoon, immediately after tea, but before tea came the traditional shotgun seminar. The institute's faculty might have no responsibility to students, but they were under great pressure to maintain standards that would satisfy their peers. Each had to be ready to give a technical seminar to the faculty on demand at the weekly shotgun seminar. The format was that all names went into a hat, and the one drawn out had to give a talk to the rest of the members.

On the day of Higgs' visit, the "winner" of the unlucky dip was Freeman Dyson. It was his exposure to Higgs' paper, and his immediate recognition of its importance, that had led to Higgs' invitation, so it was perhaps fitting that it would be Dyson who would precede Higgs in that week's event.

As well as being a remarkably gifted theorist, Dyson was an entertaining writer and speaker. He had clearly prepared a talk for the statistical likelihood that he would eventually be called upon to perform, but to Higgs it appeared to be a spontaneous tour de force on the question of why matter exists in bulk. Dyson considered the basic particles forming atoms and molecules, all held together by finely tuned forces. The same atoms that make water liquid at room temperature convert into steam when boiled or solidify in the cold of an arctic winter. This is very familiar, but the physical principles and the dynamics of phase change are complex. The physics of phase change was about to become an intense area of research in theoretical physics, in which Higgs' friend Michael Fisher would play a role. Dyson's talk was a discursive overview of the problems. The audience applauded, everyone retired for a cup of tea, and Higgs prepared to give his own presentation, in effect on how those particles in Dyson's talk become massive and have the chance to form the structures that had so stimulated Dyson.

Higgs' nerves were not helped when, immediately before his talk, Klaus Hepp—a German physicist whom Higgs had met at the Scottish Universities Summer School in 1960—told him that a paper was about to be published by three distinguished scientists which claimed Higgs' theory was flawed. Higgs entered the hall with Hepp's "encouragement" ringing in his ears: "You've definitely got something wrong."

Higgs presented his arguments carefully. Dyson was especially impressed. Fortunately, as it would turn out, it was the trio who were wrong. One of the people present at Higgs' talk was Arthur Wightman, arguably the leading expert on the formal mathematical foundations of field theory. He was convinced by Higgs' presentation and contacted the trio to inform them that they should check their calculations.

After his lecture at Princeton, Higgs travelled north to Harvard for his scheduled talk there. Before his arrival at Harvard there was intense scepticism, led by the redoubtable Sidney Coleman. Coleman was one of the most brilliant theoretical physicists of the twentieth century never to win a Nobel Prize. He had a natural cutting wit, like Oscar Wilde, and was intensely competitive. Famous for working until the small hours and then sleeping in until late morning, he accepted his professorship at Harvard on condition that he would not be required to lecture at nine a.m. As he explained, "I can't stay up that late."

Coleman's intellectual jousts with Sheldon Glashow are also legendary. I was present on one such occasion at a summer school in Erice, Sicily.

Glashow had just completed a lecture and was taking questions. Coleman, meanwhile, was due to lecture next and had gone to the bathroom. He returned to hear a heated argument raging over some abstruse point of physics. As Coleman entered the hall, he called out like a precocious child, "I know the answer! I know the answer!" As everyone turned towards him and fell silent, he continued: "Now, what was the question?" I no longer remember the question, let alone his answer, but I do recall clearly that everyone listened intently as the guru spoke.

Coleman possessed huge intelligence backed up with vast knowledge and powerful intuition about the physical universe. Like many theorists, he had spent many hours trying to circumvent Goldstone's theorem. In the process he had discovered what became known as *no-go theorems*, in effect, proofs that certain phenomena were fundamentally impossible. Convinced that Goldstone's theorem was correct and inviolate, Coleman was unequivocal when told about Higgs' presence in the United States and his willingness to give a seminar at Harvard on his apparent breakthrough. Higgs learned later that Coleman reacted with anticipation of some fun: "Oh, this idiot thinks he can get around the Goldstone theorem, does he? We'll deal with him."[17]

Instead, Higgs dealt with them. He survived the questions, and even Coleman admitted that Higgs had indeed found the loophole in Goldstone's and Nambu's construction and moved theoretical physics forwards. As for its relevance for nature, however, doubts remained. The discovery that his solution caused the photon to become massive was intriguing but also worrying. Other than in some specific cases, such as plasma, in practice the photon remains massless. Higgs seemed to have found a mathematical trick whose relevance for physics remained obscure.

In 1966 he tried to make contact between his theory and the real world. The saga had begun with Nambu's attempt to understand the strong nuclear force, which had successfully explained the existence of the pion. Beyond that, however, a robust theory of the strong force remained to be found. Higgs now decided to see if his mechanism could provide the answer.

CHAPTER 8

"PETER—YOU'RE FAMOUS!"

OR THREE YEARS after the appearance of the Gang of Six's original papers, the sextet's ideas were largely ignored. Of those that noticed the breakthrough, not everyone reacted positively. One example was Steven Weinberg, who in 1961 had worked with Goldstone in tightening the mathematical basis for his theorem. Weinberg had developed a new theory of the strong interaction—the force that binds atomic nuclei—by building on Nambu's ideas of hidden symmetry. The fundamental basis of Weinberg's approach was that pions are Goldstone bosons, and his theory of the strong interactions at low energies was so successful that when in 1964 Higgs' first paper appeared, Weinberg thought, "Well, that's nice; he's found a way of getting rid of Goldstone bosons but now I've become convinced that the pion is one." Far from being unwanted, the Goldstone boson had turned up at centre stage in Weinberg's new theory.[1]

Weinberg's theory could not be the complete answer, however, for the explosion of discoveries at the new accelerators had revealed the existence of short-lived particles about five times as heavy as a pion. Named *rho mesons*, they occur with either the standard amounts of positive or negative electric charge or with none. The electrically neutral version had properties that made it appear like a massive analogue of the photon, but with affinity to the strong interaction. So, in addition to pions there are rho mesons that experience the strong nuclear force. All of these particles would have to be accounted for in any explanation of how atomic nuclei exist and are bound together. Higgs tried the obvious route of combining his novel ideas with Nambu's original approach. This opened the prospect of building a gauge theory of the strong interactions, where these rho mesons acquired their mass through the mechanism discovered by the Gang of Six. Unfortunately, Higgs found that the pattern of particles spawned by his mathematics looked nothing like those being discovered in experiments. One example is the irony that his 1964 success in giving mass to the gauge boson—the photon, or in this latest idea, the rho meson—had no role for the pion, whose emergence as a Goldstone boson in Nambu's original theory of the strong nuclear force had motivated the entire enterprise. The algebra also seemed to need a massless electrically neutral partner to the rho meson. This could not be the photon, as it is blind to the strong force. There is a partner to the rho meson, known as the *omega meson*, but like the rho, it is massive. There was no way to make all the pieces fit. By the summer of 1967, Higgs gave up.

On 25 August of that year, Higgs went to the United States to attend a physics conference in Rochester, New York. He flew from Scotland with Icelandic Airlines via Keflavik, where he was delayed, and didn't arrive at Kennedy airport until nearly midnight. After a taxi, a train, and a second taxi ride, he finally arrived at Brookhaven National Laboratory on Long Island at about two thirty in the morning. He managed to get some sleep, but his internal clock told him it was already breakfast time back home, and he was soon in the laboratory. As Higgs recalled, "I joined a discussion which included Steven Weinberg and others on how to understand the [strong interactions], or rather how not to. I told them how I had failed to do it with spontaneously broken gauge symmetry. [I learned that] Weinberg had been having no success with something similar." Weinberg had no recollection of this meeting, but in any event it seems that both he and Higgs had reached a similar impasse.

That was the end of Higgs' attempt to build on his intellectual break-through. He visited his old friend Michael Fisher, who the previous year had moved to the United States as a professor at Cornell University in Ithaca, New York. From there Higgs went to Rochester for the conference. A chance interaction there with the theorist Ben Lee, who quizzed him about his work, would determine the course of the rest of his life.

A COCKTAIL CONVERSATION

Ben Lee—whose 1964 paper with Abraham Klein had led to Higgs' insight—had realised the significance of Higgs' work. After the Rochester conference, Lee and Higgs met at a cocktail party. "I stood with a plate in one hand and a glass of wine in the other, being interrogated by Ben about my papers." Their conversation was to have a far greater impact than either of them anticipated.

When Higgs met Lee in 1967, his theoretical work on the mass mech-anism had effectively already run its course, and he had begun to draft a paper applying his ideas to the real world. He was seeking evidence for its relevance in the domain of hadrons—particles that respond to the strong interaction, such as protons and neutrons. However, this was "too tough a problem to tackle at the time".[2] Decades later he confessed, "I went the wrong route [in trying to apply it to the strong interaction]. What I tried didn't work. I dithered."[3] Higgs gave up on the paper, unable to improve on what he had already achieved. (The opening page and references of the aborted manuscript, "Spontaneous Symmetry Breaking without Massless Bosons, II" are shown in figure 8.1.) Nonetheless, the concepts in Higgs' trio of published papers were mathematically so compelling that they had grabbed Lee's attention.

Implicitly, the key hypothesis underpinning Higgs' work was that if space is emptied of everything we know, such as matter and electromag-netic and gravitational fields, a ubiquitous essence nonetheless remains. Recall that its unusual feature is that its presence makes the vacuum more stable: if the Higgs field were removed, the vacuum would gain energy and become unstable. Higgs had shown mathematically how interaction of fundamental particles with this field can be the source of their mass and had proved that his hypothesis satisfied the tight constraints of quantum

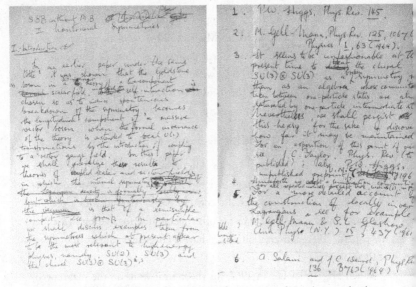

Figure 8.1: **Higgs' unfinished manuscript.** Draft manuscript of Higgs' uncompleted paper "SSB without MB [Spontaneous Symmetry Breaking without Massless Bosons] II: Nontrivial Symmetries".

field theory and special relativity. He explained to Lee an unexpected consequence of the theory: one could prove the existence of this omnipresent field by establishing the existence of the massive particle. Find this particle, and you would establish the theory as reality. Examine the boson forensically, and you might eventually understand how the ubiquitous essence is made.

That was the gist of Higgs and Lee's cocktail discussion. It must have convinced Lee that here was a momentous breakthrough which his own work had in part stimulated, and out of which surely new pathways would open. Higgs himself later reflected, "What I didn't realise was that five years later in 1972 Ben Lee would be the [keynote speaker] at the High Energy Physics conference in Chicago." By then Higgs had given up completely on trying to build on his idea. Others, however, had given it life, and in Chicago Lee devoted his presentation to what had happened in the interim, and to Higgs' contribution especially. The reason for Lee's excitement in 1972 was that in that interim, two outstanding developments had taken place, in each of which Higgs' construct played a pivotal role.

WEINBERG'S MODEL OF LEPTONS

In the summer of 1967, when Higgs had talked with Lee and with Weinberg, hopes of applying the mass mechanism to the strong nuclear forces had reached a dead end. There seemed no obvious use of this mathematical device for particle physics. Weinberg returned to the Massachusetts Institute of Technology (MIT) in Boston where, in the middle of September, he suddenly had a brain wave on how to apply the ideas that Higgs had formulated.

Weinberg recalled that while driving his red Camaro to work, he had the epiphany that he had been "applying the right ideas [but] to the wrong problem". Like Higgs, Weinberg had been trying to make the theory work for the strong nuclear force, until he suddenly realised that the *massless* photon and the still hypothetical massive W boson of the electromagnetic and weak interaction—radioactivity—fitted the theory's implications perfectly.

In this moment of brilliance, Weinberg had found the way nature uses the mass mechanism envisioned by Higgs and the rest of the Gang of Six to orchestrate the melodies of the fundamental forces. Now he needed a concrete model to illustrate his general idea.

He decided to focus on the electron and its electrically neutral sibling, the neutrino. The neutrino responds only to the weak force, and the electron feels both weak and electromagnetic forces, but neither responds to the strong force. Particles that are blind to the strong nuclear force are known collectively as leptons; those that feel it are called hadrons. For Weinberg, restricting his attention to leptons was key; hadrons, such as the proton, the pion, and the rho and omega mesons, were for him a quagmire. Today we know that hadrons are composed of more fundamental seeds known as quarks, but in 1967 this was still controversial. Leptons, however, appear to be fundamental and therefore are a direct entrée to nature's works. Weinberg duly published his idea in November 1967 in a paper titled "A Model of Leptons".[4]

In the paper, Weinberg wrote the equations for a gauge invariant field theory of the electron and neutrino, then introduced masses following Higgs' prescription (he was apparently yet unaware of the rest of the Gang of Six). When he solved the equations, he discovered that they implied the existence of four *gauge bosons*—carriers of the electromagnetic and weak forces. These are a massless photon, two electrically charged massive particles W$^+$ and W$^-$, and a massive neutral particle—the very particle that Glashow had called Z^0. So, from this fundamental starting point of hidden gauge symmetry, Weinberg had discovered the set of particles that Glashow—for different reasons—had come up with in 1961. Glashow's stillborn model had been given life. Later, the irony was not lost on Higgs that Glashow had been at the Scottish Universities Summer School in 1960 and that Higgs, the wine steward, had missed the late-night discussions between Glashow and Veltman about that very model. Had he been present, he might have been diverted from his doomed quest in 1966 to solve the strong interactions and applied his theory to the electromagnetic and weak interactions before Weinberg. As in so much of this saga, this is another "might have been".

When Weinberg drafted his paper, it seems he was aware of only Higgs' work, as "Hagen et al, Brout & Englert" was written in later (see figure 8.2). In his published paper all these works are cited, but Higgs' contribution appears first. Weinberg's paper, which set him on course for the Nobel Prize in 1979, is one of the most influential in theoretical particle physics from the second half of the twentieth century and has since been cited more than ten thousand times. The appearance of Higgs' name in

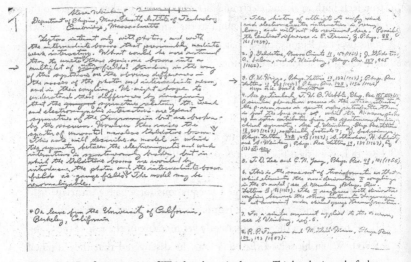

Figure 8.2: **Draft manuscript of Weinberg's seminal paper.** This handwritten draft shows how references to the rest of the Gang of Six were included as an afterthought.

pole position may be a reason why many mistakenly refer to this piece of mathematics as the *Higgs mechanism*. This is a misnomer and unfair to Brout and Englert, who got there first, a fact that Peter Higgs is the first to acknowledge. This impression on priority was reinforced by a typo in a later paper by Weinberg in 1971. In this paper, Higgs' 1964 article that appeared in *Physics Letters* is erroneously attributed to *Physical Review Letters*, and as such appears to chronologically precede Brout and Englert's paper in the latter journal.[5]

At first, it appears that hardly anyone took much notice of Weinberg's paper. As Sidney Coleman later described the response, "Rarely has so great an accomplishment been so widely ignored."[6] One person who did notice it, however, was David Wallace, who was in his first year at Edinburgh University as one of Higgs' research students. As was standard practice, Wallace's first year involved much reading towards a diploma as entrée to a doctoral research project. During this, he "came by chance on [Weinberg's paper] which looked very interesting and of course mentioned Peter's work". Wallace immediately "dashed upstairs" to tell Higgs.[7] He recalls that Higgs' reaction was to be cautious as Weinberg's work was speculative, and above all there was a need to prove that the theory was viable, free of infinities—renormalisable.

Higgs' reaction seems to have been widely shared back then in 1968, for between 1967 and 1971 Weinberg's paper was cited just four times. Then it suddenly burst into prominence. This was due to an event in 1971 that thrust Weinberg's and Higgs' breakthroughs into sharp focus and has defined the direction of particle physics ever since. A young Dutch theorist in Utrecht named Gerard 't Hooft, in his PhD thesis, confirmed that the Higgs mechanism is key to a completely viable theory extending QED to encompass the weak force of radioactivity.[8]

In Edinburgh, meanwhile, Wallace had completed his PhD on other aspects of quantum field theory and embarked on a distinguished career in theoretical physics. Higgs later recalled his reaction in 1968 and agreed, "This, in retrospect, was a mistake—I should have tried it [renormalisation of the theory] with David Wallace!"[9] In Higgs' opinion, Wallace was the best undergraduate to come through Edinburgh in his years there. Even so, he was "reluctant to give a research student, however brilliant, something I could not see through myself. I understood too little" to be able to advise on such an ambitious and technically challenging problem.[10]

Weinberg, having had his inspired insight about the possibility of uniting the electromagnetic and weak forces, speculated that the spontaneous appearance of mass in Higgs' work might be the route to a viable theory of those forces. Today we know that this intuition was correct but, unfortunately for Weinberg, even he was unable to prove that the theory was free of infinities.[11] Given the tour de force that 't Hooft produced, which rested on powerful foundations built by his thesis adviser, Martinus Veltman, and Weinberg's own inability to complete a proof, Higgs' advice to Wallace was probably sound.

THE FLYING DUTCHMEN

The breakthrough that came in 1971 had its origins much earlier, its seeds being sown by Veltman in the years following the famous 1960 Scottish summer school.

In the 1960s, as Higgs' experience illustrates, field theory was out of fashion. Veltman intuitively suspected that this was a mistake. He believed that quantum field theory would be key to the weak interaction, similar to the way that it had successfully described electromagnetic phenomena in the theory of QED. In 1960 at the time of the summer school he had not yet begun this work in earnest. It was not until 1962, when he tried calculating the electric and magnetic response of electrically charged W bosons, that his interest was piqued.

What at first sight appeared to be a simple calculation turned out to be almost intractable, as the flow of electric charge between the W and other particles complicated the accounting. Years later, in 1999, in his speech on receiving the Nobel Prize for the breakthroughs this work seeded, Veltman said he had "up to fifty thousand terms" to calculate in some parts of the algebra. In the complexity of these quantum field theory calculations, several algebraic operations were repeated as if variations on a theme. "Necessity is the mother of invention": Veltman realised this regularity would make this an excellent problem for a computer to solve. Following this insight, he became one of the pioneers of performing symbolic manipulations on computers. This is standard fare today, but Veltman was pioneering it—the first practical computer routine for performing quantum field theory calculations—more than fifty years ago. His great achievement would be to test the viability of extending QED to include the weak interaction.

When in 1967 Weinberg created his model of the weak and electromagnetic interactions, he speculated that thanks to the Higgs mechanism it might be viable—renormalisable—but couldn't prove it. Veltman used his computer programmes to investigate how the presence of a massive W boson led to the unwanted infinities, in the hope of seeing if there was a way to somehow include mass in the equations without ruining the theory. This key and final step was found by his brilliant student Gerard 't Hooft.

Like Higgs in Edinburgh, Veltman in Utrecht gave new students the task of reading and reviewing an area of the scientific literature. He instructed 't Hooft to read about theories with similar mathematical structures to QED but where the gauge bosons carry electric charge. These are known as *Yang Mills theories* after the two theoreticians who first studied them in the 1950s. Yang Mills theories are gauge invariant, so the analogue of the photon is massless but, unlike the normal photon, now has electric charge. Two questions intrigued Veltman: are Yang Mills theories renormalisable and, if so, can their analogues of the photon acquire mass without destroying this property?

Another of Veltman's students, Jan Ubbink, had been given the task of reviewing Brout and Englert's paper, which showed how the photon can acquire a mass when in the presence of a field—the ubiquitous phi-field—with the unusual property of hiding gauge symmetry by its presence making the vacuum more stable. When he heard Ubbink talk about what he had learned from that review, 't Hooft was still a young student. He didn't really understand the arguments, but the central idea that mass could be generated, at least mathematically, stuck in his mind. He told me it "came across as abstract and nothing to do with the real world" and went from his short-term memory into his subconscious.[12]

His good fortune came in the summer of 1970 when he attended a summer school in Corsica dedicated to field theory. The highlight for 't Hooft would be a series of lectures given by Ben Lee. Lee talked about a model of the strong interactions which extended Nambu's ideas about the pion, such that pairs of pions could act together, analogous to Cooper's idea of electrons acting cooperatively in superconductivity. The model was renormalisable, and hidden symmetry played a key role in its construction. As 't Hooft listened to what Lee was saying, memories of Ubbink's talk resurfaced. Years later, Lee remembered the "young Dutch student who looked always pensive and serious".[13]

Lee's lectures showed how hidden symmetry was key to the successful renormalisation of the model. Hidden symmetry had been midwife to the mass mechanism; for 't Hooft, this "strengthened my belief that the [mass] mechanism would show the same features [of renormalisability] for Yang Mills theories". He asked Lee if it would be possible to do the same for such a theory, and Lee replied he "didn't know. He hadn't looked at it!" Lee added that the person most likely to know would be none other than Veltman! This talk with Lee convinced 't Hooft that introducing mass by the Higgs mechanism was the way to make a viable theory of the weak and electromagnetic interactions. He would have to climb a huge mountain to reach that summit, but he was confident in what he would find there.

His confidence was justified, and early in 1971 he finally proved that such theories are viable when the mass of the gauge boson arises through the Higgs mechanism. This news burst into the world at an international conference in Amsterdam in the summer of 1971. Veltman was convenor of a session on field theory and used it to introduce his student to the world. It was probably the most sensational entrée into the field of physics since the arrival in 1905 of the unknown Swiss patent clerk Albert Einstein. A problem that had appeared intractable for more than a decade had been solved by a student.

Weinberg's conjecture that his model of leptons incorporating the Higgs mechanism is renormalisable was now proven to be correct. His paper suddenly became like the Michelin Guide to fundamental physics. Having taken four years to receive just four citations, it now accumulated a thousand within the next twelve months and continued to do so through the next decade and beyond.

Theoretical physicists took note of the remarkable breakthrough founded on the mass mechanism and began to apply the theory and examine its implications. Ben Lee, who with Abraham Klein had inadvertently set on course the events leading to Higgs' breakthrough, had quizzed Higgs about it in 1967, and now through his lectures he had inspired 't Hooft to the denouement of the theory. He was one of the best-placed theorists in the world to understand and develop the new paradigm. After Amsterdam in 1971, the next flagship international conference was scheduled for Chicago, in 1972. Lee was the convenor of the session devoted to this new vista.

CHICAGO 1972

The 1972 convention in Chicago was the biennial major review conference in particle physics, to which every nation would send a representative team of delegates. The keynote summaries of progress since the last conference are given by the leaders in their fields and can determine the direction of research worldwide, no less than Warren Buffett's pronouncements influence investors in the stock market. At Chicago, Lee was excited by 't Hooft's sensational demonstration that the mass mechanism is indeed key to a viable theory marrying electromagnetic and weak interactions. Lee previewed the promising new vistas this opened. The Dutchman's breakthrough was the first in a rush of disparate discoveries in the 1970s that elevated the Higgs boson from a mathematical curiosity to a key piece of physical reality. While 't Hooft was added to the list of people who had discovered this way to generate mass, only one—Higgs—had drawn attention to the boson's role in proving the mechanism's natural reality. This inspired Lee's acclaim.

Higgs described what he suspected happened at Chicago: "Ben Lee must have recalled our [1967] conversation and forgotten the wider provenance of some of the ideas, as in his talk he referred prominently to the 'Higgs' boson [which is justified] and also the 'Higgs field.'" Higgs modestly acknowledged that "Ben Lee plastered my name on everything to do with the concept despite the fact [that] my actual contribution was only a key insight right at the end of the story."

By describing his insight as being at the end of the story, Higgs saw his work as illuminating the contradiction in Nambu and Goldstone's mathematics and thereby ending four years of confusion in theoretical physics. He had not set out to discover a mass mechanism; that had been the unexpected consequence of his labour. A less self-effacing person might better have described this insight as the start of a revolution. History would concur with this view. Had the internet existed in 1972, that would have been the moment #Higgs began to trend.

Peter Higgs had not been in Chicago, however. The first that he knew of Lee's remarkable endorsement was when he met a colleague, Ken Peach, who had just returned from Geneva where at CERN he had heard people talking about the conference. "I was sitting drinking coffee after lunch at the university staff club. Ken came in, spotted me, and said, 'Peter! You're famous!' That was the beginning of hope that this idea might bear fruit."

As more news about the conference crossed the Atlantic, it became clear that mentions of Higgs' name had not been due to Lee alone. Lee had organised a session at the conference in which several theorists described their reactions to 't Hooft and Veltman's work. The presentations included applications of the ideas to possible experiments, logical tests of the theory's consistency, and pedagogic explanations or improvements in the proof of 't Hooft's theorems. The occasion was the result of a flame that 't Hooft and Veltman had lit, but every speaker who mentioned the underlying mass mechanism had uniformly attached Higgs' name to it. If anyone had tried to mount a publicity campaign for Higgs' name to be regarded as the champion of the revolution, the results could hardly have been bettered. The irony, of course, is that Higgs himself remained mostly disconnected from the entire process.

If Higgs had been unaware before that the mass mechanism was key to a viable theory of both weak and electromagnetic forces, he was certainly fully informed after the Chicago conference. I asked him why he didn't do more to apply his theory after his 1966 paper and especially after Lee's citation of his work. His reply was honestly direct:

"Let me be frank: I'm not a very competent theorist when it comes to [field theory] calculations. I struggled to understand how quantum electrodynamics had been renormalised. I never ventured into doing any [highly technical] 'loop calculations'. At that point, although 't Hooft's breakthrough had made the theory that I'd had a hand in seem viable at last, I wasn't really prepared to work on it myself. I struggled with that as it involved mathematics which was new to me. It was the younger generation—those who graduated [with a] PhD in the 1960s—who were far more competent than I. When I tried my hand at doing something, I made a fool of myself. I became a bystander."[14] In a later newspaper interview he put it more directly: "I got left behind by all the technical details and never caught up."[15]

Here Higgs' experiences perhaps epitomise the classic narrative of mathematical genius being an attribute of the young. Dirac made his major contributions in his late twenties, as had Einstein, and 't Hooft's singular breakthrough came at age twenty-four. Higgs had had his "first good idea" at thirty-five, which was relatively old though not especially unusual. Nambu, for example, had been that age when he had his insight about hidden symmetry; Weinberg had been thirty-four when he saw that Higgs' ideas applied to the electroweak interaction; and during his thirties, Veltman had developed the tools with which his student 't Hooft would complete the construct. For Higgs, now age forty-three, however, the baton had already passed to a new generation. Here too, his experience would not be unusual. Veltman, for example, became marginalised as 't Hooft—whose thirtieth birthday was not until 1976—performed computational miracles in quantum field theory. In physics, keeping at the frontier involves the energy of a young athlete, and by their forties few can maintain the pace.

A NEW ARCHITECTURE

In his 1966 paper, Higgs had presented the first identikit of the massive (Higgs) boson, including some unique features that could experimentally validate the theory. By highlighting the cardinal importance of discovering the boson as proof of the theory, Higgs had assured his place in scientific history. This and his two papers of 1964 would amount to a significant fraction of Higgs' lifetime opus of research papers, some nine on molecular physics and another nine on quantum field theory, spread over half a century. Like all but his first paper, which was co-authored with two colleagues, these papers were written by Higgs alone. All but these three would be largely forgotten.

Higgs' research bibliography is like a tidy baseball score of three hits, three runs, no errors. Whereas most careers have more hits, they have no runs—one, perhaps, if they're lucky—and many errors. But while quantity may impress the bean counters, for whom visibility of an institution in the pages of the research literature is regarded as a symbol of transient success and attracts research funds, it is quality that survives and inspires. Salieri had a much larger oeuvre than Mozart, but who cares about him? Quality fills the library of human culture. In 1964 there was a broken link in the foundations of science; it was Higgs who found and repaired it.

Higgs' insight had enabled others to build successful theories of the forces acting in the microcosm, in and around the nuclei of atoms. For the first time the mechanisms behind radioactivity and the cooking of elements in the stars had been incorporated into a grander mathematical theory. This was a theory which, amazingly, could describe the transmutation of nature's fundamental elements not just in ambient conditions on Earth but in the heart of stars and—most exciting and far-reaching in its implications—in the extreme heat of the Big Bang. By 1972 the basis of this Core Theory had been demonstrated for particles like the electron that exist naturally outside atomic nuclei, and by 1976 for *quarks*—the particle seeds of the nuclear protons and neutrons (what Weinberg in 1967 had deemed a quagmire was suddenly clarified). The moniker *Higgs boson* was becoming part of the particle physics lexicon as the capstone of the entire edifice.

Higgs had been there at the start, providing the insights that were to become key to some of the new theory's mathematics, but as experimental discoveries and theoretical advances during the 1970s began to solidify belief in the new Core Theory of particles and forces, Higgs had published no new research for a decade. Now in his forties, he might have thought his salad days were over. Having laid the foundations and mapped the plans for the structures of late-twentieth-century particle physics, he had been slow to adapt to the radical new architecture they inspired. His early work had been in theoretical physics at the periphery of biology; his mathematical strengths were in projective geometry and symmetries. He had written a student paper on helical molecules, and by the time his colleagues at King's had taken photographs of the double helix of DNA, Higgs was in transition to his first love, quantum field theory. He had not studied particle physics at PhD level, and now he felt he was playing catch-up as a new breed of theorists built on his idea. He wrote only one further original research paper, and that not until 1978. It developed mathematical aspects of quantum mechanics in "a spherical geometry", such as might be relevant to a quantum theory of gravity. His interest in the mathematical structures underlying quantum mechanics and field theory, and the search for a fabric beyond that of the Core Theory of particle physics, defined his scholarship. He did not build on his great insight of 1964. From 1966 to 1970, his work was mainly pedagogical, consisting primarily of, as he put it, "occasional seminars" where he "showed how to do things more simply than in published papers".[16] His subsequent impact on a field that would become consumed by the search for the Higgs boson was peripheral.

Instead, as a union leader in the Association of University Teachers, he immersed himself in university politics. The 1960s was a period of student unrest. Higgs, who strongly opposed apartheid in South Africa, was prominent among a group of academics who dissented with the way the principal of the university, Michael Swann, handled things. Higgs clashed with him over the university's investments in that country's companies. Into the 1970s he mounted a campaign to reform Edinburgh University's "rather antiquated constitution", agitating for greater involvement of staff members in running the physics department. His research had dried up, and he felt that to some senior people in the department and university, "I was an embarrassment, frankly."[17]

If Higgs' assessment is right, some in the university were in danger of losing sight of its raison d'être. Students from that era remember Higgs fondly as a fount of all knowledge on quantum field theory and general relativity, and as the intellectual leader of the theoretical physics group. Strikingly, Higgs was always available to students. As for his sparring with the administrative suits, his colleagues by and large seem to have regarded this with admiration and respect.

He was also putting his scientific career before his family, leading to the end of his marriage in the early 1970s. A scientist from the north-eastern United States had visited Edinburgh early in 1970, and during a dinner with Higgs and his wife, Jody, had invited Higgs to visit during the summer vacation. Jody was excited by the prospect of the pair and their now two young sons visiting her parents in Illinois. It would be their first opportunity to see the younger boy, who would be about a year old. In response, Higgs made some encouraging noises and the outlines of what were at that stage no more than a "tentative plan"; Jody, however, believed he had made "a commitment".[18] Then Higgs realized too late that he was contracted to a "hard summer professionally" because three students were completing their theses that summer and, in those days, the rules at Edinburgh University were that a student's research supervisor had to be present to oversee the examination. This was one of the university's "stupid regulations" that Higgs later argued against and managed to have changed. He proposed they all go to the United States for a shorter time, but Jody didn't want to curtail the planned visit. That summer, moreover, the International Conference on High Energy Physics was in Kiev. A member of the British delegation dropped out, and Higgs was offered the place. He said to Jody, "I'll go to Kiev, you and the children go to the United States."[19]

Higgs' primary ambition was to remain in touch with the international thrust of research in theoretical physics, even though he was no longer working at its frontier. Jody and the two children went to the United States for the summer. As Higgs put it, "At that point the marriage died completely."[20] His domestic crisis unfortunately "led to a complete lack of interest" in theoretical physics, though 't Hooft's breakthrough in 1971 "revived [his] interest a little".[21] From March 1972, he and Jody lived separately, though they never divorced.

Although Lee had made Higgs famous, finding the boson remained out of reach. "It looked as if the question would not be answered in my lifetime. In the 1980s, I began to realise that finding the boson might be possible, but the timescales were completely unclear."[22] Nonetheless, pieces of the experimental jigsaw were beginning to emerge. These then began to combine, and within a few years they were giving the first outlines of a coherent picture.

First was the discovery at CERN in 1973 of trails emerging from Glashow's cave that fitted with his assertion that the W bear had a zero-charged Z sibling. These footprints revealed hints of the Z^0—the child of Glashow's 1961 model marrying electromagnetic and weak interactions and of Weinberg's 1967 quantum field theory of the same. Recall that although the electrically charged W and neutral Z bosons were too massive to be produced in experiments at that time, their presence could be inferred indirectly. In particular, the presence of the Z implied that beams of electrically neutral ghostly neutrinos can bounce off matter. This had now been observed in experiments.

Meanwhile, away from the nuclear cave in another region of the particle landscape, new trails led to the discovery of an exotic species of particles possessing a quantum property known as *charm*. This convinced even the most sceptical physicists that theorists had found the golden path to enlightenment. By summer 1976 these charmed particles were confirmed to behave as predicted by the new theory marrying the weak and electromagnetic forces, and proof of their existence completed a pleasing balance between the varieties of fundamental quarks—the seeds of strongly interacting hadrons—and the leptons. The basic ingredients for a viable theory of matter and of weak and electromagnetic forces were in place thanks to the Higgs mechanism. Meanwhile, 't Hooft had shown that this theory gives sensible numerical predictions; the bouncing neutrinos gave indirect support to the reality of the Z (direct observation of the Z and W would remain out of reach for nearly a decade), while the discovery of charm helped complete

Peter Higgs and Gerard 't Hooft, whose independent discovery of the mass mechanism led him to create the theory of quantum flavourdynamics. (Photo: Frank Close, 2012)

a well-crafted, mathematically balanced theory. Key to its construction was that nature reads the mass mechanism named after Higgs.

Science had a beautiful candidate Core Theory. Individual pieces of the construction had been confirmed experimentally, but the pinnacle to all this structure would be the discovery of its key implication: existence of the Higgs boson. In the absence of the boson the construct would remain just a mathematical theory. A decade after Higgs had first drawn attention to the massive boson, ideas on how to establish its reality now began to form.

PART 2

PART 2

CHAPTER 9

THE FIRST DISAPPEARANCE—1976

IN THE SUMMER of 1976, twelve years had passed since Peter Higgs had what he called his one and only "really original idea". After publication of his 1966 paper with its portrait of the boson, Higgs' sole appearance in the scientific literature was in the form of two lectures on the background to his breakthrough, which he gave at a Scottish Universities Summer School in 1973.[1] Peter Higgs' metaphorical ascent of Everest was still largely unnoticed, and most of us were as yet unaware there was even a mountain. The theme of the 1976 Scottish Universities Summer School, held at St Andrews University, was the major experimental breakthrough of the time: the confirmation of charmed particles. The basic pieces of the Core Theory of matter and forces were appearing, and interest in its deeper foundations was beginning to mount. No one knew, of course, that in another two decades the hunt for its crown, the Higgs boson, would consume physicists' attention. Even so, awareness of the significance of the Higgs boson was slowly growing.

I had been active in research for seven years, two of which had been at CERN. I had by now heard of the Higgs boson but had no idea who Higgs was, nor whether he was alive. Although the concept of the boson was out-side my mainstream research, the names of leading theorists in that area were familiar and, in the case of their British members, known to me per-sonally. Higgs was not among them. Initially I assumed that the postulate, which I had begun to hear about during the previous couple of years, must have emerged sometime at the dawn of quantum mechanics, back in the 1930s.

Many pieces of quantum lore, discovered in the theory's infancy, have entered the lexicon of the subject with the name of their original creator attached—for example, Dirac's equation, which describes the electron, named for theoretical physicist Paul Dirac, who had influenced the entire field for many years. I assumed Higgs and his boson also came from that era.

When I was invited to lecture at the 1976 Summer School, it was a pleas-ant surprise to learn that the co-director and opening speaker would be none other than Dr Peter Higgs of Edinburgh University, he of the boson. For the first time I realised Higgs to be a scientist still living in our midst. I was full of expectation, fascinated at the prospect of learning about this latest "must-know" of physics from its creator. Turning the virtual Higgs into reality proved hard, however. As I enrolled for the school, I became aware that col-leagues from Edinburgh were gathered in an agitated conclave. Their theme: Where was Higgs? He hadn't arrived; some personal crisis was preventing him from facing an audience and speaking. It became clear that he would be unable to give the keynote speech, and even that we might spend the entire fortnight of the school waiting for him.

It turned out that Higgs was experiencing a severe bout of depression because his estranged wife, an academic specialising in phonetics, had taken a six-month appointment in the United States and had recently moved there with their two children. Worried that they wouldn't return, Higgs had taken a severe downward turn and couldn't write his lecture. In the end, the trauma incapacitated him to the extent that he never appeared. The school proceeded without him.

A VISIT TO CERN

After missing the summer school, Higgs felt he had to get out of Edinburgh for a while. He asked Nick Kemmer, head of the mathematical physics department, for two months' leave to recover. Almost a year previously he had received an invitation to visit the theory division at CERN, and so in mid-October he took up the offer.

These days we tend to think of CERN—the Conseil Européen pour la Recherche Nucléaire—by association with the Large Hadron Collider and the discovery of the Higgs boson, but the facility in the outskirts of Geneva had been founded in the 1950s as a collaborative research centre of twelve European nations. Originally it comprised a particle accelerator and offices for staff, covering an area akin to that of a moderate industrial site, but the ambitions and the hardware grew. By 1976 CERN was on the way to becoming a world centre of particle physics where the E in its name might more accurately signify *Everyone*; with a smorgasbord of accelerators, the facility now spread over several square miles and straddled the border of Switzerland and France. Vast hangars enclosed the experimental laboratories, and near the main entrance to the site were blocks of offices—a matrix of rectangles containing three storeys of long anonymous identikit corridors. Here was housed a group of theoretical physicists, and perhaps appropriately the first general assessment of how the Higgs boson might be found was a paper by three young CERN theorists: John Ellis, Mary Gaillard, and Dimitri Nanopoulos. It was published in 1976, but Peter Higgs already knew of it via a preliminary manuscript in 1975. The CERN trio's paper signified to Higgs that people were now starting to take his idea seriously. Even so, as Ellis recalled decades later, many at that time saw the mathematics as "a trick to give mass to the W and Z bosons [the carriers of the weak force]. They did not necessarily believe in the [physical reality of the] mechanism and thought that science would come up with a better idea without need for a scalar [Higgs] boson."[2]

In his 1966 paper, Higgs had discussed a surprising amount of phenomenology, including the boson's decay and interactions, which indicated that he was very serious about the particle's reality. Beyond that paper, however, Higgs had not sought to advance his ideas. He later admitted to me, "My tendency [is] to go my own way and be a loner. I never mind what other people think."[3] He made no research collaborations that could have interested others in moving the field forwards. Indeed, except his very first paper in 1951, his entire oeuvre of research consisted of papers written alone.

Nevertheless, during that time at CERN he saw the first plans made for the vast expedition towards discovery of the Higgs boson.

The overwhelming problem was that no one knew where to look. Indeed, the paper by Ellis, Gaillard, and Nanopoulos reminds us how uncertain the whole idea of the Higgs boson still was in 1976. There was as yet no general belief that it could be the panacea to make a viable theory of the weak interaction. In the introduction to their paper the trio admitted that the Higgs boson "may well not exist" and pointed out that a consistent theory could arise from dynamics without need for it, but they did outline a strategy for establishing whether the boson exists.

Their biggest problem was that there was no way to know or to calculate the mass of the hypothesised particle, so they covered the range of masses that might be accessible to experiments (existing or foreseeable) and evaluated the best way to detect the boson. This would depend on how light or heavy the boson turned out to be. If its mass was less than about 10 GeV—roughly ten times the mass of a proton—it would decay into known particles, such as pions, electrons and positrons, or muons. However, if the mass ranged between 10 and 100 GeV, the boson's decay preference would be for heavier particles because the relative chance for the Higgs boson to decay to one variety of particle or another was predicted to be proportional to the masses of those particles' constituent quarks.[4] This implied that the Higgs boson would most likely decay into the new, massive, charmed particles that had been discovered earlier that year. In effect, the CERN theorists were highlighting the property first mentioned in Higgs' 1966 paper—that the eponymous boson distributes its favours in proportion to the mass of its progeny.

This unusual affinity for mass could, they suggested, be used to tell if some newly discovered particle was a Higgs boson or some more conventional particle composed of quarks and antiquarks. The CERN theorists recalled that the heavy charmed quarks had first been sighted in a combination known as *charmonium*, which had been produced when protons collided with matter at high energy.[5] A charmonium particle can decay into an electron and a positron whose total energy equates to the rest energy (mass) of their charmonium parent. In a typical experiment of this sort, there are many electrons and positrons, and the amount of energy they possess is somewhat random. The evidence for the charmonium having been present arises when one value of the total energy of an electron and a positron occurs in many independent measurements; this magnitude identifies the mass—energy at rest—of the parent charmonium. The CERN trio proposed that the spectrum of energies of the electrons and positrons in this experiment should be compared with the analogous spectrum of muons, which are like electrons but 207 times as heavy. A charmonium type of particle would decay pretty much the same in each of these cases; a Higgs boson, by contrast, should have much greater affinity for the heavy muons than for the light electrons, so a very pronounced signal would appear in the muon experiment but not the electron experiment.[6]

Being electrically neutral, the Higgs boson could be produced directly by the annihilation of an electron and a positron in a head-on collision if their combined energies equalled the rest energy—mass—of the boson. Unfortunately, as the Higgs boson was predicted to couple to particles in proportion to their masses, and as the electron and the positron are exceedingly light, the CERN trio judged that the probability of producing the Higgs boson this way "seems negligible". They pointed out that there might be a way of producing it, nonetheless, if the electron-positron annihilation had first produced a massive particle, such as the neutral Z boson. If the Higgs boson was lighter than the Z, which was itself predicted to exist with a huge mass of around 90 GeV, then it might also be produced alongside a Z boson.[7]

After forty-two pages of closely argued analysis, the trio concluded their paper "with an apology to experimentalists, for having no idea what is the mass of the Higgs boson". With a sense of anticlimax, their final words on the issue were "we do not want to encourage big experimental searches for the Higgs boson, but we do feel that people performing experiments vulnerable to the Higgs boson should know how it may turn up".[8]

Such was the state of play early in 1976. Bear in mind that the W and Z bosons, whose existence and masses were confidently predicted, had yet to be experimentally confirmed. Looking to the future, meanwhile, plans were afoot to build gargantuan machines capable of producing the Z by annihilating electrons and positrons, and perhaps opening a route to the Higgs boson—or even one day producing the Higgs boson directly in collisions of protons.

During his visit to CERN in the autumn of 1976, Higgs sat in on a discussion of plans for the first of these: the Large Electron-Positron (LEP) collider, a ring of magnets with a circumference of twenty-seven kilometres in the underground tunnel that today houses the LHC. The idea was that LEP would produce annihilations of electrons and positrons simulating the intense heat of the Big Bang. Director John Adams, whose background was in building proton accelerators, agreed to adopt the project so long as the tunnel would be spacious enough one day to house a proton beam. The planners agreed to make the tunnel suitable for such a behemoth in case the Higgs boson was out of reach of LEP. That far-sighted vision eventually led to the Large Hadron Collider and its momentous achievements.

WILCZEK'S BRAIN WAVE

So much for the theory of detecting the Higgs boson, but how could it be produced in the first place? The paradox is that the theory implied that Higgs bosons prefer to couple to massive particles, not to light ones, yet the commonly available particles that experimentalists were using—such as electrons, positrons, and protons—are among the lightest of all. We now know they are light because they abhor interacting with the Higgs field, and so are very unlikely to produce the Higgs boson.

The breakthrough came the next summer, 1977, at Fermilab in Chicago, thanks to American theorist Frank Wilczek, who later would win the Nobel Prize for his thesis work on the nature of the strong interactions and quarks. His insight was inspired by a sequence of discoveries the previous year, climaxing with one at Fermilab in July 1977.

Contemporaneous with the confirmation of charm in spring 1976 had come the discovery of a heavier sibling of the electron and muon, known as the *tau lepton*. This discovery of a third variety of charged lepton, and a massive one—some four thousand times heavier than an electron—led theorists to anticipate the existence of further heavy quarks, to maintain a symmetry between the emerging pattern of quarks and leptons. These heavy quarks were named *bottom* and *top*. The top quark was eventually found in 1994, but the discovery of the first particle containing a bottom quark came at Fermilab in July 1977. Wilczek was visiting Fermilab that summer, and the focus on heavy quarks stimulated his breakthrough.[9]

Wilczek's expertise in the strong interaction had taught him that when protons collide at high energy, the strong fields gluing quarks to one another inside those protons should be able to fluctuate momentarily into heavy quarks and antiquarks thanks to quantum uncertainty. These transient heavy particles could then mutually annihilate to make a Higgs boson. That last step should in effect be "easy" because, according to the theory, the Higgs boson likes to couple to heavy particles—the greater their mass, the more affinity it has. Wilczek was using the gift of quantum uncertainty to determine a way up the ladder of energy from the light-mass proton to the transient presence of heavyweight quarks, which could then become the portal to the Higgs boson.

The next challenge would be to detect the boson itself. Here Wilczek had his second insight. A Higgs boson can decay to two photons by a process that is in effect the reverse of its creation. First, the Higgs boson decays or fluctuates into heavy quarks and antiquarks, or perhaps into W bosons or Z bosons, which in turn mutually annihilate, yielding two photons. Detecting these photons is technically relatively easy. Experimentalists could measure a spectrum of the photons' energies and then seek correlations among them. If the energy of pairs of photons tends to cluster at some specific value, its magnitude would indicate the mass of a particle that had spawned the photons.

To confirm that this new particle is indeed the Higgs boson would require detecting it in some other decay channels, such as those that Ellis, Gaillard, and Nanopoulos had investigated. But with Wilczek's insight came a novel possibility. The Higgs boson decaying into two Z bosons, each of which in turn could decay into a pair of muons or into an electron and a positron, gave the possibility of the Higgs boson spawning four leptons, consisting of two pairs, one pair at least clustering around the mass of the Z. This would be an unusual way for particles to behave, and forty years later experiments at CERN would indeed use this very pattern to confirm the existence of the Higgs boson, which had first shown up in the two-photon channel. Bear in mind that the Z was not itself discovered until 1983, so the idea of using its decays as a litmus test for the Higgs boson was visionary.

So, by 1977 theorists were already identifying a way both to produce the Higgs boson and to confirm its identity. But there was still no idea of its mass.

BANQUO AND THE BOSON

It is easy to get lost at CERN, both literally and metaphorically, as Higgs was to discover. Three corridors in the labyrinth of offices and experimental laboratories housed the theory division, which in 1976 consisted of about a dozen permanent members plus some fifty research fellows on temporary contracts—young postdoctoral scientists who had won national competitions to be their nation's representative for one or two years. Smaller nations tended to be allocated a single position, larger ones two per year. CERN is like a huge university of advanced science and technology whose members each have a special claim to be there, as the intense competition to win one of the national CERN fellowships in the theory division ensures. There is an extreme form of Darwinian selection at work. You may have been top dog back home—anything less, and you would not have been shortlisted—but now you are among your equals, or superiors, in the European pack. To be noticed and have a chance of surviving, you must take initiative and advertise your wares. This can be a positive and rewarding experience, for if you have a good idea, it is very probable that someone among the galaxy of talent will respond and a research collaboration will develop. That is how progress is made.

Higgs' presence at CERN would—should—have been a paradigm of this process. In fact, he was barely noticed by the laboratory at large, like Banquo at the feast in *Macbeth*. Higgs' absence at the St Andrews summer school was matched that autumn by his near invisibility during his two-month visit to CERN to escape from the pressures of his failed marriage.

Years later, Higgs told me his time at CERN was "not as successful in terms of interaction with people as it could have been because I was completely ignorant about the organisation of the seminar series. . . . I didn't know how the system worked."[10] There are innumerable seminars at CERN, varying from highly specialised technical ones for a tiny group of experts to a weekly colloquium aimed at a wide audience. Speakers for the colloquium are invited from around the world and stay at CERN for a few days, with their presentation as the focus of the visit. Many of the technical seminars are also the result of invitations to outside scientists, as a means to bring them in for consultations. For a scientist who is already at the lab or there on an extended visit, the normal procedure is that if you have something to talk about, you ask the person organising the seminars for a slot. Higgs didn't realise this. His retiring persona waited for an invitation and, as he "only discovered too late", this left him overlooked; no one asked him, and so he didn't speak about his work.

That no one at CERN took the initiative to invite Higgs to speak seems remarkable given that a trio of CERN theorists had just written about how best to pursue the Higgs boson. Why did his presence at CERN not give the stamp of authority to the study by Ellis, Gaillard, and Nanopoulos? Why was the father of what would become a revolution not automatically invited to give a presentation to the scientists at the laboratory? Perhaps in 1976 this was less anomalous than it now seems. The quest for the Higgs boson would eventually occupy CERN and much of world physics, but that would only come later. Higgs himself remained a spectator as other physicists took the initiative forwards.

John Ellis, who later became head of CERN's theory division, was one such person. He played a leading role over the subsequent decades in focusing the attention of CERN and world physics on the quest for the Higgs boson. He remembers the hesitant reaction to the concept and the first discussions as to whether the boson might be found at the proposed LEP. But when I asked him about Higgs' visit to the laboratory, he admitted: "I honestly don't recall Higgs at CERN in 1976 at all."[11]

Higgs' quiet persona may well have contributed to his being overlooked, but that may be only part of the story. By 1976, Higgs had little new to say. His theorem on mass generation and prediction of the Higgs boson was more than ten years old. His singular insight had created the field, but he was now a spectator as others advanced its frontiers. Lee's résumé at the Chicago conference in 1972 had focused attention on the breakthrough by 't Hooft and Veltman and the exciting prospect of a viable theory of the weak force. Their masterpiece had established the new direction for particle physics, and their lectures were not to be missed. Higgs' mechanism was an essential component of 't Hooft's part in the triumph, admittedly, but by 1976 for most people Higgs was just a name, the prefix to a boson, not the name of an instantly recognised celebrity scientist. Similarly, the three younger CERN theorists had charted a possible search strategy for the boson and laid out the challenge to produce it in an experiment.

This lack of awareness of Higgs would be evident three years later, in 1979, at his own university, when, following Kemmer's retirement, the Tait Chair of Theoretical Physics became vacant. Higgs was not even shortlisted for the post. It is telling that a future Nobel laureate was so completely passed over, even though his seminal paper was well known and already starting an international quest for the eponymous boson. (He was, however, awarded a personal chair in 1980.) The sad reality, of course, is that while he was a deep-thinking, well-read scholar who had kept abreast of developments in theoretical physics, he had made no further inroads at the frontier of the subject. For over a decade he had devoted much energy to nuclear disarmament and revitalizing the university.[12]

Over subsequent decades, Higgs' name would become increasingly associated with the quest, to such an extent that the wider public were largely unaware of Brout and Englert, let alone that they had beaten Higgs to the mass breakthrough. For several decades this misconception even permeated much of the physics community. Weinberg's hugely cited model of leptons and his subsequent 1971 paper with its erroneous attribution of Higgs' 1964 paper to *Physical Review Letters*, giving Higgs implicit priority over Brout and Englert's paper in that journal, had become a standard entrée to the field for theorists. Among these were Ellis, Gaillard, and Nanopoulos, whose 1976 paper became a touchstone for experimental physicists. Here too, the erroneous citation of Higgs' paper implying its chronological priority was repeated.[13] Over the following decades, as generations of theoretical and experimental papers appeared, the false chronology spread like a genetic mutation. The moniker *Higgs* became attached to the description of the mechanism by which gauge bosons acquire mass, whereas he was actually among the runners-up in discovering it. It was the significance of the Higgs boson in proving the mechanism, however, that had been mentioned by no one before him.

Higgs was thirty-six years old when he described the boson, and another thirty-six years would yet have to pass after his visit to CERN before the experimental proof would emerge from the LHC. Yet throughout most of this saga, Peter Higgs—the inspiration behind this vast enterprise—would be absent from his own story.

And not just Higgs. Apart from Tom Kibble at Imperial College, who in 1967 produced an extension of the original mathematics and by inspiring Weinberg stimulated the birth of the Core Theory of particles and forces—what is now mundanely called the Standard Model—no one else in the Gang of Six built on their original work of 1964. For years, decades even, the significance of the work seems to have escaped even some of its authors.[14] In the opinion of John Ellis, the "ideas were never sold at the market price".[15]

CHAPTER 10
EVERY JOURNEY BEGINS
WITH A SINGLE STEP

AT CERN IN 1976, Higgs had sat in on the first discussions about a new particle accelerator. Three decades later, this initiative would culminate in the machine known as the Large Hadron Collider (LHC), built to search for Higgs' boson. The first step came soon after this seminal meeting, in 1978. Italian physicist Carlo Rubbia, a bear of a man with huge energy and a forceful personality, convinced Adams and the CERN management to modify an existing machine so that it could collide protons and their antimatter counterparts, antiprotons. His idea was that the annihilation of matter and antimatter, protons and antiprotons, might occasionally produce a W or Z boson in the debris, and in so doing provide the first piece in the new paradigm, en route to the Higgs boson.[1]

Today, forty years later, we can isolate Rubbia's decision to modify an existing machine as the moment when the scale and ambitions of particle physics entered a new era. Two thousand years ago, the philosophers of ancient

Greece had proposed that matter is made of small indivisible pieces which they named atoms. The identity of those basic pieces evolved—especially during the nineteenth and twentieth centuries—but the central question remained the same: what are the basic components of matter? The first signs of change in the focus of this quest had been in 1932 with the discovery of antimatter in the form of the positron, the heavy analogue of the electron known as the muon, and strange particles—forms having no obvious place on Earth, of which we would have remained ignorant but for studying the cosmic rays that bombard the upper atmosphere and building machines to replicate them.

The study of terrestrial matter through the nineteenth century had almost always been conducted by lone experimenters working with small apparatus on a bench top. These scientists were cashing in on a five-billion-year investment: over eons nature sealed its basic pieces into complex structures—crystals, molecules, atoms, and subatomic particles—and human ingenuity was now teasing out their mechanisms.

The first particle accelerators in the 1930s could each fit in a single room. At Cambridge University, this was a disused lecture theatre; at Berkeley in California, an empty building adjacent to the physics department sufficed. Particle accelerators developed further after World War II; by 1960 they were typically a circle of magnets about half a kilometre in circumference, but their application had stayed the same. Typically, intense beams of protons would blast targets made of earthly liquid and solid matter ever more violently to expose their deepest pieces. But when matter is annihilated by antimatter, the obliteration converts their substance into radiant energy, intense heat, in effect a pale imitation of the conditions in the Big Bang. From this mini bang, new forms of matter and antimatter may emerge. Where previously the focus had been on the makeup of matter, now the goal moved to understanding how its basic constituents originated, what exotic varieties these include, and how they evolve into the templates of stable substances. And increasingly the focus would move towards the act of their creation: how that radiant energy coagulated into material particles with mass.

The use of proton-antiproton annihilation to try to produce W and Z bosons not only opened a new stage in particle physics but also revolutionised the engineering of particle accelerators. At CERN, atoms can be ripped apart by intense electric fields and the resulting protons injected into an accelerator, the seven-kilometre-circumference super proton synchrotron. Once inside the accelerator they can be focused together to form a narrow beam and steered by magnets in a circular path. Previously these protons had been smashed into static targets of nuclear material, much of their energy going into recoil of the nucleus and doing relatively little damage. Rubbia had the ingenious idea of storing antiprotons—the antimatter analogue of the proton—and then of guiding this beam of antiprotons in the opposite direction around the ring to smash it head on into the first one, the beam of protons.

First, the antiprotons had to be created in a customised facility, then stored in a near perfect vacuum to avoid premature annihilation, and finally corralled into beams steered by magnetic fields around the circumference of a circle. Antiprotons and protons have the same mass but opposite signs of electrical charge, and so the same magnets can swing the two beams counter-rotating along juxtaposed paths.

If theories of radioactivity were to be believed, W particles occasionally occur deep in atomic nuclei at room temperature and trigger radioactive decays. In that environment they vanish before they can be detected, with the radioactive decay being a remote consequence of their passage. But in the cauldron of the CERN experiment, when protons and antiprotons annihilate, there was planned to be enough energy concentrated at a point to materialise the W and Z particles. Rubbia was confident that if the theoretical predictions were right, out of this fireball the elusive W and Z bosons should emerge. Although the W and Z are highly unstable, they can be detected by surrounding their birthplace with 2,000 tonnes of sophisticated electronic equipment, and the products of their decays captured at the instant of death. Thus would their brief lives be studied and their properties measured and compared with the theory.

Whereas Rubbia's machine was much smaller than the eventual LHC, which in 1980 was but a distant dream, at seven kilometres in circumference and just over two kilometres in diameter the proton-antiproton collider was nonetheless monumental compared to previous attempts to harness and annihilate antimatter. Those earlier devices had collided electrons and positrons after first sending these particles on a lightning-fast 100-metre sprint around a circle. Scaling this up to control bulky protons and antiprotons—each about 2,000 times heavier than an electron—required prodigious effort. This was a new push in Big Science, soon to be matched in scale, at least, by another proton accelerator at Fermilab near Chicago. By 1981 the CERN machine was ready.

The collider was to become a key element in CERN's development from a leading European laboratory with limited successes in frontier particle discoveries to the world-leading centre it is today. During the 1970s, the United States was where the most notable discoveries in particle physics were made. The tau lepton and charmed quark had been discovered at Stanford University's linear electron accelerator, while the first hadron made of bottom quarks was discovered at Fermilab. CERN, to outsiders, appeared to be lagging. It had discovered the neutral weak interaction, where electrically neutral neutrinos bounce off a target in accord with Glashow's original model, and thereby added confidence to the electroweak theory, but the sharpest experimental verification of that also came from the United States.

CERN's main contribution to particle physics, though no one yet knew it, was that it was "inventing the future".[2] That, at least, is how a young scientist working on particle acceleration remembers it. Lyn Evans, a Welshman from Aberdare, had joined CERN on a temporary fellowship when he graduated with his PhD in 1970. CERN was building the Intersecting Storage Rings (ISR), the world's first proton collider. As the ISR used only protons, it needed two separate rings to steer its beams in opposite directions. One ring of magnets guided protons clockwise around a circle while a second ring of magnets, with their poles reversed, steered protons in the opposite direction. Where the rings intersected, the protons collided head on. The ISR ran from 1971 to 1984. The ISR must have produced many particles containing charmed and bottom quarks, but the detectors were not configured to detect particles produced at large angles to the beamlines and thus were blind to them. As a piece of machinery, however, the ISR was a technological triumph both in bringing protons into collision and in developing a means of intensifying the beams by *stochastic cooling*, a technique invented by Dutch engineer Simon van der Meer.

At about the same time as Evans was coming near to the end of his tenure, in 1972, CERN decided to build the Super Proton Synchrotron (SPS), and he was offered a contract to work on its construction. Six years later, he was already a leading accelerator physicist when, in 1978, Rubbia convinced the CERN·Council to modify the SPS, building on experience with the ISR, into a proton-antiproton collider. His idea that the single ring of the existing SPS could in principle swing protons one way and antiprotons along a similar circuit but in the opposite direction was brilliantly simple on paper but technologically a huge challenge.

Evans worked on the design and construction of the collider. By 1981, it was ready to be tested for the first time. He told me how uncertain everyone was about the likelihood of success. "There was just Carlo [Rubbia] and me in the control room in the middle of the night and nobody else. This was for a good reason because we were not sure that it would ever work."[3]

Fortunately, the collider did work, and so began four decades of triumphs in particle physics discoveries and innovation in accelerator design at CERN. During the autumn of 1982 and the spring of 1983, millions of collisions between protons and antiprotons were recorded at the collider. In most of these the debris consisted of known particles, such as pions and photons. Very occasionally, if theory was correct, a W or Z boson should appear transiently among the maelstrom; the task of detecting it from the trails left when it decayed was like looking for the veritable needle in a haystack. Within a few months a handful of examples had been isolated. Data accumulated and were analysed until the team was sufficiently confident enough to go public. On 24 January 1983, the discovery of the W^+ and W^- was announced, and during the first week of June the Z^0 was reported. Rubbia's vision had been rewarded with the discovery of both W and Z particles. Their large masses—the W bosons at about 80 GeV and the Z slightly heavier at 91 GeV—agreed with theoretical predictions. The first pieces of evidence confirming the new theory uniting weak and electromagnetic forces were in place.

A THEORETICAL HINT OF THE HIGGS

For theoretical physicists, the confirmation of W and Z was akin to having climbed the tower of enlightenment to a higher floor, where the elevated perspective inspired new vistas. Theory papers written earlier, based on the assumed reality of those particles, took on a deeper significance. One such paper was by British theorist Chris Llewellyn Smith, a tall, lean former captain of cross-country running at Oxford University, who in 1973 had shown that situations could be imagined in which beams of these novel particles collided. Although no one knew how to make such beams, let alone dash them together, nonetheless collisions could be pictured taking place and the ensuing possibilities evaluated. The technique of making "thought experiments" has a long history, notably when Albert Einstein imagined what he would experience if he were travelling at the speed of light, which helped him to conceive his special theory of relativity. His musings on how to distinguish between the force of gravity and the sense of weightlessness in a free-falling elevator led him to the general relativity theory. Einstein and Niels Bohr had several discussions about quantum theory, based upon some of these thought experiments.

So, Llewellyn Smith's approach had a well-founded pedigree. Now he used the logic of quantum field theory to posit what the outcome would be when massive W or Z particles met one another. What he found was a paradox. Having included all known quantum trickery, he found that were one to make such collisions, as their energy was increased the probability of the particles interacting would also grow until it exceeded 100 percent. This was obviously nonsensical and showed that the theory was incomplete.

Far from being a disaster, Llewellyn Smith's result was very exciting, because while the W and Z were present in his algebra, the Higgs boson was not. His equations also showed that if the Higgs boson existed, the quantum waves emerging from the collisions of two W bosons could interfere with waves from the Higgs boson, leading to mathematically sensible results—probabilities never exceeding 100 percent. With the W and Z now confirmed, here was further proof that the Higgs boson—or something like it—was needed to consummate the marriage of electromagnetic and weak forces.

In the theory of the weak and electromagnetic interactions there are two pivotal masses that control the phenomena. The effective strength of what was originally known as the "weak" force is controlled by both. The first mass is that of the W and Z bosons, which for both is slightly below 100 GeV.

Processes where the amount of energy transferred from one particle to another is around 100 GeV, the same order as the masses—energies at rest—of the W or Z, have the same strength or probability as electromagnetic inter-actions. Under these conditions the two forces are indeed united—a situa-tion known as *electroweak symmetry*. The W boson mass is like a fulcrum on the energy scale because the chance of an interaction between particles taking place depends upon the amount of energy transferred among them relative to the mass of the W: M_W. This dependence is very sensitive, in some cases being in proportion to the ratio of this energy to the mass of the W multiplied by itself four times: $(E/M_W)^4$. When the energy transfer is small and this ratio is very tiny, the effect of the force is feeble. For example, in naturally occurring radioactive decays, which were discovered at the end of the nineteenth century, the energy liberated at atomic level is a trifling 1 part in 100,000 of M_W. This is what gave rise to the naming of the force responsible as *weak*.[4]

By the 1980s the production of W and Z bosons at the CERN proton-antiproton collider confirmed that the previously known weak processes—weak because of their perceived rarity relative to electromagnetic phenomena—had increased their likelihood dramatically such that they happen at roughly the same rate as their electromagnetic cousins. The unifi-cation of the two forces at such energies was thereby verified; the historical identification of the weak force was due to all experiments in the early twen-tieth century being restricted to energies that were small compared to the W rest energy of 81 GeV.

All this is in line with the theoretical expectation that the chance of par-ticles interacting is proportional to energy scaled by the W mass—E/M_W. What does that imply for experiments at energies much higher than 100 GeV, where this ratio becomes large? The chance of interactions between particles happening at extreme energies would be so big that the mathemat-ical technique involved—*perturbation theory*—would break down. In extre-mis, the theory would violate common sense—chance being greater than absolute certainty, for example. This is where the second mass scale—that of the Higgs boson—takes control. The mass of the Higgs boson effectively determines when the strength of the force stops growing, preventing chance exceeding 100 percent and enabling sensible results to emerge. If the Higgs boson's mass is small, this restriction in growth will happen at relatively low energies and the effects of the force will remain relatively feeble. If the Higgs boson's mass is very large, however, emasculation of the previously weak interaction is much delayed, and its power will continue to grow up to extreme energies.

With confirmation of the W and Z, all this too was now understood and brought a calculation by Ben Lee and his colleagues Chris Quigg and Hank Thacker at Fermilab to the fore. Back in 1977 the trio had produced a paper that brought the Higgs boson's role in moderating the weak force into sharp focus. They made thought experiments similar to what Llewellyn Smith had done in 1973.[5]

Llewellyn Smith had already concluded that a Higgs boson was needed for the theory to cohere but had not computed implications for its likely mass. Five decades later, he recalled: "I knew that if you supposed [the Higgs boson mass is infinite] the cancellation would fail but at a then unimaginable energy, so I did not attempt to quantify it." The American team's equations described the chance that W or Z bosons would interact with one another, and when solved they discovered this would exceed 100 percent—in other words, be nonsense—if Higgs boson masses exceeded about 1,000 GeV, that is, a teraelectronvolt or 1 TeV. When Llewellyn Smith had made his calculation, the heaviest established boson was barely 2 GeV in mass, about twice as heavy as a proton. The American result of 1,000 GeV was in practical terms unimaginable, as Llewellyn Smith had already realised, and it would remain so for thirty-five years, but he later added, "I kicked myself for not following it up."[6]

Martinus (Tini) Veltman, in Utrecht, also was making computations about how a Higgs boson could affect quantum fluctuations in the vacuum and contribute to precision measurements of, for example, the response of an electron or its heavy sibling, the muon, to a magnetic field—its *magnetic moment*. The agreement between theory and experimental data and the mathematical consistency of the theory together limited the mass possibilities for the boson. These complementary investigations came to similar conclusions: something had to intervene at energies not larger than about 1 TeV to prevent the continued growth of probability and logical inconsistency.

The Americans did not claim this to be a theoretical argument for a Higgs boson, however. At this stage many theorists regarded the mass mechanism as an interesting mathematical trick but expected that something other than a massive boson would be revealed as the true agent responsible for breaking electroweak symmetry. The Americans made the more general inference that "new phenomena are to be found in addition to the [W and Z] bosons". Either a Higgs boson "of mass well below 1 TeV" had to exist or the "weak" interactions would have to exhibit features akin to the strong interactions, with new levels of structure, resonances, and more besides. Either way, exciting new phenomena were assured, and the 1 TeV energy scale was the region to explore.

At the time when Lee, Quigg, and Thacker wrote their paper, the W and Z had not yet been discovered. There was then still a real possibility that the Higgs boson would be lighter than about 100 GeV and thereby within reach of LEP—but the question of how to proceed beyond that, above 1 TeV, began to concentrate physicists' minds. The Fermilab trio's paper mentioned the Higgs boson and was built around the existence of this still hypothetical particle. However, nowhere did they cite Higgs or indeed any of the Gang of Six. By 1978 the Higgs boson and even the (erroneously named) Higgs mechanism were becoming trade names among particle physicists for what the American trio called "the weak interaction paradox at 1 TeV".

Following the discovery of W and Z, in agreement with electroweak theory, attention focused on making precision studies of the Z at LEP, which was due to commence operation in 1989. That the Higgs boson might be found at LEP was still a possibility, but with no theoretical guide other than that some new discovery must solve the paradox, the long-term horizons of high-energy particle physicists became set on exploring the TeV energy scale.

CHAPTER 11

A MACHINE FOR 1 TEV

AFTER TWO DECADES of complexity and confusion during the 1950s and 1960s, the discoveries in particle physics during the 1970s culminating in the discovery of W and Z particles in 1983 had cleared the mists and presented a vista of how nature configures the fundamental electromagnetic, weak, and strong forces. The most exciting realisation was that a common mathematical structure governs the dynamics of these forces, each of which according to quantum field theory is transmitted by packets of energy. In the case of the electromagnetic force, these bundles of electromagnetic radiation are photons; for the weak force this role is taken by the W or Z—particles so massive that it is almost impossible for them to play their role. Recall that this improbability is the root cause of the force appearing to be feeble— hence the name *weak*. Thanks to discovery of the mass mechanism, by Higgs and the rest of the Gang of Six, the source of the W and Z particles' great mass and the perceived imbalance between the strengths of electromagnetic and weak forces was now understood, at least in theory.

Discoveries in astronomy and cosmology had added confidence in the Big Bang theory of genesis and established that the universe evolves. The microwave background radiation, discovered in the same year as the mass mechanism, was recognized to be the echo of an intensely hot Big Bang that occurred some 13.8 billion years ago. The intense cauldron of energy liberated within a volume smaller than an atom when protons and antiprotons were annihilated at CERN replicated those conditions to give a laboratory simulation of the Big Bang's immediate aftermath.

Thanks to this new perspective, particle accelerators were now akin to telescopes that could peer into the Big Bang and reveal the dynamics of the early universe. Rebranding the field as *experimental cosmology* also liberated particle physics from years of public scepticism. Previously it had appeared as an arcane stamp collection of unimaginably small particles, most of such fleeting existence as to have no obvious relevance to the world at large. The machinery and detection equipment were often out of sight, hidden behind radiation shields consisting of tons of concrete blocks, making the marvels of engineering and technology inaccessible too. Now a sense of purpose had arrived, and particle physics began to attract attention from the media and the wider public.

Its costs were drawing criticism, however, and in 1983, when construction of the electron-positron collider LEP was about to begin at CERN, the British authorities set up an inquiry into whether the UK should stay in CERN—an international collaboration whose existence and finances relied on the cooperation of, by then, fifteen nations. If the UK pulled out, the funding of the whole organization would be severely diminished. Worse, LEP's construction would be threatened and the future of particle physics as a global endeavour put at risk. Rubbia's discoveries of the W and Z at CERN's Super Proton-Antiproton Collider confirmed that particle physics was indeed heading along a route towards enlightenment, and this proved timely for supporters of CERN in Britain. The UK remained a member and the future of CERN was assured—at least in the short term.

When the idea of LEP had first been mooted in 1976, the then director-general, John Adams, had presciently insisted that the tunnel be made large enough to include a proton machine one day.[1] In 1983, Lyn Evans wrote the first technical paper with a rough design of what would eventually become the LHC. However, as he later remarked, "it was not at all ripe for approval".[2] That same year, at much the same time as Rubbia in Europe was establishing the existence of the W and the Z, the Americans started designing a machine known as the Superconducting Super Collider (SSC), capable of finding the Higgs boson—assuming, of course, that it existed—or identifying the fundamental dynamics of the weak force above 1 TeV. Discovery of the W and Z bosons at CERN had taken leadership in the field away from the United States, and the aim was to leap ahead of the Europeans. Meanwhile plans were already in hand to upgrade the accelerator at Fermilab. A set of superconducting magnets was installed in the four-mile-long tunnel of the accelerator (the Tevatron), which would be capable of doubling its energy to near 1 TeV. Initially the beams could only smash into static targets, but by the end of 1986 a beam of antiprotons had been constructed enabling head-on collisions with protons at energies higher than at CERN. While the Tevatron enabled production and forensic study of the W and Z at a level beyond what CERN could achieve, it could not reach the ambition where a TeV of energy is used for exploration with total efficiency. To achieve that and solve the weak interaction paradox above 1 TeV would require an entirely new machine. That was the strategy behind the SSC, in which beams of protons could each reach energies of 20 TeV and then be brought into head-on collisions.

The SSC's ambitious approach involved building two concentric gargantuan rings of magnets underground in a tunnel circling for eighty-seven kilometres. Evans described it as a "technological dinosaur",[3] because in effect it simply took the basic ideas of the ISR from 1970 and scaled them up in size. But it was science on a scale that made Rubbia's seven-kilometre machine seem puny by comparison. The length of the SSC could have enclosed a major city—half as long as the M25 motorway encircling outer London, for instance, and only a few miles short of the Beltway around Washington, DC. The American strategy was for the SSC to produce the boson by means of conventional machinery and brute force.

Word began to spread of the plans to build the huge machine, in a project as ambitious as the heroic Apollo lunar landings of the 1960s. Whereas the Apollo programme had released humans from the gravitational shackles of Earth, the SSC would effectively transport us billions of years into the past, to replicate the heat of the universe as it was within fractions of a second of the Big Bang. The Americans were designing the SSC simply, their idea being to use proven technology and push it as far as necessary to achieve the goal.

In January 1987 President Ronald Reagan endorsed the SSC as an American machine with a price tag of $4.4 billion, and the decision was taken to build it in Texas. The commitment made international headlines. Higgs told me that "for the first time it began to look as if I might see the answer after all".

When the Americans came up with the idea of the SSC, CERN quickly responded by preparing a first outline for Adams' proton machine: the LHC. Four years after questioning whether membership in CERN was the best use of UK resources, funding agencies in the UK now raised problems regarding CERN's plans to follow LEP with the LHC, because the SSC promised to be an even more powerful machine.[4] In the UK the mantra was *value for money*. For them the decision was clear: why build the LHC if the SSC is going to exist? On the other hand, for many other European nations this was a matter of pride: "if the Americans can do this, then so must we." This feeling was especially strong in France and Italy, whose enthusiasm was enlivened by off-the-record hints that Germany might be prepared to bankroll the construction. Rubbia, with the stature by then of Nobel laureate, became director-general of CERN in 1989 and a powerful advocate of the LHC.

The media informed the general public that the goal was to find something called the Higgs boson, though few understood what a boson is, and fewer knew of the eponymous Higgs. The man whose insight seeded the international boson hunt had disappeared from view while others had embraced his idea, built new theoretical structures upon it, and transformed perceptions of the physical universe. But now, as the world of particle physicists prepared their strategy for finding the particle—a quest that would take thirty years—and as in Europe the ambitions to build the LHC matured, Peter Higgs was reluctantly thrust into a starring role. The life of a quiet, unassuming, intense scholar was appropriated to promote a vast international project.

He recalled: "The earliest media attention was as far back as 1988. Some of the better science correspondents in the broadsheet press picked up that there was something interesting happening." The first person to come to Edinburgh was Robin McKie, science editor of *The Observer*. Higgs had never given an interview before and didn't know how to organise it. He told McKie, "'We'll meet in the staff club, and I'll find a quiet corner'—it turned out to be in the bar!" McKie wrote up an account. They sent their star photographer, who lived in the Edinburgh coastal suburb of Portobello. McKie had a biological background and, as Higgs recalled, "I left him quite baffled. Communication [in the bar] was quite tricky, and I don't think it worked very well." Thirty years later, McKie's memory remained fresh as he confirmed to me that Higgs' assessment matched his own. He hadn't understood Higgs' idea in any detail, but thanks to years of experience in reporting science McKie was able to appreciate its importance. With "considerable difficulty" he produced what turned out to be a superb report, the first article alerting readers that something revolutionary might be brewing.[5]

Next, also in 1988, two Americans came: Peter Menzel, a photographer from California, and Charles Mann, a writer from the East Coast. They had an assignment to visit CERN, and while there they learned about Higgs. They came over to Edinburgh to film him. This time Higgs was better prepared and met them in his office in the university's physics department.

LEP

The interest of McKie and the media at large was piqued not just by a vision of a future SSC or LHC but by the impending start of physics at LEP at CERN. On Bastille Day, 14 July 1989, LEP began operation. This was the culmination of the discussions that Higgs had sat in on at CERN in 1976. LEP was an engineering marvel. First a tunnel had had to be built 50 metres below the surface of Switzerland and France, of similar dimensions and identical length—twenty-seven kilometres in all—as the Circle Line on the London Underground. Inside the tunnel, 3,500 separate magnets bent the beams of electrons and positrons around the curves of the ring. The tubes within which the beams travelled formed the longest ultra-high-vacuum system ever built. The insides of the tubes were pumped down to a pressure lower than that on the moon to preserve the precious positrons—the pieces of Dirac's antimatter that would be destroyed if they touched even a single atom of matter before reaching their intended goal.

Each beam moved at almost the speed of light, the positrons travelling clockwise and the electrons counterclockwise. At four points around the twenty-seven-kilometre circuit, small pulses of electric and magnetic forces deflected the beams slightly, so that their paths crossed. The beams were so diffuse that almost all their individual particles missed one another and carried on circulating. However, occasionally a positron and an electron made a direct hit, leading to their mutual annihilation in a flash of energy. For an instant, in a small region of space, this makes a miniature representation of what the entire universe was like in the first moments after the Big Bang. Huge detectors encircled the four collision sites, capturing and recording the primaeval particles of debris as they emerged from these mini bangs. Composed of an enormous number of individual pieces of electronics, the detectors' components had been built at universities and research institutions around the world, shipped to Geneva, and finally assembled at LEP.

LEP was specially tuned to produce the Z—the particle with zero electrical charge that had first emerged in Glashow's tentative model of the weak nuclear force, and whose existence had been confirmed at CERN's proton-antiproton collider. The Z is electrically neutral and so can be produced when beams of electrons and positrons are suitably tuned and annihilated. Their opposite electrical attributes, electrons being charged negatively and positrons positively, cancel to zero, matching the neutral Z; their combined energies, when the two beams are correctly tuned and meet each other head on, at the same speed, equal the energy of a Z at rest. That was the thinking behind LEP. With the reality of the Z now confirmed, the conditions for creating it in vast quantities, enabling forensic examination of its properties—despite its almost instantaneous decay—were agreed. By repeating the annihilation of electrons and positrons over and over again across a decade of LEP's operation, tens of millions of Z particles were made, their death rattles carefully recorded by LEP's huge detectors.

These data were then compared with the predictions flowing from the complete theory of the weak force that Gerard 't Hooft and his thesis supervisor Tini Veltman had built. As we saw earlier, Veltman had devoted years of work to reach the point where his student finally cracked the problem in a work of remarkable technical brilliance. Unfortunately, the huge publicity given to the wunderkind 't Hooft had led Veltman to feel that his own contribution was not properly appreciated, and the resentment soured their personal relationship.

Their theory had been inspired by quantum electrodynamics, and 't Hooft's breakthrough was his proof that the mathematical structures of QED could be applied to the short-range weak force too, thanks to the insight of Higgs. In essence, he started with the equations of QED, made a simple adjustment to allow for the W^+ and W^- analogues of the photon to carry electric charge, and then made the profound extension in which these force carriers acquire mass from the mechanism that Higgs had found. Agreement was remarkable and their theory gained a name: quantum flavourdynamics.[6] Within a few months, experiment matched theory to an accuracy of one in a thousand. This encouraged optimism that the entire theoretical construct of quantum flavourdynamics was correct, and that the Higgs boson did in fact exist. What's more, with the masses of the W and Z experimentally established, more confident predictions could be made of the conditions needed to find the Higgs boson.

ROBERT BROUT

By 1992, belief in the mass mechanism's physical reality was gaining traction. Now for the first time Higgs met one of the other founders of the idea: the American theorist Robert Brout, one of the theorists who in 1964 had independently shared Higgs' insight. They were brought together—Brout from the Free University at Brussels, and Higgs from Edinburgh—by a conference on the rise of what was becoming known as the Standard Model of particles and forces, held at the Stanford Linear Accelerator Center (SLAC) in California. As Higgs told me:

> I was in a motel a few miles from SLAC. The motel didn't serve food, so a minibus came to take us for breakfast at SLAC. I was waiting for the bus when I realised the tall man next to me and talking to a third party must be Robert Brout. I did some quick thinking because I knew from years before that another scientist, Lalit Sehgal, had told me of his experience at Brussels. While giving a talk at the university, without thinking, he had referred to the Higgs boson. He became aware that someone in the front row was displeased. He realised it was Brout. He tried to correct himself by saying, "I

appreciate that in this work there were several people involved but as is the custom in my theoretical community I refer to it by the shortest name." The voice in the first row exclaimed, "My name has five letters."

Higgs introduced himself to Brout: "I think we have a lot to talk about. I have a lot of things attributed to me that you did first."

After that, they got on extremely well and by the time they walked onto the sunlit terrace at SLAC with their breakfast trays they were like old friends. "As we went out through the door, we met Veltman, whose jaw dropped. He really couldn't believe that Brout and I could be on such good terms."[7]

BOSON POLITICS

Meanwhile in the United States, the SSC was running into problems. Winning congressional support for the budget had called on American leadership and national pride, a favourite invocation for big science projects in the United States being "This has nothing to do directly with defending our country, except to make it worth defending."[8] The possibility of such a big-ticket item coming to their own state made congressional representatives very positive—for a while. Once the decision was taken to build in Texas, however, political support from other states dwindled. Costs also escalated. Financial pressures were mounting for the LHC project as well. At CERN, Rubbia's tenure as director-general came to its end, and in September 1992 Chris Llewellyn Smith became his successor. He quickly discovered a hiatus with LHC planning: Rubbia, having realized that the LHC's costs were becoming untenable, had effectively washed his hands of it. When Llewellyn Smith asked for the long-term plan, he later told me, he "found a completely empty cupboard".[9]

With senior management he made an emergency plan, paring costs to the limit. Even so, the UK and German governments said that CERN must come back with something cheaper. British physicists suspected that their Euro-sceptic government would have been happy to kill CERN and hold on to all the money. In the United States, too, events were coming to a critical stage. In October 1993, with about twenty kilometres of the SSC's tunnel already dug beneath the Texas soil near Dallas, the US Congress withdrew funds, and the project was terminated. The future of particle physics, including the quest for the Higgs boson, was now in jeopardy. Higgs, naturally, was discouraged: "The cancellation of the SSC was a disappointment because they should have been able to find [the boson] with their technology."[10]

It was then that British physicists suddenly found an unexpected ally in their science minister, William Waldegrave, a politician blessed with intellect and a profound wonder about science. Waldegrave's parliamentary constituency was Bristol West, the town of Peter Higgs' youth and scientific awakening at Cotham School. A wave of publicity about the LHC, and of excitement that if it discovered the Higgs boson a son of Bristol might win a Nobel Prize, spread outwards into national attention. Waldegrave became so interested that in 1993 he challenged the British physicists to help him explain the Higgs boson and make the case for funding the LHC during discussions with other cabinet ministers, including the Chancellor of the Exchequer, of an upcoming budget. He offered a bottle of vintage champagne as prize for the best effort.

A winning entry by David Miller, a professor of particle physics at University College London, cleverly used a political analogy to grab Waldegrave's attention. He imagined the Higgs field as a crowd of political workers at a cocktail party. Former prime minister Margaret Thatcher played the part of a massless particle that enters the room and encounters the field of acolytes. She tries to traverse the room, but the occupants want to shake her hand. This interrupts her, creating inertia. Her interactions with the gathering have altered her from a flighty massless particle into a massive lumbering one. In similar fashion, a massless particle gains inertia—mass—because of its interactions with the ubiquitous Higgs field.[11]

In the analogy for the Higgs boson, imagine that instead of the prime minister appearing at the door, someone arrives with an important message: perhaps that the PM has resigned. The news propagates across the room: those nearest the door lean in close to one another to hear the news, and in turn pass it on to colleagues who are farther away. The wave of compression, as people cluster together momentarily, move away, and regroup, is analogous to the wave whose particle manifestation is the Higgs boson.

In the UK, Waldegrave's challenge generated huge publicity for science. In consequence, the government maintained its support, and the media discovered CERN and decided that thirty years of particle physics had been orchestrated by the genius of a lone Englishman, turning Higgs into a celebrity.

EMOTIONAL ROLLER COASTER

In Europe the long-term strategy for experimental particle physics was based on the vision that CERN director-general John Adams had expressed in 1976: build LEP, the machine colliding electrons and positrons, and then later upgrade it to use beams of hadrons—protons—making the Large Hadron Collider. Compared to the SSC, the design of the LHC was relatively compact, and to have any chance of success it would require innovation in a wide range of technologies. There was no guarantee that it would be possible, which created huge worries when the SSC project was prematurely terminated in 1993.

After much political manoeuvring, in December 1994 the LHC project was approved by the CERN Council. Physicists had many wide-ranging visions for how the machine might be used, but as politicians know only too well the public responds to easy slogans. Following Waldegrave's challenge, the perception developed that the machine would be built to find the Higgs boson. Physicists shared that hope and designed the LHC to have the best chance of doing so. Higgs' hopes were raised again: "Given some years of technological development, I began to hope again [that] maybe [discovery of the boson] might happen after all while I was around to see it."[12] Many were worried, however, as no one could rule out that Higgs' boson might be up to a thousand times heavier than a proton and, if so, its existence would be difficult to establish, even at the LHC.

Following the go-ahead, and twenty-four years after joining the team building the ISR, Lyn Evans was appointed director in charge of the division responsible for constructing the LHC. Early in 1995, he visited Edinburgh to give a seminar in the physics department. This was shortly after Waldegrave's competition challenging physicists to give a pedagogic description of the boson, which gave a background to the occasion. The university set up a press conference for Evans and Higgs as a means of highlighting Edinburgh's involvement in the adventure. They put Peter Higgs in front of a collection of journalists, including the BBC and science editors of several broadsheets. The assembled media eagerly anticipated a popular explanation of the physics background to the LHC project; instead, Higgs gave them a lecture on spontaneous symmetry breaking. As a colleague recalled: "In those days he was Peter the physicist and that's what you got. The press must have wondered why we had dragged them all the way up to Edinburgh to listen to someone who spoke a foreign language."

Richard Kenway, Tait Professor of Mathematical Physics at Edinburgh, heard a story that one journalist, at least, had a success. This reporter went to the city's main thoroughfare, Princes Street, and asked people if they had heard of the Higgs boson. The first person replied, "I'm pretty sure it's a nautical term"; the second said, "Oh, it's an elementary particle." The journalist was so impressed that a member of the public in Princes Street recognised that the Higgs boson had something to do with particle physics that the credibility of the physics department was salvaged. Public awareness of the boson—not the nautical bosun—and of the reclusive scientist whose name it carried began to grow.[13]

Following the demise of the American machine and approval of the LHC at CERN, the roller coaster continued for Higgs. As he told me, "Perhaps I was more optimistic [than I should have been in 1995] as I was ignorant of some of the technological challenges facing the LHC."[14] There were any number of possible technological barriers that could ruin the project, and the LHC eventually took twenty years from conception to design and construction. Not least, scientists and engineers from around the world would have to build detectors the size of ships to record the results—all with the aim of teasing out the Higgs boson, a particle which would live for less than a billionth of a billionth of a second.

QUANTUM ROLLER COASTER

Through the 1990s, LEP continued to accumulate data, and as the precision of the results improved, the first signs began to emerge of a slight mismatch between the theoretical predictions and what the experiment was finding. Far from showing the underlying theory to be wrong, these surprising results turned out to be the first hint of another track in the snow of a previously unknown, and hitherto undiscovered, variety of quark—the *top quark*. The Standard Model and the successes of the electroweak theory implied that leptons and quarks match one another in number. For the leptons, six were known: the electron, muon, and tau being electrically charged, each paired with a neutral neutrino (the tau-neutrino's existence had been implied but was not directly observed until July 2000). For the quarks, two pairs—down and up, strange and charm—had been known since 1976. The discovery of the bottom quark in 1977 had convinced physicists that a partner, the top quark, must exist, and they had been searching for it for nearly two decades. The top quark was too heavy to be produced at LEP but had revealed its presence thanks to quantum effects. Energy is conserved over ordinary timescales, but according to quantum theory the energy account can be overdrawn for brief moments. This allows the Z^0 to transform momentarily into a "virtual" top quark and antiquark, which then coalesce back to a Z^0 during its brief lifetime. Such quantum fluctuations leave imprints, which were being manifested in the experimental measurements. Much as the dawn heralds the sunrise, these quantum effects preview phenomena that lie beyond the current energy horizon. Their magnitude gave an indication of how much more energy would be needed to bring the top quark into existence—in analogy, to work out when the rim of the sun will actually appear. The answer was that the top quark's mass will be somewhere in the range of 160 to 190 GeV.

The subsequent production of the top quark, with a mass of some 175 GeV, in 1995 at the Fermilab Tevatron, was in line with those predictions. The reason it took so long to discover is that its mass is so huge, similar in magnitude to that of a gold nucleus, which contains nearly two hundred protons and neutrons. The top quark is nearly twice as heavy as the W or Z bosons, which until that moment had been the heaviest known fundamental particles.

This discovery gave huge impetus to Frank Wilczek's 1977 insight that quantum uncertainty could provide a portal to the Higgs boson. Key to his idea was that the strong fields gluing a proton together could transiently fluctuate into heavy quarks and antiquarks, which would then fuse to make the boson. The Higgs boson's affinity for heavy particles meant that the heavier the evanescent particles are, the greater the chance of producing the Higgs boson. When Wilczek first proposed this mechanism, charmed and bottom quarks were the heaviest known. But now, discovery of the hugely massive top quark made production of the Higgs boson through the intermediate role of a top quark and a top antiquark look plausible.[15]

The precision of experiments at LEP continued to improve, and by the end of the century it exceeded one part in ten thousand. By then the discovery of the top quark meant its mass was precisely known and could be included in the quantum calculations. The result was that further subtle discrepancies began to show up between LEP's data and the theoretical predictions. Once again, quantum fluctuations were giving a foretaste of new phenomena, as yet out of reach. Excitement mounted when it was realized that here, possibly, were the first experimental hints of the Higgs boson. In 1976, when serious interest in the Higgs boson had first begun, many feared it might be up to a thousand times heavier than a proton and out of reach of experiment in any realistically foreseeable future. Now, to everyone's relief and huge excitement, it began to look as if the Higgs boson might be lighter than that. Higgs recalled: "The surprising thing perhaps was how light the thing turned out to be."[16]

The precision measurements of the Z boson's properties, analysed by the mathematics of quantum flavourdynamics and incorporating the quantum fluctuations associated with the transient top quark, whose mass was now known, led to a prediction for the mass of the Higgs boson somewhere in the range of 110 to 130 GeV. It appeared that producing the Higgs boson in the laboratory was tantalizingly just beyond LEP's reach but would be achievable at the LHC.

LEP had been designed originally with the energy of each beam being 45 GeV so that their collision would produce the Z particle, mass 90 GeV. By May 1999, extra accelerating features had been installed in LEP which doubled the energy to nearly 100 GeV per beam.

LEP's career was due to end in 2000, to make way for construction of the LHC, which would occupy the same underground tunnel. The accelerator engineers managed to increase the energy to 104 GeV per beam. In a nail-biting climax to LEP's career, the scientists on one experiment thought they had a possible sighting of the boson and requested more time to pursue it. CERN's management now had a major decision to make: should they continue running LEP longer at this extreme energy for more months in the hope of establishing the existence of the Higgs boson, or should they follow the agreed plan of closing LEP and begin construction of the LHC?

This dilemma reached far beyond those who had to make the decision and was the coffee-time gossip of physicists around the world. It became a topic of discussion at a physics meeting in Korea attended by, among others, Stephen Hawking and the American particle theorist Gordon Kane. Kane recalled how he was sitting at a big round table at dinner next to Hawking. The topic of LEP's continuing operation came up. Kane knew more than the others about that branch of physics and was explaining the arguments to the assembly. In the middle of Kane's exposition, Hawking spoke up: "I'll bet you $100 there is no Higgs boson." As Kane recalled, "I immediately took the bet." He and Hawking spent some time discussing the conditions of the wager. The bet was not that there would be no discovery of the Higgs boson at LEP, but that there would be no Higgs boson, period.[17]

It was to Kane's good fortune that the wager did not refer to a discovery at LEP because after much soul-searching CERN's management decided to stick with the original plan to terminate LEP and get started on constructing the LHC. This proved to be a wise decision, as the sighting was later realised to have been spurious.

For their successful theory of weak and electromagnetic forces—quantum flavourdynamics—'t Hooft and Veltman were honoured with the Nobel Prize in 1999. LEP had confirmed their theory: the top quark had been discovered in agreement with its predictions. The mechanism of Higgs and the Gang of Six, which was used in the construction of the theory, was also implicitly confirmed. From the quantitative precision of LEP and application of quantum flavourdynamics, a signpost towards discovering the Higgs boson and validating the entire structure had been found. As LEP closed to make way for the LHC, the first real chance of discovering the Higgs boson had at last arrived.

CHAPTER 12

FATHER OF THE GOD PARTICLE

URING THE LONG buildup to the start of the LHC, media interest had come in waves. Higgs' fame with the media had started back in the late 1980s when LEP started up—Robin McKie of *The Observer* and the first interviews with Higgs. But these were forgotten by all but interested parties as soon as the following week's editions came along. LEP produced exciting physics, but with no immediate bearing on the Higgs boson, at least at first. Plans for the LHC to replace LEP in about a dozen years matured, but these were not mentioned much outside the professional journals. Then in the mid-1990s, three unrelated events occurred which put Higgs' boson at the top of the agenda and thrust the reclusive scholar into the limelight.

The demise of the American super collider, the SSC, was a major upheaval, with huge political and scientific implications, which the world community of particle physicists realised could threaten their quest for the boson, but the news made no big impact on the public at large. In the UK, science minister William Waldegrave's challenge raised awareness of the Higgs boson and, for the first time, of its British creator. Internationally, the most significant publicity for Higgs' boson was a popular book by American Nobel physicist Leon Lederman titled *The God Particle*.[1] The physics community almost uniformly hated the description, and as an atheist Peter Higgs found it hugely unsatisfying. The media, of course, loved it. Three decades later, the boson is still widely referred to by this sobriquet.

For the particle physics community, a seminal moment came in March 1995 when Fermilab discovered the sixth and—according to theory, at least—final variety of quark: the top quark. This completed the quest for the basic seeds of matter begun nearly one hundred years previously, in 1897, when Cambridge professor J. J. Thomson announced his discovery of the electron in a formal letter no longer than this page. The electron was the first member of what we now know to be a family of fundamental varieties of matter—the leptons, fermions that are blind to the strong force. When the final member of the sextet of strongly interacting fermions, the top quark, was announced, the accompanying paper ran to 150 pages. The journey from electron to top quark illustrates the progress of a century in science: from a lone Victorian gentleman with a starched collar working at a table to hundreds of women and men from around the world collaborating at a vast particle accelerator. Fortuitously, the news of the top quark's discovery hit the headlines just a month before European governments were due to deliberate on the LHC project. The confluence of the massive top quark's discovery—the final piece in a century-long quest—with the imminent decision to build a machine to establish the capstone of the theory, the Higgs boson, brought Higgs to centre stage.

In 1996, Higgs retired from his tenured job as professor at the University of Edinburgh. His life was now increasingly taken over by media and public interest in his boson and, with it, personal fame. The following year he won the European Physical Society prize for High Energy and Particle Physics. In 1999 he was offered a knighthood in the millennium honours by the British government. "But," he told me, he "didn't want any sort of title" and, in any event, felt "anything of that sort" was premature, so he declined it.

Higgs knew that his big idea remained to be proved. Billions were being spent building the LHC and its detectors to make it an adequate telescope into the dynamics of the Big Bang. Whether the Higgs boson would turn out to be part of that vista no one yet knew. Meanwhile a media circus had focused on the "God Particle", giving the impression that Peter Higgs' idea was at the vortex of the whole enterprise. Higgs knew that the purpose of the LHC was for much more than that, and that its real heroes rarely made the headlines—Lyn Evans, the machine's lead engineer; Jim Virdee, architect of one of the two huge detectors; and the thousands of invisible technicians working towards the LHC's common goal in universities and research institutions around the world. Some younger research students might spend their entire career on the LHC, first a decade planning and testing the software programmes while the machine was being constructed, then massaging the apparatus until confident of its operation, before finally performing the experiments, accumulating terabytes of data and then analysing the results for years. If none of this revealed a Higgs boson, if Higgs' insight was not after all part of nature's scheme, then so be it. His life's work and place in history was now in the hands of others.

HAWKING HIGGS

Becoming a figure of interest to the world's media was unsettling for Peter Higgs. Born in the age of radio, he had done his major work in the year when BBC television split into two channels, and the climax of the search for his boson would be in the modern celebrity-obsessed era of the internet. Higgs was as yet unaware of the new media's rules; his first introduction to the cavalier reality came on Monday 2 September 2002, when his name was linked to the world's most celebrated scientist, Stephen Hawking, in a headline controversy.

That year, the Edinburgh Festival Fringe hosted a Geneva dance company which had developed a show around the concept of antimatter, the brainchild of Peter Higgs' hero, Paul Dirac. The UK Particle Physics and Astronomy Research Council (PPARC, the funding body) thought it would be a good idea to stir up some publicity through this for what was going on at CERN and raise the profile of Peter Higgs. It bought tickets to the show for a small group including Higgs and the science correspondent of *The Scotsman*.

At that time, 2002, the newspaper was suffering the consequences of purchase and restructuring by the businessmen twins David and Frederick Barclay, with Andrew Neil installed as editor-in-chief from 1996 to 2005. Financially run down, the paper had combined the positions of correspondent for science and transport. Higgs had a low opinion of the journalist given that bifocal role who was "not much interested in real science, maybe more interested in transport".[2]

After the show that night, the group moved on to dinner at a restaurant on Edinburgh's Royal Mile. The wine flowed, and conversation became relaxed. Not everyone was happy, however, for as Higgs recalled, "all the so-called science correspondent was interested in was Stephen Hawking. He didn't give a damn about particle physics." Hawking, while unquestionably an outstanding scientist famed for his work on black holes and how quantum theory might affect them, was no expert in particle physics. His bet with particle physicist Gordon Kane that there would be no Higgs boson had been widely publicised and inspired the journalist. Growing irritated, Higgs eventually said, "Listen. I think you should appreciate not everyone thinks all Stephen Hawking's pronouncements come from on high and carry absolute authority", adding that "Stephen Hawking doesn't know as much about particle physics as he thinks he does."[3] Higgs had been piqued by media reaction to a calculation Hawking had made that seemed to imply that the Higgs boson wouldn't be found. He explained that Hawking had done the calculation without understanding technical details of the theory. Naïvely, he assumed he was speaking in confidence.

Next morning, the front page of *The Scotsman* reported Higgs' comments. National papers in London then picked up the story, *The Independent* reporting that Higgs had "launched what appeared to be a deeply personal attack on Professor Hawking, who is confined to a wheelchair and speaks through a voice synthesiser." In what it described as a "battle of the heavyweights of theoretical physics", it quoted Higgs as saying that "it is very difficult to engage him [Hawking] in discussion, and so he has got away with pronouncements in a way that other people would not". Higgs' conclusion, these articles said, was that Hawking's "celebrity status gives him instant credibility that others do not have".[4]

The episode gave Higgs a stark tutorial in the way media stories can escalate. Unnamed scientists were quoted, as if in Higgs' support, unintentionally fanning the flames. One cosmologist reportedly said: "To criticise Hawking is a bit like criticising Princess Diana—you just don't do it in public."[5]

As *The Independent* summarised: "Professor Higgs only said what many other scientists say about Professor Hawking in private, but its prominence in a newspaper article makes it appear a planned, personal attack, which is clearly not what Professor Higgs intended." The latter was certainly true, as another anonymous scientist expressed surprise: "It's not [Higgs'] style at all. Physics is full of vindictive, nasty people but Higgs is not one of them." In so doing, however, the unnamed source inadvertently portrayed Higgs as a spokesman for those "many other scientists" who were privately critical of Hawking's celebrity but, lacking Higgs' stature, were unable to speak out. In the fevered atmosphere, another scientist's innocent reference back to the theme of the evening's theatrical performance, Paul Dirac, seemed belittling of Hawking: "Paul Dirac made a far bigger contribution to physics than Hawking, yet the public has never heard of him." Stephen Hawking himself was drawn in, quoted in *The Independent* as "surprised by the depth of feeling in Higgs' remarks. I would hope one could discuss scientific issues without personal attacks."

These were Higgs' first encounters with the media in the new era where his name was becoming almost as well known as that of Hawking. The experience led to renewed caution. Meanwhile he wrote Hawking a letter explaining what had happened, and eventually this episode was smoothed over. Hawking accepted that Higgs simply disagreed with what he'd said and had solid scientific grounds for doing so. It didn't damage their personal relationship, but it left Higgs nervous about the media and protective of his privacy.

One ironic consequence was that the spat brought an excitement about and public interest in Higgs himself. Having Higgs' opinions of Hawking identified in media headlines immediately aligned the pair in public perception. Peter Higgs was now spoken of in the same breath as Stephen Hawking; the father of the still elusive God Particle was fast becoming one of the scientific gods.

"THIS IS GOING TO BE HUGE"

Nearly eight years passed while the infrastructure of LEP was removed from the underground tunnel and replaced with the customised magnets designed for controlling beams of protons, the fuel of the LHC. When at last all its components were in place, in 2008, a new burst of interest placed Higgs in the spotlight. In celebration of the LHC's impending inauguration, on 5 and 6 April 2008 CERN hosted an open house weekend. James Gillies, my successor as head of communications and public education at CERN, explained that "the open [house was] at the peak of some conspiracy theorist hype that the 'LHC will destroy the planet by making mini black holes'. The guides—many of whom weren't physicists—were trained that the simplest way to assure concerned people was to say: 'If cosmic rays don't do it, the LHC isn't going to do it.'"[6]

When Higgs' colleagues at Edinburgh learned that CERN planned an open house, they thought it would be a nice idea if they could persuade him to visit the LHC before the machine started work and became inaccessible. Although Higgs and Jody had separated years earlier, they remained on good terms, so Higgs' academic colleague and aide-de-camp Alan Walker sought her advice first. She thought Peter might not want to go as "he did not like big machines, but she would see what she could do". Walker recalled how "within twenty minutes Peter had called me to say he would be delighted to go as long as we kept the visit 'private'".[7]

Higgs duly went, accompanied by Walker and Richard Kenway, Edinburgh University's Tait Professor of Mathematical Physics. As Kenway recalled, "The visit to CERN first awoke us to the realisation that interest [in Higgs and his boson] was huge and [was] going to attract a lot of public attention."[8]

About fifty thousand people were expected to visit CERN over the weekend. Higgs and his colleagues didn't take part in the formal events. Kenway explained, "We avoided it. The whole idea was to take Peter to see the experiments, meet the people who were looking for the boson, and see what was going on. It was totally focused on giving Peter a private visit. The [teams at the] experiments stuck to that extremely well."

Early on Friday 4 April, they flew to Geneva. Upon arrival, they rented a car and went off first to visit the two main experiments designed to be sensitive to the Higgs boson: CMS (Compact Muon Solenoid), where they spent two hours, and then another two hours at ATLAS (A Toroidal LHC Apparatus). At 25 metres in diameter and 46 metres long, ATLAS is about one-seventh the height of the Eiffel Tower or the Empire State Building. The

CMS is compact only in a relative sense; it is 15 metres in diameter and 21 metres long, and it contains 14,000 tonnes of magnets and electronics in the length of a cricket pitch.

Kenway recalled the excitement felt by the technicians. The young physicists were of course interested, but they were already used to seeing the creators of the theoretical architecture in specialist conferences; the presence of world-leading physicists was a regular feature at CERN, though for almost all of them this was their first sight of Peter Higgs. For the technicians and engineers who had spent decades designing and building the equipment to find the Higgs boson, meeting the eponymous scientist was an even more memorable experience. There was "a nice set of one-on-one meetings down in the experimental area. Higgs signed several of their hard hats."[9]

On Saturday morning they visited the French side of the CERN site, where the control centre is, and then in the afternoon they visited ALICE (A Large Ion Collider Experiment), which was designed to study the interactions of heavy nuclei and the physics of strongly interacting matter at extremely high energy densities, akin to the early universe. This is an example of the wide reach of the LHC and a counter to a growing perception that its sole purpose was to discover the Higgs boson. Although that was ALICE's primary goal, if it succeeded it would also be able to produce Higgs bosons and potentially complement the results from the primary experiments of ATLAS and CMS.

The next day, Sunday, was the most popular of the open house weekend at CERN; thirty thousand visitors were expected. The Edinburgh group had already visited the experiments and now planned to mingle with the crowds and see the various exhibitions on site. Kenway recalled what happened next, as they had their first taste of the celebrity fame about to overwhelm Higgs. "The point where everything changed was at the open day. There were school visits. We were having a beer in the CERN cafeteria that afternoon when a bunch of American schoolchildren spotted Peter and ran over. 'We'd like a photo with you,' they cried, and he obliged."[10] Higgs recalls they had a video camera, and "asked me to wave, and to say 'Hello to America' on video".[11] Then like wildfire, word spread among the visitors that the progenitor of the Higgs boson was there among them. As he visited the exhibits, visitors would stop him and crowds would gather. Higgs recalled he "had nowhere to hide" when people realised that he was present. His visit was like that of an aging rock star. Kenway started to feel the pressure as they were "chased" out of the cafeteria. "The rest of the visit we had the sense that people were on the lookout for him. It's an exaggeration to say 'paparazzi' as it was mostly schoolkids, but we had a sense of being pursued. That's the moment when I began to realise this was much bigger than just a physics event. The general public was interested and excited."

Newspapers and magazines from all over the world wanted interviews, and the CERN press office was inundated with requests. Higgs, mildly panicked, stalled them: "I said yes, but not in the open days." Edinburgh University arranged a press conference the next day at a hotel near the airport, chaired by Kenway. At his first press conference in 1995, Higgs had in effect given a technical precis of his work; now, thirteen years later, he was better prepared, his presentation being "more understandable, and short".[12]

The world community of particle physicists was focused on the quest for the boson because of its role as capstone of the Standard Model, aware that if it was discovered this would be a singular moment in the history of science. Peter Higgs and his Edinburgh University colleagues felt likewise. Then, at the CERN open house, other implications of the Higgs boson became apparent too: "This was going to be a huge episode at a human level."[13]

CHAPTER 13

THE "DOOMSDAY MACHINE"

A FTER FIFTEEN YEARS of planning, design, and construction, Big Bang Day—the starting up of the LHC—was scheduled for 10 September 2008. Edinburgh professor Richard Kenway's prophetic vision was already coming into focus as the world's media gathered in the control room of the LHC to watch the first beams circulate around the machine.

This launch of a metaphorical journey back to the Big Bang was scientifically as risky as a NASA space launch. NASA achieves much positive public support by showing these live, and when CERN announced the date of the switch on, it had an experience akin to that of Higgs at the open day. The world's media were phoning, not to ask, "Can we come?" but to say, "We're going to be there!" James Gillies advised the director-general, Robert Aymar, "I think it's better that we invite them in rather than have them outside." Aymar agreed. "We had huge numbers of media here."[1]

It proved to be a wise decision. If CERN had not invited the media on site there would have been fewer people, so not only would the coverage have been less, but, Gillies judged, "Those outside the fence would have been the ones saying, 'they're starting up the doomsday machine and they won't let us in.'" The welcome result was that CERN had media inside "who realised this wasn't a doomsday machine but an incredibly complex piece of engineering that we were trying to get working. Also, from feedback afterwards, I think they appreciated that we were being quite brave having them here because these things don't always work first time."[2]

Whereas the American design of the SSC had been a "technological dinosaur", the LHC has two major innovations.[3] First are the two-in-one magnets, a single ring of magnets capable of curving one beam of protons clockwise and the other one anticlockwise around the circuit. The second is the use of superfluid liquid helium to power the magnetic fields to 9 tesla, three hundred thousand times stronger than the Earth's magnetic field.

If the LHC eventually achieved its full energy, the collisions between the beams would momentarily create temperatures unknown since the Big Bang, making the LHC the hottest place in the universe. Ironically, to do so would require the LHC magnets to be colder even than outer space. This is because the beams are steered by superconducting magnets made from niobium and titanium, and to maintain them as superconductors requires them to be cooled to −271.3°C, which is 1.9 degrees above absolute zero Kelvin. This was done with liquid helium, making the twenty-seven-kilometre ring the world's largest refrigeration plant. There are smaller-scale experiments in technical laboratories that reach temperatures lower than this, so the LHC is not the coldest place on Earth, but the exciting physics it promised to do would, in the opinion of Gillies, make it the "coolest".[4]

The LHC engineers had built a 100-metre-long test cell with superfluid helium and confirmed that the technology worked. In laboratory science a small beaker of liquid helium in a cryostat is usually sufficient for most experimental purposes. For the LHC proper they would need 100 tonnes.

To bring electric current into your home it's sufficient to flick a switch. To get an intense current of protons around the LHC takes much more. Each proton's journey begins in an insignificant bottle of compressed hydrogen gas, about the size of a fire extinguisher, which symbolises the extremes of scale involved in the LHC. When fully operational, the machine will circulate about five hundred trillion protons in its beams. To get some idea of this magnitude, if each proton were a grain of sand 100 microns across, then this number would half fill an Olympic-size swimming pool. This sounds like a lot but is nonetheless trifling compared to the numbers of protons in everyday objects. The bottle of compressed gas, for example, contains more atoms of hydrogen than there are grains of sand in the Sahara, more than enough to satisfy the LHC's needs for centuries (though in practice, for safety reasons bottles are replaced twice a year). Each hydrogen atom provides one proton for the LHC. Protons are cheap; it is putting them to work that is expensive—in money, intellectual effort, and equipment.

To energise some of these protons and focus them into intense beams capable of replicating the hot Big Bang takes not just the twenty-seven-kilometre ring of the LHC but a means of transporting them from the hydrogen bottle five kilometres across the CERN site to the injection portals at the LHC. And along the way a sequence of computer-controlled preparations must take place. Thousands of individual elements must work in harmony, with timings of magnetic switches and the passages of bunches of protons synchronized to better than a tenth of a nanosecond.

First, hydrogen atoms are fed from the bottle at a carefully controlled rate into a linear accelerator. Each hydrogen atom contains a single positively charged proton encircled by a single negatively charged electron. An intense electric field strips the proton in each atom of its neutralizing electron and accelerates a packet of positively charged protons until it is moving at about one-third the speed of light. This is like getting a car moving in first gear. When a carefully monitored number of protons has been collected in the packet, the machine automatically moves them up a gear. At CERN this second gear involves a *booster* accelerator.

The goal in this second stage is to accelerate the protons to just over 90 percent of the speed of light. Straight acceleration is impractical, so instead magnets push the protons in a circular path with a circumference of about 160 metres, while electric fields in regular pulses thrust them—analogous to the way you might push a child repeatedly on a swing.

The packets are squeezed, increasing the intensity of the protons' current. Now CERN moves them up to third gear by injecting the packets into the proton synchrotron, some 630 metres in circumference, where they circulate for about one second, reaching 99.99 percent of the speed of light. Nothing can speed through the light barrier, and the protons are now so near this natural speed limit that any added energy doesn't appear as increased speed but as larger mass, a phenomenon described by Einstein's special relativity theory.

When the protons exit the synchrotron, they are about twenty-five times more massive than at rest. Now they enter the Super Proton Synchrotron (SPS). The machine that in 1983 provided the tools with which Carlo Rubbia discovered the W and Z bosons, confirming physicists' faith in electroweak theory and the Standard Model, is now merely the launch pad for the protons as they make their final thrust to the gateway of the LHC itself. The SPS energises the protons until they are nearly five hundred times more massive than at rest. Only now are they ready for injection into the LHC. Although as the crow flies this is only five kilometres away from the source, in making millions of circuits round the booster accelerators en route, the protons' total journey has been about three million kilometres, a distance equivalent to five round trips to the moon.

There are two vacuum tubes in the LHC, one for each of the counter-rotating beams, each with its own injection portal. The goal was that eventually over 2,800 packets of protons should be injected during a half-hour period through special gates to direct them clockwise or anticlockwise around the machine, and for the LHC to energise them so that each proton was up to seven thousand times more massive than at rest. They would then be moving so near to light speed that each packet would go around the twenty-seven-kilometre ring eleven thousand times each second. The engineers would have to synchronise the flow of the packets so that at four points[5] around the ring, where huge detectors await in underground caverns, the paths of the two beams cross and the counter-rotating packets arrive from both directions at the same moment to make head-on collisions. The precision required for this is itself a challenge. Each beam consists of packets of protons about 7 metres apart, in pencil-thin bunches about 60 centimetres long—in other words, most of the tube at any moment is empty space. The electronics must be tuned so that these counter-rotating pieces of ephemera reach the crossover at the same moment, precise to within better than one-tenth of a billionth of a second. The energy of the resulting collision would be twice that of the individual opposing protons.

The debris from those collisions is what the detectors aimed to record, and hopefully they will occasionally detect a Higgs boson.

That was all for the future. On 10 September 2008 the challenge was to see if, after all the planning, checking, construction, and assembly of the components, this interlinked set of machines and the LHC complex itself—the largest scientific experiment in history—would work in practice. With the SSC long abandoned, the LHC was the world's best hope for ever knowing if we are immersed in a ubiquitous Higgs field. If there had been an oversight in the planning so that the machine did not come to life, the hunt for the Higgs boson would have been at an end, with billions of euros wasted in addition to the dollars already spent on the aborted SSC. The immediate challenge was: will packets of protons successfully reach the LHC and then complete an entire circuit, first in the clockwise direction and then anticlockwise?

The LHC consists of eight arcs, each 2.45 kilometres long, and eight 545-metre-long straight sections. The plan was to feed the beam into the LHC one octant at a time and steer it around the arc before crashing it into a copper block placed in the line of fire at the end of that octant. The role of the metal was to absorb the beam and protect the magnets farther downstream in the circle. The first attempt was scheduled for seven in the morning, so CERN had to get the press into the media centre by six. They watched video screens showing the scene in the LHC control room, where the day began with Director-General Aymar wishing the assembled throng of technicians and senior scientific kibitzers "*Bonne chance*".

For the head of the project, Lyn Evans, whose boyish grin hid the bout of nerves he was experiencing, this was the moment of truth. All the scientists' computer simulations confirmed that the machine should work, but until Evans initiated the first test, no one could be totally sure. He was confident, however: his team included some of the world's foremost experts in the technology of particle acceleration, magnets, and cryogenics.

Evans had arrived early and recalled, "When I arrived at CERN, I was astonished by the number of TV trucks. I walked into the control room to see a battery of cameras with a whole crew from the BBC and their reporter Andrew Marr standing in a corner drawing doodles." This was all in dramatic contrast to his experience three decades earlier, when he and Carlo Rubbia had turned on the proton-antiproton collider in the middle of the night with no one else present. He drew the contrast: "This time with the LHC it was different, but I did not expect the kind of coverage there was."[6]

Evans spoke with a musical lilt as he explained to the packed room what should happen. He sounded confident, but there were no certainties; it could happen, or maybe not. Then, all checks having been completed, the engineers prepared for injection of a beam. A cheer erupted as the computer monitors revealed that the first pulse of protons had been injected into the LHC and been recorded at the measurement site.

Over in the media centre, a commentator explained what they were seeing on the screens: "We are at the beginning of the process with the first proton beam being injected." The picture shifted to Evans as he explained to the watching world what was visible from one of the monitors in the control room. It showed a white splodge wobbling slightly from side to side relative to a matrix of markers. This was a cross-section of the beam showing its shape and position relative to the controlling magnets. "So here you can see the position of the beam with respect to the centre of the vacuum chamber. That scale is plus or minus 10 millimetres, so you can see the beam is oscillating, but it's travelled three kilometres from point of injection," he said. In other words, it had completed the first octant successfully. The commentator explained that this was "massive progress. The beam is into its clockwise trajectory this morning very much earlier than expected." Evans added, "We are working step by step through all the eight sectors of the LHC machine." The copper block at the end of the first octant was removed, allowing the beam to continue to the second stage. As this process was repeated and the beam successfully progressed from one stage to the next, there were cheers and applause. The next moment of excitement came when they had managed to steer a beam to the halfway point. It was barely ten o'clock.

Like musicians bringing an orchestra into perfect harmony, Evans' technicians tuned the machine, carefully adjusting the magnetic fields that focus and steer the beams. A computer graphic recording the progress showed where the beam had reached, and in less than another half an hour, a beam of protons was being guided around seven of the eight sections. Now came the first goal of the day. Injection of a beam into the LHC was akin to demonstrating that you can open the doors of a car and get inside. Guiding it around the sections was like checking that the ignition key turns, but not yet that the engine will start and keep on firing. Could they now steer the beam around a complete circuit and keep it circulating? Only then could they be sure the machine would work.

There was a small screen in the line of the LHC's protons, which would register the beam's passage by illuminating a small indicator light on a monitor in the control room. A single spot had shone regularly through the morning, indicating the successful entry of the beam into the LHC. Now, all being well, when the beam came all the way around the LHC it would hit the screen again, 90 microseconds later. This is too small an interval for anyone to see the difference in one spot flashing off and on again, so Evans' team had designed it so that when the beam made it all the way around, the second coming would trigger a second light. Everyone watched intensely for the second spot to flash and prove that the LHC was running.

Evans' mellifluous Welsh tenor voice counted down the seconds as the pulse was first energised in the SPS, was transferred to the LHC, and then made—hopefully—the first complete circuit: "Five! Four! Three! Two! One!" But instead of the climactic launch of the LHC, there followed silence as Evans first paused, and then with a gentle nervous laugh said: "Err, . . . Nothing."

Have you ever been in an elevator when, having arrived at your destination, the doors remained closed long enough that momentarily you feared you were really stuck? If so, you can imagine the atmosphere in the CERN control room at that moment. Fifteen years of effort in building the machine that would fulfil a half-century-long quest for the Higgs boson had seemingly come to a catastrophic halt. "OK. Let's try again," he said, and suddenly everything worked. "Yes! Oh yes!" he exclaimed.

It was 10:28 a.m., just three and a half hours after the day had started. With genuine excitement, the news commentator told viewers in the media centre, "The beam is now all the way around the LHC." The automatic word graphics initially mistranslated this as "all the way round the galaxy", which was unwittingly an appropriate metaphor given the euphoria being exhibited by those in the control room.

Afterwards, Gillies received a lot of positive messages from media. As he recalled, they had found it "refreshing to see something that was real.

It wasn't rehearsed. It was clear that this was live, and they experienced the excitement of what was happening." CERN hadn't turned anybody away, so when the media centre was full, they put latecomers in the main auditorium with the physicists. Those reporters later told Gillies they had "the best seat in the house" because they could "see the emotion of the physicists when the monitor lit up showing [that] the beam had gone all the way round the machine once."[7]

So much for the clockwise direction; now they had to attempt it all again with the anticlockwise beam. Being able to complete a circuit proved that the machine was running, but the engine was not yet fully tuned. After some further tests, correcting the magnetic fields to steer the beam more precisely, they launched the second beam shortly after two in the afternoon. As had been the case in the morning, it made a controlled journey around the LHC, being stopped at various stages to improve its quality. By mid-afternoon both circuits—one clockwise and the other anticlockwise—had been successfully completed. At 4:30 p.m. the celebrations properly began because that is when the alcohol ban at CERN was lifted.

As the beam passed through the four underground caverns housing the experimental detectors, its passage was registered, confirming that the detectors' timing mechanisms were right. Evans announced, "We will be continuing to work through the night and through the day tomorrow, which is an official holiday at CERN, and we will be going full speed at getting this machine up to the design energy and getting collisions for the start of the scientific programme as soon as possible." Even if there were no major problems, it would take many days before the beams would be stable and intense enough to satisfy the LHC designers, and weeks before they could guarantee two counter-rotating beams capable of colliding head on.

Frontiers-of-knowledge physics experiments at the LHC would not be possible for some time yet. Even so, in many people's minds, the quest for the Higgs boson began that day. Evans only learned later the extent of the public's interest: "Eurovision told us that at some time in the day there was a total of one billion people watching. It was probably because they thought we were going to blow up the universe."[8]

HAWKING ROCKS THE BOAT

In addition to a billion people watching, there was a vast radio audience. In Britain, with a sense of proprietary interest in the Higgs boson, the BBC had built up Big Bang Day as a special event, with the quest being promoted as if it were a British analogue of the Apollo moon landings. The overture to the day began at breakfast time with BBC radio's flagship programme, *Today*. The station proudly announced the ambitious goals of the LHC and briefly mentioned the Higgs boson, but it was not Higgs but Stephen Hawking with his singular genius for playing the media who managed to grab public attention. In a prerecorded item, Hawking told *Today*'s millions of listeners: "The LHC will increase the energy at which we can study particle interactions, by a factor of four. According to present thinking, this should be enough to discover the Higgs particle, the particle that gives mass to all the other particles." So far, so good. But then Hawking introduced echoes of the spat that had erupted between him and Higgs six years earlier: "I think it will be much more exciting if we don't find the Higgs. That will show something is wrong, and we need to think again. I have a bet of $100 that we won't find the Higgs."

Hawking then raised the stakes by moving into areas that were almost science fiction. He mentioned that the LHC might reveal hidden dimensions, gateways to multiple universes and parallel worlds. The possibility that the LHC could also produce miniature black holes was an idea which excited Hawking. He was quick to promote this, having argued back in 1974 that primordial black holes created during the Big Bang could "evaporate" by a theoretical process known as Hawking radiation, in which particles of matter would be emitted. Hawking then added, "If the LHC were to produce little black holes, I don't think there's any doubt I would get a Nobel Prize, if they showed the properties I predict."

That Hawking speculated on the possible production of miniature black holes touched a raw nerve for many involved with the project. There had been fevered speculation by some media that what started as "miniature" might grow and devour the planet. That the theory implied no such thing, even in the unlikely event that miniature black holes could be produced at all at the LHC, did little to calm those who were convinced that CERN was building a doomsday machine. Hawking did come down to Earth, however, adding: "However, I think the probability that the LHC has enough energy to create black holes is less than 1 percent, so I'm not holding my breath."

Naturally, the media looked to Higgs for a comment about Hawking's views on the boson. Higgs duly obliged. The following day, this made headlines as a "row between two of the world's most famous scientists" which "threatened to overshadow the celebrations as the world's greatest scientific experiment got underway".[9]

At a press conference in Edinburgh to celebrate the LHC's successful start and to brief the media about prospects—not least that it would be a few years before there would be any real hope of confirming Higgs' boson—the question had come up whether the particle was impossible to find. Higgs reacted to Hawking's remarks by saying, "I solved the theoretical problem to show how to turn . . . a massless particle into a massive one. This was slightly surprising but was important."

This was true, and hardly sensational. In what London's *Times* described as a "withering attack", however, Higgs said that Hawking's work, which was behind his claim that the Higgs boson doesn't exist, was "not good enough". The reports were that Higgs dismissed the views of "the man generally considered to be the greatest physicist of his time", saying that no other particle physicist would view Hawking's approach as correct. According to *The Times*: "Both men are contenders for the Nobel Prize depending on the outcome of the experiment, and their spat is likely to send shock waves through the scientific establishment."[10]

In 2002, Higgs had been annoyed by remarks downplaying the Higgs boson made at a private dinner party. Now, six years later, he was being confronted by widely publicised statements attributed to Hawking and being questioned about them in a public press conference. Small wonder that he reacted with visible irritation.

What Higgs actually said was more measured than the impression from the headlines. As Higgs carefully explained to the press:

I have to confess I haven't read the paper in which Stephen Hawking makes this claim, but I have read one he wrote which I think is the basis for the kind of calculation he does and frankly I don't think the way he does it is good enough. My understanding is he puts together theories in particle physics with gravity in a way which no theoretical particle physicist would believe is the correct theory. From a particle physics quantum theory point of view, you have to put a lot more than just gravity into the theory to have a consistent theory and I don't think Stephen has done that. I am very doubtful about his calculations.[11]

What was the line that Hawking was pursuing here? Although the grand theory uniting quantum field theory with Einstein's general relativity theory remains to be established, some qualitative features of that theory are generally agreed upon. Hawking started with one of these. He assumed that at the Planck scale of extremely high energy and short distance, space and time are no longer continuous but become a foam of virtual black holes popping in and out of existence. This will have profound implications for phenomena at extreme conditions far beyond our reach, but what interested Hawking was whether there could be some implications visible at much lower energies, such as those being investigated at the LHC.

This is quite a remarkable quest if one realises that in terms of energy, the Planck scale is some fifteen orders of magnitude greater than the highest energies which can be reached at the LHC—in other words, a factor of one million billion. To put this in context, the Planck scale of energy relative to the maximum reach of the LHC is like the energy of a collision in that machine as compared with the amount liberated by a molecule when you digest your food. Given the multitude of phenomena that have been discovered over the centuries as we have reached from the energies of molecular biochemistry through atomic and nuclear physics to the extremes of the Big Bang as manifested in the LHC, it would be surprising if there were not similar riches awaiting discovery between the current frontier and the extremes of the Planck scale. But as we have no idea what these might be, it was a leap of faith to hope for signs of Planck-scale physics at the LHC. The physical relevance of this exercise was regarded with scepticism by most other physicists; one leading theorist advised that it "should be taken with a large pinch of salt".[12]

Nonetheless, Hawking had made the calculation and discovered that within the confines of his model, some fundamental features of quantum mechanics could be modified in a way that would affect the behaviour of particles with no spin—in effect, would make them nonexistent. The still hypothetical Higgs boson was a particle with no spin, and as such was subject to Hawking's analysis. His conclusion: "We have not yet observed an elementary [spinless] particle and I predict we never will."[13]

Even when Hawking wrote this paper back in 1996, he faced an immediate empirical problem. Although the Higgs boson was yet to be found, other spinless particles had been known for years, decades even; the pion, which had stimulated Nambu and Higgs back in the 1960s, is but one example. None of these particles are fundamental, however. The pion is made of quarks and antiquarks, which spin individually but are choreographed in such a way that their spins annul one another. Hawking then included a possible way of avoiding his conclusion by adding, "If we do detect the Higgs particle it will turn out to be a bound state of [spinning constituents]."[14]

So, although Hawking publicly stated that he did not believe the Higgs boson would be found and had made a highly advertised bet to that effect—two actions that grabbed media attention—his actual paper did not make that extreme claim. He had in fact concluded that a Higgs boson could exist if it was made of spinning constituents. Many particle physicists were quite happy to suspect that the Higgs boson might be composed of a deeper level of structure. After all, the history of particle physics shows that what one generation believed to be the fundamental constituents—atom, nucleus, proton—was proved later to be a composite structure. Hawking's prediction that the Higgs boson would not be found raised more excitement in the media than among the scientists at the LHC.

CATASTROPHE

By the end of September 2008, the tuning of the LHC was complete. Beams of protons circulated, and as the LHC's operators gained experience and confidence with the new machine, its acceleration systems were brought into play and the engineers expected that they would soon be able to bring beams into collision. Before the research programme could begin in earnest, there would then be a period of measurement and calibration for the LHC's experiments. All being well, results would start to appear in around a year.

Higgs at last had real hopes that discovery of his boson—or its refutation—was now only a matter of time.

Then there was a catastrophic component failure. A faulty electrical connection between two of the accelerator's magnets caused mechanical damage. The beams had been injected at the same energy at which they left the SPS, and to increase their energy tenfold in the LHC required powering up the magnets to their maximum strength. This had been successfully achieved for seven octants, but as the final octant was ready to be tested, there was an electrical short circuit. The accelerator technicians had made a risk analysis on the joints between electrical cables and concluded that there was only a one-in-ten-thousand chance of failure. The problem is that in the LHC there were a total of ten thousand joints. The vagaries of chance had conspired against them. Liquid helium started to escape and immediately vaporised in the atmosphere. The temperature rose, and the magnets ceased to be superconducting. This caused the current to heat the magnets further, vaporising the helium even faster, and the system failed catastrophically. The sudden release of magnetic force ripped the LHC's ten-ton magnets nearby from their mountings, bolted to the floor, with explosive force. Fortunately for the technicians the safety systems performed as expected and no one was put at risk, but the insides of the tunnel looked like an underground grotto filled with a collection of stalactites and stalagmites of frozen water vapour and other detritus.

The whole assembly had to be warmed up to room temperature before an assessment of the damage could be made and repairs begun. Ninety of the LHC's 1,600 magnets had to be replaced. The quality assurance demands on the entire construction were raised. The destruction was so serious that the renovations took over a year to complete.

Finally, all was well, and on 20 November 2009 proton beams were back in the LHC. The engineers had put the intervening months to good use, learning more about the quirks of the machine's control system and understanding its operation much better. Within three days the first collisions took place, and a week after that the protons' energy had been increased to the point where the LHC was now the highest-energy accelerator in history.

By 2010 the machine was ready for experiments. Since the crash, not only had the LHC's technicians used the intervening months to fine-tune their operating systems, the scientists also had continued running tests on their detector software. So when the first data began to pour in, everyone was well prepared to respond and start analysing the results. By March the LHC had reached its initial energy goal of up to 4 TeV per beam and Higgs suspected that "my way of life was about to change."[15]

CHAPTER 14

"WE SHOULD GO TO CERN"

EVERY TIME TWO protons collide at the LHC, the mysterious behaviour of quantum mechanics is revealed. The bizarre uncertainty inherent in quantum physics makes it impossible to guarantee the conditions required to produce a Higgs boson, even if you knew its precise mass in advance.

The best you can do is to smash the beams of protons into one another time and again and rely on chance—though not random chance. When a proton in one beam hits one from the other beam, head on, it is impossible to predict with certainty what will happen. Billiard balls bounce off one another in a determined way, but beams of protons scatter in some directions more than others, forming areas of intensity or scarcity like the peaks and troughs of water diffracted through an opening. The direction of bounce in any individual collision is uncertain; the distribution of millions of such bumps, however, can be predicted with certainty.

That, at least, is what happens when protons bounce off one another gently. When smashed together at the LHC, they are more likely to shatter, spawning new particles. Most often these particles are familiar, like photons, electrons, and pions. Among the hordes, occasionally a Higgs boson may be expected. It lives for such a brief moment, about one ten-thousandth of the time it takes for light to cross a single atom, that it is impossible to see it directly.[1] The best hope is to capture the particles that emerge in its death rattle, and to derive from them forensic proof of their transient parent. The task of the vast detectors, such as ATLAS and CMS, is to record the passage of these particles.

Even now you're not done. How can you be sure that the set of particles indeed came from the demise of a Higgs boson? What if they are instead some random correlations that by chance look like the real thing? To decide between genuine signal and random chance, you must have a huge number of such examples, which means gathering data for years.

In jargon, one is trying to distinguish between signal and noise. The amount by which a possible signal stands out against the background noise is described by a statistical measure known as *sigma*. All we need to know is that 1-sigma is defined as random chance—in other words pure noise—while 2-sigma is the first hint of possible interest, with 3-sigma becoming more significant. Particle physicists regard 5-sigma as indicating a discovery.

The easiest way to illustrate the difference between chance and signal, and the role of sigma, is by tossing a coin and seeing how often it lands heads rather than tails. If the coin has not been tampered with—for example, by being magnetised—we would expect it to land equally heads and tails. In reality this doesn't happen precisely, but how do we assess whether the difference from 50:50 is significant—indicative of a biased coin—or not? Suppose for example our coin landed heads three times as often as tails. Is that mere chance or is it significant?

The answer depends on how many times we have tossed the coin. In this simple example, the mathematics of probability theory implies that the magnitude of 1-sigma equals the square root of the number of trials. A difference between the number of heads and tails that equals 1-sigma is pure chance. When the spread becomes larger than this, the implication is increasingly likely to be a real signal. The likelihood that 3:1 is a real signal grows as the number of trials increases. To see how, start with four throws. The square root of 4 is 2, so 1-sigma is 2. A threefold bias to heads in this case is 3 heads to a single tail; the spread is 2 and so the significance—the spread—equals 1-sigma: it is pure chance.

That it is indeed pure chance is easy to see if we imagine that after two throws there is one head and one tail—pure chance. The next throw could be either heads or tails; let's say it is heads. Now for the fourth throw. It will be random whether this is heads or tails, so whether we end up with a total of two heads and two tails, or three and one, is pure chance. In the jargon: it is 1-sigma and not significant. If we increase the number of throws, however, we can test whether this preference for heads tends to even out, meaning pure chance, or continues to build up, implying a signal.

For example, after 36 tosses, a three-to-one split becomes 27 heads to 9 tails. One sigma is now 6—the square root of 36. The difference between the number of heads and tails is 18 (27 minus 9), which equates to 3 times sigma. The imbalance of 27 heads to 9 tails certainly looks very unlikely, but whether you would bet your fortune against that, I doubt. After 100 tosses, the three-to-one spread is 75 to 25. Most rational people would be prepared to wager by this point that there is something askew with the coin. One sigma is now the square root of 100, namely 10, and the difference between the numbers of heads and tails is now 50, which is 5 sigma. The odds of this result being pure chance are like the chance of betting successfully on the same number coming up on a roulette wheel four times in a row (in an honest casino!)

At the LHC the beams circulate eleven thousand times a second, and two independent teams of physicists—the collaborations of thousands working with the ATLAS or the CMS detectors—can accumulate data. The longer the LHC runs, the more data they obtain and the more confident they can become in discriminating signal from noise. But how long would it be before the scientists were certain enough to go public?

Early on, luck was in. During the delay caused by the damage to the LHC, the technicians had improved the precision and stability of the beams, while the physicists had tested and recalibrated the detectors. When the LHC started up again in November 2009, it worked more efficiently than expected. Throughout 2010 and into 2011 the LHC performed well, and data from the collisions began to accumulate in the huge detectors. In the spring of 2011 Peter Higgs was contacted by two near neighbours whose son was a senior scientist working in the ATLAS collaboration. Rumours were circulating that the experiments might be seeing something interesting, and

Higgs' neighbours told him that their son had sent an enigmatic message that he should "watch out for an announcement" at a conference being held in Grenoble in July. There turned out to be no announcement on that occasion, but the episode typified the nervous tension in the physics community, which was desperate to find the boson, and the rumours that alternately raised and then dashed hopes.

By the end of 2011 there was a hint that the data were giving a signal that seemed more than mere chance, but more data would be needed to establish this with confidence. If there were no breakdowns and the LHC continued to work well, then the winter of 2012 seemed to be the earliest that a clear answer would emerge.

POPULARISING HIGGS

As the news story looked likely to break in 2012, the challenge became how best to get Higgs to popularise his creation. Higgs' talent had been in manipulating algebra, solving equations, and interpreting their meaning to describe the physical universe, amplified by intellectual stamina which enabled him to focus on a given problem for months or even years. This is a special genius far removed from the skills required to carry an audience of the general public. Few premier-league research physicists have succeeded at both; Richard Feynman was a rare example of a Nobel laureate who also charmed with his popular expositions. Higgs was at home lecturing on advanced theoretical physics to a class of university students or to professional colleagues but had no experience in how to do a stand-up popular performance in a large theatre. But it turned out that he *was* happy to be interviewed on stage, allowing his story to emerge during a conversation, and that such a performance could be split into three or four segments, allowing natural breaks for the audience to ask questions and, in effect, help orchestrate it. That's how on 15 June that year, at the Borders Book Festival in Melrose, he and I made the first of a series of joint appearances that were to extend over the next three years. These discussions spanned anticipation of discovery, the Nobel Prize, and latterly a retrospective of what all this implied for the future of particle physics.

Among the participants at the festival was Jim Naughtie, the celebrated commentator on international affairs and experienced questioner of world leaders. As I had never played the role of interviewer on stage before, I asked him how he would approach a discussion with Higgs, if the goal was to help the audience understand the significance of the eponymous boson. He thought for a moment and then said, "Contextualise it." That very morning there had been a leader article in *The Times* anticipating that discovery of the boson would soon be announced. Naughtie explained his remark: "Is this being hyped up by science and the media, or will discovery be a seminal moment in human culture?" If the latter, he added, what would it mean? What would we know of fundamental importance that we hadn't before? In that brief homily Naughtie had encapsulated the key feature of the challenge and the singular importance of the quest.

We explained that according to Higgs' theory, we are immersed in some mysterious medium known as the Higgs field. The relationship of the Higgs boson to the Higgs field is like that of a photon to the electromagnetic field. Add energy to an electromagnetic field and you will generate an electromagnetic wave, which in quantum field theory occurs as a burst of particles— photons. Analogously, excite the Higgs field and you can produce Higgs bosons. The difference is that whereas you can excite vast numbers of photons by striking a match, to excite even one Higgs boson needs the LHC.

We explained further that contrary to a common misunderstanding, the Higgs field is not the source of all mass, only that of the most basic particles. It is the atomic nuclei in your body that give you about 99.5 percent of your weight. The mass of an atomic nucleus comes from the large kinetic energy of quarks within its protons and neutrons, which manifests as mass thanks to Einstein's equivalence of mass and energy. This has nothing to do with the Higgs field. What the field does is give *structure* by acting on the fundamental particles, such as the electrons found in the outer reaches of atoms. Your weight has little to do with the field, but your size does. In quantum mechanics the size of the atom is inversely proportional to the electron's mass; in other words, if this mass were zero, the hydrogen atom would have infinite size—that is, it would not exist. Thus the finite mass of the electron gives the measure of atoms, setting the scale for molecules, crystals, and the world at large.[2]

Whereas the photon, the agent of the electromagnetic force, has no mass, the key feature of its analogue for the weak force—the W boson—is that it is massive. This matters for us because the weak force controls the first stage of the solar fusion cycle, in which protons transmute through a series of processes to form helium, liberating the energy that has spawned life on Earth. The weak force is so feeble that if you were a proton in the sun at its birth, today—five billion years later—there would still be only a 50:50 chance that you had undergone fusion. If the W had no mass at all, like the photon, the "weak" force at work in the sun would instead have been as powerful as the electromagnetic force. The transmutation of hydrogen into helium, which is the key process in driving the sun's fusion engine, would have happened much faster than in reality, and the sun would have expired very quickly. Thus, the fact that intelligent life has managed to evolve is, not least, because the sun has lasted for billions of years, which in turn is because the W has mass. Our existence is consequential on the Higgs field.

We had to admit, however, that much of this was still all a hypothesis and would remain so until experiment either proved Higgs correct or destroyed the theoretical construct. Higgs assured the audience that thanks to the LHC, we hoped soon to know the answers.

We punctuated the conversation with two opportunities for the audience to put questions to him. The first—"What inspired you to become a scientist?"—led Higgs to relate his memory of seeing the name of Paul Dirac on the honours board at Cotham School. This, he said, was his first awareness that his school had educated a Nobel laureate.

Four weeks earlier, on 16 May, Higgs had returned to Cotham for the first time in more than sixty years; the head teacher had invited its distinguished alumnus to open the Dirac-Higgs Science Centre. Dirac's biographer, Graham Farmelo, who was present that day, was struck by Higgs' genuine modesty. The head teacher invited Higgs to open the centre by unveiling a plaque commemorating the occasion and the names of the two scientists. Higgs did so, saying: "I'm not worthy to be on this same plaque with Dirac."[3]

PREPARATIONS

In April 2012 Stephanie Hills, the vivacious thirty-seven-year-old media manager at the Science and Technology Facilities Council (STFC) in the UK, convened a meeting in London of press officers from all the nation's universities involved in LHC experiments. STFC funded the nation's particle physics research, and at the meeting draft plans were made for how to maximise the publicity should a discovery be announced later that year. It was clearly crucial to know when and where the experiments might go public. Hills and her colleagues drew up a list of all the big particle physics conferences for the next twelve months. The major International Conference on High Energy Physics (ICHEP) was scheduled to run from 4 to 11 July 2012 in Melbourne, Australia. This was the biennial conference series where Higgs' name had first come to prominence forty years earlier, in 1972. Hills recalled, "We absolutely ruled out ICHEP in Melbourne because the time differences were so awful." An announcement of discovery of the Higgs boson would be an international news story, and the sessions at Melbourne would not fit with the major news bulletins in Europe or North America. The timescales to possible discovery and major conferences led the STFC meeting to conclude that "all the logic was that it would occur at a conference in Katowice, Poland, in September".[4] This judgment that any discovery would probably not be announced until autumn reached Peter Higgs in Edinburgh. That is what he, and I, anticipated in June when we talked on the platform in Melrose.

Meanwhile, the organisers of ICHEP drew up a timetable for the conference. This included a half-day session on 6 July at which the latest results from ATLAS and CMS would be presented and discussed. As July approached, media reports and gathering rumours on blogs of an imminent announcement became a metaphor for the physics: did hearing the same rumour from different sources imply signal or mere noise? Everyone had known for more than a year that the ATLAS and CMS experiments at the LHC were seeing data that had the characteristics of the Higgs boson but could also be the result of other mechanisms within the Standard Model. Separating signal from noise was the challenge, for the public and physicists alike.

On 3 June 2012, shortly before Higgs appeared on stage at Melrose, I discussed the situation with Rolf Heuer, the director-general of CERN. He told me that the LHC had taken as much data in the previous six months as it had accumulated previously in total. From this alone, the expected statistical significance of any genuine signal could be expected to increase by about 40 percent. Given increased understanding of the experiments, potential backgrounds, and other intelligence that always grows during an ongoing experiment, they could hope for somewhat greater than that. So simple statistics brought one up to a sigma around 4 or above. That was what should happen if the previous signals were real. However, until the data were unblinded, no one could be sure.

On 15 June the experimentalists in one of the research collaborations took the first look at their results. What they saw made them gasp. When the data files had last been opened, months previously, there had been a small tantalising hint of something new—possibly the Higgs boson—with a mass around 125 GeV. Not only had this signal remained, but it had grown. There was still much analysis to be done before they could be sure, but the leadership agreed to include James Gillies, the head of CERN communications, in the small circle privy to the news, and alerted him to prepare for a possible announcement in the summer. Gillies recalled being at home, near CERN, gardening when he received a phone call from a scientist on one of the experiments which included the prophetic remark: "What I've just seen is not going away."[5]

Coincidentally, this happened the same day that Higgs and I made our presentation in Melrose, though we knew none of it, of course. Meanwhile, the experimentalists were preparing to report their latest results at ICHEP in Melbourne. Gillies had plans in place to relay all presentations from Australia to CERN's main auditorium so that CERN scientists could hear the updates. The phone call Gillies had received in his garden had made him aware of the excitement from one experiment, but there seemed to be too little time for any formal announcement of an actual discovery to be made at ICHEP. In addition, there was still the possibility that the ATLAS and CMS experiments would disagree, revealing that the hints were nothing more than the vagaries of chance after all.

The supreme decision-making body at CERN is the CERN Council, which includes delegates from each of the twenty-three member states. Their regular summer meeting took place on 21 and 22 June. At that meeting they judged that whether there was a discovery or not, the update on the Higgs search was too important to be announced at the Melbourne conference and should first be presented at CERN. Gillies issued a press release to that effect on 22 June: "CERN to give update on Higgs search as curtain raiser to ICHEP conference". No one yet knew whether there would be enough signal to announce a discovery, but the press release and the CERN Council's role fuelled speculation that a discovery announcement was imminent.

Although no one yet knew what would happen, to Gillies a discovery "was looking pretty likely at this point because the experiments were showing the director-general independently—as was the right thing to do—what they had". Even if neither experiment on its own was going to be able to say it had 5-sigma (the agreed statistical measure for discovery), only Heuer, the director-general, knew in outline both teams' results. Gillies' intuition was that Heuer must have judged, from what he had seen already, that there was enough for him to informally weigh the two sets of data and to say there had been a discovery. Otherwise, why call such a high-profile announcement only to have anticlimax?

A few days later I met Peter Higgs again, this time at a physics summer school held from 25 June to 2 July in the remote Sicilian hilltop town of Erice. The fact that CERN planned to give a progress report was by now common knowledge. Higgs was understandably anxious. On the one hand, he wanted his life's work to be confirmed; on the other, he accepted that if it was, he would be thrust once more into the media spotlight. I arrived at Erice to lecture the new generation of young particle physicists a couple of days before Higgs was due. The students were full of anticipation. Many were doing PhDs on one or the other of the two huge CERN experiments looking for the boson. All had heard of Peter Higgs, but none had ever met him, and most didn't know what he looked like.

THE SICILIAN HIDEAWAY

CERN planned to make the progress report on 4 July, the only day that they could have the spokespeople of the two big experiments present and leave them enough time to get to Melbourne in time to give talks at the conference on 6 July. The world of particle physics was turned on its head as the previous plan to relay talks from Melbourne to CERN was replaced with a morning transmission of the CERN event in Geneva to conference delegates arriving in Melbourne in the evening. Physicists close to the experiments, meanwhile, were teasing their favourite media contacts with hints that something big might be announced—or then again, that it might not.

As rumours about a possible birth announcement of the Higgs boson swelled, Higgs himself was in the haven of Erice, still believing that although his boson was very likely real, it was too early for its confirmation. Erice was far enough away from the media to give him peace, and yet near enough to the LHC's central players to glean some insight as to what might happen. When he arrived in Sicily, I found him confidently looking forward to eventually being proved right, and maintaining a level of equanimity.

On 30 June, the temperature was scorching and the midday sun reflecting off the white stone of Erice's narrow alleys assaulted the senses. Most residents had retired to their private shaded courtyards for siestas. A Dutch film crew, who were making a documentary about Higgs and the boson, had come to Erice for three days and were lunching with him and his charismatic Yorkshire colleague Alan Walker in the air-conditioned restaurant Venus. Walker, a retired physicist from Edinburgh University, had become in effect a personal assistant to Higgs, helping organize the many demands on his time and accompanying him on visits abroad. For some days he had been trying to find out how significant the 4 July event might be, as Higgs was due to return to Scotland with no plans to go to CERN. Walker had contacted the CERN press office that morning to ask: "What should we do?" Suddenly the lunch was interrupted when his phone rang. Alan Walker recalled: "I saw the code +41, which is Switzerland, so I thought it was the CERN press office calling me back, but it was John Ellis" (the senior theorist at CERN whose paper in 1976 had first brought the quest for Higgs' boson to life). So as not to disrupt the lunch, Alan left the table and went over to the window to take the call. He turned around to see that the film crew had set up their equipment and were filming. They motioned to him "to continue acting naturally", so Alan "started a conversation with Peter saying—'It's John Ellis saying we should go to CERN'". Higgs replied: "If John Ellis says that, then we should go."[6]

If there was a moment when Higgs knew, that was it. That evening, after a communal dinner with the lecturers and special guests, Alan pulled me aside to tell me what had happened at lunchtime. After the diners dispersed, we joined Peter Higgs in one of Erice's small piazzas, where over drinks and late into the night he spoke freely in a way I had never heard him do before. More at ease, less reticent than usual, he told us that after forty-eight years of waiting, when Alan had told him of the CERN summons he had experienced a momentary sense of relief, even of triumph, followed almost immediately by panic. "I had in a way been dreading the occasion and been preparing for how to cope with it," he said, all the while maintaining a distance through the belief that this would not happen before 2013, or in the winter of 2012 at the earliest. But as the Sicilian night calmed the day's heat, he accepted: "I have now suddenly realised that I am going to have to face up to this event in my life some months earlier than I had expected."

Only a handful of scientists within ATLAS collaboration knew the final state of its data. A similarly small number within the CMS team was party to that experiment's overall result, and no one among these privileged few knew any details of the other team's conclusions. This firewall between the experiments was to avoid the analysis of either being influenced by unconscious bias, which can all too easily result from hearing what the other might be finding. There was total secrecy until the results were to be presented on 4 July: only then would each experiment learn of the other's evidence, and only then would the world at large see for itself.

Although Higgs had received a clear indication that something big would happen at CERN on 4 July, he still had no idea how robust this would be. There are countless examples of media headlines anticipating some major announcement, which become letdowns when they actually happen, when caveats are aired, or when critical questions remain unanswered. After so many years of waiting, the approach of 4 July meant the tension was if anything growing rather than being assuaged. What further clues could we find?

Thousands of research scientists were working on each experiment, and agreement on the solidity of the analyses required wide consultation within each team. Like cryptographers reading a coded message by what at first seem trifling insights, there were clues that enabled those of us outside the experiments to assess the likely outcome. Conveniently, some of CERN's experimenters were students who were now with us at Erice. In the bar before dinner, two had been comparing notes. At that stage I was still unaware of what had happened in Venus at lunchtime and was excited when I learned from the students that ATLAS had finalized its presentation near the critical 5-sigma value. Later that evening, I told Higgs. "That sounds good enough"

was his understated response, "provided that CMS are more or less in agreement".[7] But did the two experiments agree?

The leader of CMS was due to arrive at Erice the next day but cancelled at
the last minute. This seemed a positive sign. That he might have discovered
a flaw in some computer programme seemed unlikely. So Walker rebooked
tickets for Higgs and himself to fly from Palermo to Geneva via Rome. Having originally planned to return to Edinburgh that day, Higgs had no Swiss
francs with him, and his travel insurance was about to run out. I was due to
return to the United Kingdom via Milan. Aware of the approaching media
storm, and in the hope of protecting Higgs for some while further, Alan
Walker photographed Higgs and me together after check-in, and this was
tweeted to social media referring to our separate travels but worded to suggest that Higgs would be arriving in Geneva from Milan rather than Rome.
This bought him one more day of privacy away from the paparazzi. From 4
July, everything changed.

Peter Higgs and the author at the Palermo airport, 2 July 2012. (Photo: Courtesy Frank
Close)

CHAPTER 15

THE FOURTH OF JULY

STEPHANIE HILLS, WHO in April had convened the meeting in England to plan a future announcement of the discovery of the Higgs boson, had subsequently been appointed to the post of UK communications officer at CERN. Her first day was Monday 2 July. All the communications people, about sixty in total, had gathered to plan for the media storm anticipated on 4 July. One of the jobs would be to guide Peter Higgs through the press briefing and look after him during his visit. She heard someone say, "You'll be doing that", and she "looked round to see who got that plum job" and discovered it was her. Having only just arrived at CERN, "I really didn't know where anything was". However, that was the job she had just taken on: "I got the gig."[1]

Higgs and Alan Walker had their first clue to what lay in store when they went to the CERN cafeteria for a meal soon after their arrival on 2 July. CERN hosts a summer student programme for select undergraduates from around Europe, which had just begun. More than a hundred students had discovered that a big announcement was expected on 4 July, and as word spread that Higgs himself had arrived, many of them came to his table wanting selfies and autographs. For the Edinburgh duo, this was an eerie replay of what had happened in that same cafeteria during the open days in 2008. Hills first met Peter Higgs on the morning of 3 July when he and Walker came to see Jane MacKenzie, head of the UK liaison office, and asked how CERN could help Higgs survive being swamped by excited students, physicists, and media.

As MacKenzie recalled, "It was clear that we needed to put some protection in place for Peter" as the reaction in the cafeteria had been "quite intimidating".[2] The discovery of the Higgs boson was a well-kept secret within the community, but everyone at CERN suspected what was going to happen. Higgs' presence itself was enough to get people excited. For the young students, he had become a "rock star of physics".[3]

The entire CERN communications team was involved—press office, outreach people, everyone was mobilised to have a role on the day, whether it was crowd control, making sure the microphones worked, or taking photos. In effect everything was planned to ensure that one of the biggest occasions in CERN's sixty-year history would work smoothly and be recorded for posterity.

Two press officers from Edinburgh University had flown in on Monday evening and helped MacKenzie and Hills draw up plans for the two days of Higgs' visit. The Edinburgh team wanted to go out to lunch with Higgs and other Edinburgh scientists at CERN, so MacKenzie arranged a table at Le Smash—a restaurant just off the CERN site. That evening, 3 July, Higgs and Walker had been invited to dinner at the home of CERN theorist John Ellis in Tannay, in the canton of Vaud about twelve kilometres north of Geneva, and MacKenzie promised to drive them there and back. Ellis, a former head of theory at CERN, was one of the trio of theorists who in 1976 had realised the importance of the Higgs boson and written the first survey suggesting how to look for it. The group would be joined by Chris Llewellyn Smith, the sole surviving British former director-general of CERN, whose paper in 1973 had highlighted the need for the Higgs boson if the electroweak theory was to be mathematically consistent.

The convivial evening sealed any lingering doubts about what was likely to occur the next day. Higgs learned that CERN director-general Rolf Heuer had invited Llewellyn Smith and the other former DGs to the event. CERN had also invited François Englert as well as other surviving members of the Gang of Six. Of these, Tom Kibble chose to watch the presentation from London, but Englert, Gerald Guralnik, and Carl Hagen were coming. This was a key argument that Ellis had deployed in his phone call to Walker on 30 June to persuade Higgs to come also. Englert and Higgs had never met in the fifty-six years since Englert and his colleague, the late Robert Brout, had unveiled the mass mechanism. The fourth of July promised to be momentous for personal reasons, not just for physics.

Did Ellis or Llewellyn Smith have inside knowledge that could now be shared? Ellis said he had not seen any data since that released at the end of the previous year where there had been hints of a signal. As for what would happen the next day, "I had no doubts that there was something there." He recalled to me later his thoughts that evening: "The fact the management had invited Higgs, Englert, and others meant there had to be something very significant and positive. They wouldn't be invited if ATLAS and CMS ended up saying 'we don't see anything', nor if they were going to stand up and say something different to one another. The whole event would not have been scheduled if the two collaborations were not consistent."[4] Llewellyn Smith confirmed that he hadn't seen any of the latest results either, but for him too "it was obvious what was going on. The way the invitation arrived from Rolf [Heuer]. They had to be ready to announce a discovery."[5]

Ellis recalled that it was a cheerful evening as they confidently anticipated the end of a half-century quest, in which he and Llewellyn Smith had played parts in making Higgs' idea a reality. The conversation was intense but, he recalled, "Rather modestly we only got through one bottle of champagne." Subsequently he was asked by London's Science Museum if he would kindly donate the empty bottle. He did, and it was on show there for a while, and then later it went on a world tour where Ellis' daughter saw it on display in Singapore. They had gathered like members of a family the night before a wedding, the empty bottle of champagne its sole physical remnant. As Ellis recounted the occasion, he paused, and then suddenly exclaimed: "I don't think we signed it!"[6]

ONCE IN A GENERATION

The director-general was mindful that this was going to be a once-in-a-generation moment for all the staff at CERN. Back in the 1960s, everyone at

Cape Canaveral, including the people who emptied the litter bins, felt they were part of the Apollo project. Now at CERN, Heuer wanted all the rank-and-file members of the organisation who had been involved in building the LHC and the detectors and in helping to fulfil the dream of finding the Higgs boson to be able to participate rather than just have the leaders of the experiment present the results to a select audience of physicists. Relatively few seats in the auditorium were reserved. These were set aside for former DGs and people who had led the data analyses or been otherwise centrally involved in the quest. Of the five surviving theorists whose work had seeded it, Guralnik, Hagen, Englert, and Higgs would also be present. Tom Kibble chose to stay in London, where he could follow the webcast at a VIP session for the minister of science and the British science media in Central Hall Westminster near the Houses of Parliament. Higgs and Englert would meet for the first time as they took their reserved seats in the auditorium. Beyond these few, it was to be first come, first served.

On 4 July the plan was for Higgs and Walker to meet Stephanie Hills to be briefed about the day at a quiet breakfast in a conference room well away from where everything else was happening. Hills needed to be in top form after just forty-eight hours at the laboratory, so she rose at dawn, "very excited but also very nervous as I knew how many press crews were coming". She arrived at CERN at about six in the morning, which was when she had the first indication of what the day promised.

CERN's main auditorium is on the mezzanine of its main building. In front of it is an open area, the Salle des Pas Perdus. A bridge connects this landing to the labyrinth of corridors housing the offices of research physicists. The name has its origins in civil law, where it designates the central space for lawyers and clients to consult one another in a courthouse. At CERN, the Salle des Pas Perdus is where people normally gather to discuss events taking place in the surrounding conference rooms, the two ends of the mezzanine hosting the Council Chamber and the main auditorium. On the night of 3–4 July, however, the Salle des Pas Perdus was a scene of total mayhem. Hills recalled that when she arrived at six a.m., "I walked into the main building and there were people lying on the floor. On the mezzanine by the entrance to the lecture theatre there were sleeping bags, duvets, piles of blankets, and more sleeping people. These people had been there all night.

There was already a queue to get in, mostly summer students but not exclusively. Within probably half an hour to an hour the queue went all the way round the mezzanine, down the stairs, and snaked through the main restaurant." In another direction another queue headed along the bridge connecting the auditorium to the physicists' offices. The atmosphere was like that before a rock concert or to get the best place in London's Oxford Street sales. There was real excitement at the expectation of being present at a moment in history when scientific epochs change.

A MOMENT IN HISTORY

I was in England, watching on the internet, with a crowd of physicists at the Rutherford Appleton Laboratory in Oxfordshire. Even as kibbitzers, we felt we were living through a historic moment. The camera lingered on Peter Higgs, sitting next to François Englert, whose collaborator, Robert Brout, had sadly not lived to see this fulfilment of their journey. In the front row was CERN's director-general, Rolf Heuer, accompanied by a phalanx of former DGs—Herwig Schopper, Carlo Rubbia, Chris Llewellyn Smith, Luciano Maiani, and Robert Aymar—who had overseen the epic enterprise: Rubbia's discovery of the W and Z, construction of LEP, and finally the LHC. Surely all these people could not have come together to witness an anticlimax?

Nor had they.

Joe Incandela, spokesperson of the CMS team, first described the CMS search for the Higgs boson in two-photon events. These showed a clear peak at 125 GeV, which was sharper than the previous year but not good enough to claim a discovery. Then he showed data for events containing four charged leptons, which could arise from a Higgs boson decaying into two Z bosons. Here again there was a tantalising peak around 125 GeV, but not enough to be certain. After over half an hour of painstaking analysis he revealed that when the CMS team combined the two sets of data together, the significance of the peak exceeded the key 5-sigma. At last: CMS had strong evidence for the Higgs boson.

The extraordinary tension broke, and the audience burst into prolonged applause. When Fabiola Gianotti, the ATLAS spokesperson, announced that ATLAS too had found the same phenomena, independently, and with the same conclusions, there was cheering. Former DGs, including staid octogenarians, were slapping one another on the back like excited children. So here was the answer to Jim Naughtie's question: We *were* witnessing a seminal moment in human culture. What had been conjecture for so long was now knowledge, knowledge about the fundamental nature of the universe that would be there for as long as humanity itself, passed down the generations, as we ourselves have been taught about the insights of Isaac Newton and other scientists from past ages. The mysterious power of mathematics had been confirmed once more: the ability of equations written on pieces of paper to know nature.

The long lens of CERN's photographer caught Higgs and Englert dabbing their eyes with handkerchiefs. For all his belief that his ideas were correct, and that the boson was there to be found, Higgs was not prepared for the overwhelming emotions that erupted when confirmation came. "It was very moving. I burst into tears. It was partly the result of the audience reaction, their euphoria. There was a huge buzz."[7]

Higgs had seen an equation written on a long ago July afternoon spawn a global enterprise involving some ten thousand scientists all working to a common goal. Taxpayers around the world had underwritten their efforts. Although rationally Higgs could not be blamed had nature chosen some other mechanism than his theory and the quest for the boson come to nothing, nonetheless the confirmation was a huge release. Many scientists had devoted twenty years to the endeavour. Higgs had waited for more than half a lifetime.

At the vortex of the storm, Peter Higgs as always was modest but unable to avoid the immense public reaction. The world media had sent reporters to witness the event, and Gillies had arranged for over a hundred of them to watch the proceedings on a video feed in the Council Chamber, a hall on the far side of the Salle des Pas Perdus. Gillies recalled how earlier that morning, for all the sense of anticipation when the doors of the auditorium opened, proceedings were remarkably orderly, not like the experience at airports where people rush to get on an overbooked plane. The real problem was afterwards, getting Higgs from the auditorium across the 30 metres or so of the Salle des Pas Perdus to the Council Chamber. Stephanie Hills and Jane MacKenzie were waiting at the auditorium door to help guide him. They ran a gauntlet of press cameras while Gillies pushed people back to make space to get him across. It wasn't very far but "there must have been four or five camera crews plus I don't know how many journalists. They were all thrusting microphones in his face, and shouting 'Professor Higgs, Professor Higgs!' Everybody was wanting a comment from him."[8] It was like having to fight your way through a rush-hour crush, with the crowd additionally carrying microphones attached to extendable boom poles, or powerful arc lamps—television cameramen jostling one another for the perfect shot.

Higgs found it "utter madness",[9] MacKenzie concurred, describing the experience as "insufferable" and a "nightmare". The media, wanting certainty that the discovery was indeed the eponymous boson, kept asking, "Have we got it, Professor Higgs?" Higgs maintained a steady line: "It's not appropriate for me to comment at this stage. This is an occasion to celebrate the experiments and congratulate the people involved."[10] He declined to say much more.[11]

THE PRESS CONFERENCE

Physicists in the auditorium had erupted with joy when they saw arcane bumps in graphs or peaks in histograms, or heard phrases such as *5-sigma* and other technical pieces of jargon. Over a hundred journalists and photographers, including many of Europe's leading science correspondents, were now waiting in the Council Chamber, preparing to play their role in bringing the news to the world. At a table facing them sat CERN's director-general, Rolf Heuer; the spokespersons of the CMS and ATLAS collaborations, Joe Incandela and Fabiola Gianotti; and Sergio Bertolucci, CERN's director of research and scientific computing. In the front row of the audience sat François Englert and Peter Higgs, Englert with his balding head leaning slightly forwards, peering keenly at the stage through heavy rimmed spectacles, and Higgs slumped back in his seat looking exhausted. The media were aware of Englert's name from their briefings, but their interest was on Higgs, whose name was given to the boson. Reporters continued to press him with "Have we got it Professor Higgs?", to which Higgs, somewhat embarrassed, persisted with the formula that it was inappropriate for him to comment as this was a day to celebrate the experiments. Higgs then sank lower in his chair, his body language clearly indicating that he wanted to observe the proceedings without being called upon to perform.

First, the reporters needed to know what had been discovered, what it meant, and why anyone outside a club of particle physicists should care. The first question went straight to the point: "For six billion laymen out there—what is the best shorthand explanation of what this means?" Heuer took up the challenge with a clever play on the winning entry to the Waldegrave competition, which back in 1993 had compared the mass mechanism to British prime minister Margaret Thatcher trying to pass through a room full of political supporters. He gave as an analogy a room full of journalists. If you are someone unknown to them, you pass through the room at the speed of light. The more famous you are, the more journalists cluster around you—the more massive you are. He added, "You saw that when you came in here. Peter Higgs was pretty heavy." He continued, "I open the door and whisper a rumour into the room. The journalists cluster. That clustering is the Higgs boson."

Fabiola Gianotti, who would later succeed Rolf Heuer as DG of CERN, showed both her aptitude as a scientist and her interpersonal skills when she described what the discovery meant to her team. "The last few days have been extremely intense, full of work and emotions. At the same time, we had to be extremely focused in order to be able to analyse very quickly huge amounts of data that were coming out of the LHC." The analysis had continued until the last moment, ensuring that there were no oversights, that all checks had been made. She portrayed the experimental team of thousands as a living organism and explained how the data emerge and are analysed and interpreted. "It's essentially a chain which is extremely complicated that goes from the detector in the underground cavern all the way through trigger data acquisition, data calibration, then processing and distribution to the worldwide centre. Then the data is analysed [in universities and laboratories around the world] and then the graphs and plots are made. This is a very long chain." It had to work perfectly with "oil everywhere and no friction". She summarised the achievement as being the result of thousands of individuals each committed to "hard work, dedication, high competence, team spirit".

Joe Incandela was asked how he felt at the moment when he made the first announcement of the discovery. He described the audience response as "overwhelming, a really magnificent moment to see the reaction of the community, like I was walking on air". He too remarked on the "unbelievable amount of work done by a huge number of people. I don't think people realise it's very hard for us to express what's involved. It's so complicated." He explained that there are so many pieces of the whole organisation that have to work correctly. The team cannot have any mistakes in hundreds of different areas, so subsets of scientists cross-check and scrutinise the analyses, and all the chain must work. There are billions of events involved, heavily processed, distributed all over the world, and they all have to come in to CMS central, and all the files have to be tracked down. He revealed the human side of science when he remarked, "It didn't really hit me emotionally until today because we have to be so focused, and there was so much work to do, and so many people to work with. I'm just super proud of my collaborators for what they've done."

Heuer reinforced this by describing it as an example of *coopetition*. "Everyone within each experiment is collaborating, and also competing. There is a lot of scrutiny inside the experiments. We are lucky to have two equally performing experiments working side by side, competing but also collaborating." Cooperation and competition: coopetition.

The journalists wanted to know why this boson is so special, more than just "another particle". Incandela explained: "This boson is very profound. We are reaching into the fabric of the universe in a way we haven't done so before. It's telling us something that is key to the structure of the universe." One journalist raised "that dreaded phrase, 'the God Particle'" and remarked that "although we all know you hate it, it has captured the imagination of the general public and it does kind of describe what's going on in a way." The panel agreed that the Higgs boson has a unique place among the known particles. Incandela commented, "This famous description of the 'God Particle' is because it actually embodies the substance of all the other particles that exist." As to its relationship to those other particles, he said, "These particles are not isolated. They talk to each other. Their properties are interwoven within certain frameworks, so if this boson turns out to have properties that are quite discrepant from the Standard Model, this would also be a very big clue about constraining other models that are out there."

These discussions about the Higgs boson continued for an hour without any comment from Higgs himself. Then Geoff Brumfiel of *Nature* asked a question, his voice strained with frustration: "I know, Professor Higgs, we're not allowed to ask you questions, but can I ask you to say something? Anything! Your name is transcribed there on all the billboards. Not all of us work for Reuters. A brief statement would be wonderful, thank you." There was a brief pause. People looked at Higgs as he turned on his microphone. Then, speaking uncomfortably, as if he had just had his paper rejected rather than his work confirmed, Higgs replied slowly: "You can ask. But again, as I say, this is not the occasion for this discussion. So please let's continue on the main topic." In the silence that ensued, Heuer lightened the atmosphere: "Okay, but you cannot deny that this was a statement."

What no one at CERN knew at the time was that the news had already been broadcast to the world from London. The person who first made the announcement was John Womersley, chief executive of the UK's funding agency for particle physics, at Central Hall Westminster. Womersley had been at the CERN Council meeting that decided the news should be announced at CERN, and "although Rolf [Heuer] was careful in not saying anything that could be written up as a story in advance, it was clear this was going to be 'it'. I knew that sufficiently far ahead to book [Central Hall and] to invite people."[12] In the hall was a select gathering of senior scientists, including Tom Kibble of the original Gang of Six, and all the British science media. The minister of science, David Willetts, would only be there for a short time, not long enough to listen by video feed to the two technical presentations being made in Geneva on particle physics with a still uncertain outcome.

Media stories, press releases, and even scientific papers normally carry the revelation in the headline, with a summary of the main facts followed by more measured details. The presentations at CERN would be utterly different—almost the reverse, in fact. Womersley knew that there were going to be two long and methodical scientific talks, each carefully making the case like a counsel in a law court, only at the end of which would the speaker assert, "We've discovered a particle compatible with the Higgs boson." After the first speaker started displaying data on figures filled with histograms, Womersley recalled, "It was clear that the minister was getting restless." A once-in-a-blue-moon opportunity for a senior member of the government to experience a huge triumph for British science was in danger of slipping away. When he realised "it was going to take about another hour before they got to the denouement, as soon as the first speaker said something like '5-sigma significance', I said, 'That's it. We've reached the point where a discovery can be claimed and so I'll interpret this for you, Minister', and at that point we cut away from the video feed." He then briefed the minister and the VIP audience on the significance of what they had heard—that the Higgs boson was confirmed. He explained, "I judged it was a political necessity, because there is no way we could have got these people to sit there for the whole duration of the event. To get on the news you need to be timely."[13]

And thus all the British press got the news before anybody else, including Peter Higgs, and posted it on the internet. The best laid plans of CERN that communications officers in the CERN member states would put out press releases later that day came to nothing. But those at CERN didn't notice any of this because they were rapt, listening to Joe Incandela and Fabiola Gianotti give their reports.

NOT IN MY LIFETIME

Stephanie Hills had been intimidated by the experience of getting Peter Higgs through the crowd from the auditorium to the press conference. By the time they were settled in the Council Chamber, Higgs looked anxious. She stayed in the conference while Jane MacKenzie arranged for CERN security guards to clear the way for them afterwards, when they would escort Higgs to a private lunch in a room nearby.

MacKenzie recalled, "As soon as he came out of the [press conference] door into the corridor, the paparazzi were there again, with all their lights flashing. Thankfully the security guards were with us immediately." The melee was "like he was some kind of massive celebrity or a teen pop sensation. Cameras were looming in our eyes; they were right in our faces. Steph[anie] and I kept saying to them all, 'Would you please step back; please create some space.'"[14]

Hills was grateful for the presence of the security people who "took us to the door of the [lunch] room with what felt like the whole universe shouting 'Peter, Peter, what do you think? Can we have a comment?' We were bundled inside, Peter and me and no one else." A security person stood guard outside while MacKenzie searched for the guests.[15]

The door shut and there was relative peace and quiet. They could hear the madness of the world outside, now slightly muffled. Hills suddenly thought: "This is most bizarre! In all of this crazy day I'm in this little room on my own with Peter Higgs." They were sitting on opposite sides of the table facing one another. Peter "gave a wry smile" and Stephanie said, "Well, did you expect them to find it?" and he replied, "Not in my lifetime." Unwittingly she had got his best quote of the day.[16]

Jane MacKenzie and Stephanie Hills guiding Peter Higgs across the Salle des Pas Perdus at CERN, 4 July 2012. (Photo courtesy Jane MacKenzie)

PART 3

PART 3

CHAPTER 16

"TIME TO PLAN MY ESCAPE"

Although Peter Higgs is not recognised as a TV personality might be, in his home city of Edinburgh he is regularly stopped on the street. I had noticed how this changed between Melrose in June 2012, when the boson was still an idea, a reality as yet inaccessible, and when I interviewed him at the Edinburgh Book Festival in August that same year, just four weeks after the confirmation. The reaction of the August audience spoke volumes—in all senses. In June everyone was thrilled that Higgs was there on stage; the applause was loud but not exceptional. In August it was singular. When an audience applauds before an event, it's as if there is a timer in your head, which tells you when you expect the clapping to die down. But it didn't. It went on—and on. "This is their boy", I thought. "We don't need to say anything. We can stand here for an hour, let them applaud, and they will leave happy."

With the boson confirmed, speculation inevitably grew about the 2012 Nobel Prize. The Prize for physics is traditionally announced on the Tuesday of the first full week in October, at about midday in Stockholm. As it approaches, a highly selective epidemic breaks out: Nobelitis, a state of nervous tension among scientists who crave the Nobel Prize. Some of the larger egos will have previously had their craving satisfied, only perhaps to come down with another fear: will I ever be counted as one with Einstein? Others have only a temporary remission, before suffering a renewed outbreak the following year.

Straight after the discovery in 2012, the authorities in Edinburgh University started paying attention. The university's principal for fourteen years had been Tim O'Shea. Years earlier, as a research fellow in computer science at Edinburgh, O'Shea had heard Higgs talk about hidden symmetry, so in 2012 he was well prepared and immediately began to organise how Edinburgh University might benefit from Higgs' discovery. The press officer, under the impression that Higgs would win the prize that year, prepared two draft letters, one for Higgs to sign and another for the principal. Higgs said, "Put them in storage. It's not going to happen this year. I know how the Nobel committee works and by this time it's already made up its mind about the 2012 prize. It might happen next year."[1] This wise judgement did not prevent a media circus speculating how to select at most three out of a cast of worthy characters. The question became not so much "Will Peter Higgs win it?" as "Who will share it with him?"

Three people at most can share a Nobel, and at least six had had ideas like Higgs' in the halcyon days of 1964 when this story began. Adding to the conundrum, the discovery of the boson, which gave experimental proof of the hypothesis, involved teams of thousands of physicists from all around the world, drawn together in a huge cooperative venture at CERN, using a machine that is itself a triumph of engineering, led by Lyn Evans and designed and built by hundreds of others. The 2012 Nobel Prize for physics was announced on Tuesday 9 October and did indeed go elsewhere—to French experimentalist Serge Haroche and American physicist David Wineland for taking the first steps towards a quantum computer.

On Thursday that week, 11 October 2012, I went to Edinburgh. By some irony, I had been scheduled to talk to a colloquium at the university physics department on the history of the boson, and although no one (except perhaps the press officer) had seriously anticipated the prize that year, there was still a feeling of anticlimax.[2] Higgs joined me for coffee beforehand and I asked him how he felt now that the moment had passed, at least for this year. The great physicist Richard Feynman once remarked that he didn't need any prizes; discovery itself was reward enough. Higgs had a similar attitude. Having been incessantly in demand for months, he remarked: "I'm enjoying the peace and quiet. My phone hasn't rung for two days."[3]

NOTHING IS GUARANTEED

On 30 June 2013, Higgs and I were once again in Erice in Sicily, a year to the day since he had received the call to CERN, and in the same restaurant. I asked him how the reality of the discovery had compared with the anticipation. By then evidence was accumulating that the particle is indeed the source of mass, as the theory had posited. Its decays into different varieties of quark and lepton and to the W or Z bosons show a universal affinity for all fundamental particles in proportion to their masses. That the sensational discovery of 2012 was indeed of Higgs' boson was, by the summer of 2013, beyond dispute. That Higgs was in line for a Nobel Prize also seemed highly likely. Higgs himself, however, knew from experience that in the Stockholm stakes, nothing is guaranteed.

Back in 1982, at dawn on 5 October in the Midwest and the eastern United States, preparations were in hand for champagne celebrations in three departments at two universities. At Cornell, the physics department hoped they would be honouring Kenneth Wilson, while over in the chemistry department their prospect was Michael Fisher. In Chicago, the physicists' hero was to be Leo Kadanoff.

Two years earlier the trio had shared the Wolf Prize, the scientific analogue of the Golden Globes to the Nobel's Oscars. That fuelled speculation that a Nobel would soon follow, a suspicion reinforced in late summer of 1982 by what appeared to Higgs to have been "a premature leak from Stockholm".[4] Full of hope that this was to be their year, the three scientists and their colleagues awaited the official confirmation.

At the appointed hour in Stockholm, the chair of the awards committee announced the result. He began: "The 1982 Nobel Prize for physics is awarded to Professor Kenneth Wilson. . . ." If anyone was surprised in that microsecond, as the names are usually given in alphabetical order, the question was answered definitively as the announcement finished. The award was to Wilson alone. No Fisher, no Kadanoff.

The hurt was especially keen in the case of Michael Fisher, whose experience and teaching about phase transitions, illuminating the subtle changes in states of matter such as melting ice and the emergence of magnetism, had inspired Wilson, five years his junior. The omission of Kadanoff and Fisher was a sensation at the time and has remained one of the intrigues of Nobel lore.

Fisher's agony was no secret to Peter Higgs, for as undergraduates they had been like brothers and close friends for over sixty years. They had maintained contact, both personal and professional, throughout all that time. Fisher's influence was not far away the day in July 1964 when Higgs, while examining how some ideas from statistical mechanics were applied to particle physics, had the insight that would become the capstone to the theory of particles and forces at the cusp of the twenty-first century.

For this, in 2004 Higgs had shared the Wolf Prize with François Englert and Robert Brout. Now, as October approached in 2013, he became a hot favourite to win, or at least share, the Nobel Prize for physics, and the bookmakers would only take bets at extreme odds-on. Unlike Peter Higgs, they were not aware of Michael Fisher's previous disappointment.

In 2013, 8 October was the day when the Nobel decision would be announced. Higgs' experiences the year before had helped him to prepare: "I already had some attention from the local press around the time of the 2012 announcement. So I was forewarned about what to expect when it was for real. 2012 was like a dress rehearsal. I did a bit of forward planning. I decided not to be at home when the announcement was made with the press at my door; I was going to be somewhere else."

Higgs' first plan was to disappear into the Highlands by using the north Highland and west Highland railway lines to do a round trip connecting through Skye and stay somewhere like Plockton, on the west coast, on the way. Then he realised this wasn't a good plan at that time of year, early October, and also decided it was far too complicated: "I can hide equally well in Edinburgh. All I would have to do is go down to Leith early enough. I knew the announcement would be around noon so I would leave home soon after eleven, giving myself a safe margin, and have an early lunch in Leith about noon."[5]

Richard Kenway, the Tait Professor of Mathematical Physics and by then also one of the university's vice principals, confirmed the tale. "Peter managed to propagate a story that he was going to head off to the Highlands on the day before the announcement and he was not going to be contactable. That was what we all were told, and he completely convinced us. Right up to the actual moment when we were sitting waiting for the [Nobel] announcement, we thought he had disappeared off somewhere into the Highlands."[6]

None of Higgs' colleagues knew of his change of plan. As Kenway recalled, "So quite genuinely we all attended at the university to watch the broadcast of the announcement. We sat through the long wait as it was delayed." And not just those in Edinburgh. Scientists on every continent—even some at Antarctica's polar research station—were tuning in on video screens, laptops, and smartphones to the live feed from Stockholm. An event which for more than a century was associated with timing akin to that on Swiss railways took on an uncertainty more familiar to passengers watching delays announced on airport video monitors. The Nobel committee had been struggling to reach the famously reclusive physicist. The announcement of his long-awaited crown was delayed by about half an hour until they decided they could wait no longer and must go ahead. Meanwhile, shunning it all without a phone, and unaware of the ructions taking place, Peter Higgs sat at his favourite table in The Vintage, a seafood bar in Henderson Street, Leith, drinking a pint of real ale and considering the menu.

I was watching online as the committee announced the award, explaining in arid prose that it had given the prize to François Englert and Peter Higgs for the "theoretical discovery of a mechanism that contributes to our understanding of the origin of mass of subatomic particles. . . ." As messages flooded social media and my inbox, it seemed that the whole of the physics world was watching too. Except one.

Almost immediately, phones started going off in the Edinburgh physics department. Kenway recollected, "We were saying to all the journalists, 'He's gone! He's gone off into the Highlands. We don't know where he is. We can't contact him.' From that point of view the bluff worked—whether it was deliberate or not I don't know—and we didn't find out until later in the day, when he'd been spotted coming back to his flat, that he was in Edinburgh. We were as fooled as anybody."[7] Some newspapers got the fake news from the department, and one reporter even went up into the Highlands to look for him.

Meanwhile, Higgs finished his lunch. It seemed a little early to head home, so he decided to look in at an art exhibition. At about three o'clock he was walking along Heriot Row in Edinburgh, heading for his flat in the next street, when a car pulled up near the Queen Street Gardens. "A lady in her sixties, the widow of a high court judge, got out and came across the road in a very excited state to say, 'My daughter phoned from London to tell me about the award', and I said, 'What award?' I was joking of course, but that's when she confirmed that I had won the prize. I continued home and managed to get in my front door with no more damage than one photographer lying in wait."[8] It was only later that afternoon that he finally learned from the radio news that the award was to himself and François Englert.[9]

After the anticlimax of my talk about bosons in October 2012, the Edinburgh physics department had repeated their invitation to come and give a public talk about the significance of Higgs' discovery. This took place two days after the announcement of the Nobel Prize. We gathered beforehand for coffee in the hall facing the lecture hall as before. There was no sign of Higgs, who had not been seen by more than a handful of his colleagues since the news broke. Then, a few minutes before the start, he was suddenly there, having arrived unnoticed like a participant in an illusionist's trick. Given the fifty years that it had taken to get from the idea to the discovery of the eponymous boson, and Higgs' disappearance at the climax of his success, the title of my lecture had of course chosen itself: "Searching for Higgs".

PRINCE OF ASTURIAS: NOBEL REHEARSAL

In June 2013, Higgs had learned he had won the Prince of Asturias Award for science, jointly with François Englert and CERN.[10] The actual awards ceremony was held on 29 October, by which time Higgs and Englert also knew they had won the Nobel Prize. The Spanish awards cover science and arts, and the elaborate ceremony in the presence of the royal family is an echo of the Nobel event. For Higgs and Englert, the ceremony in Oviedo, Spain, would be in effect a dress rehearsal for Stockholm in December.

For Asturias as for the Nobel, winners can invite a small number of guests. The etiquette of where to make the cut in the invitation list for a family wedding is minor compared to the sharp decisions necessary in these select events. In Stockholm the guests include a handful of immediate family and traditionally some scientists who were integral to your accolade or colleagues of long standing. For Oviedo, Higgs chose a more maverick handful, focusing on friends who lived nearby. One was Jane MacKenzie, who had helped him at CERN when the discovery of the boson was announced and now lived in France near the Pyrenees. Another was a brewer of real ale from Barcelona.

After the big announcement, Higgs had been contacted by the brewer, who was trying to introduce real ale into Spain. Traditionally, Spanish beers are lagers, although brown beers were becoming more popular. The brewer asked for permission to create a Higgs boson ale. Not many brewers would even have known what the Higgs boson is or cared. Higgs gave the permission and invited the brewer to the award. His other invitee was an academic physicist from Spain.

After the ceremony there was a grand reception where the prince and princess were present. Formal occasions where he is thrust in the limelight are not Higgs' style. He asked his Spanish guests if they knew anywhere less formal where they could go. There was a bar nearby, which the brewer knew because it also had some real ales. They spent a pleasant evening there, away from the formalities, but as they were on their way through the streets of Oviedo, MacKenzie found herself doing the same job that she had done in CERN, pushing people back as they came towards Higgs. His face was familiar because it had been in the Spanish press and it was the evening of the Prince of Asturias Awards. It was one more reminder that Higgs was now a celebrity, and his stardom wasn't going away.

CHAPTER 17

THE GLITTERING PRIZES

ONE AFTERNOON IN 2015, two distinguished retired particle physicists were drinking tea in the stately grandeur of the Royal Society, in London's Carlton House Terrace, when in walked Peter Higgs. Wondering what brought the somewhat frail eighty-six-year-old scientist to London, they learned he was en route to Moss Bros. to be fitted for a morning suit. They were surprised to learn that he had not invested in one of his own by this stage.

He was already a Freeman of Newcastle, his birth town, and of Bristol, where he had grown up. Edinburgh, his home of six decades, had presented him with their Edinburgh Award in 2013 and engraved his handprints in Caithness stone in the quadrangle of the City Chambers. Higgs, long cynical about the way the honours system "is used for political purposes by the government in power", had as we have seen turned down a knighthood in 1999. In 2012, however, he accepted membership in the Order of the Companions of Honour, having been assured that the award was the gift of the queen alone. The order confers no title or precedence, but recipients are entitled to use the postnominal letters *CH*. (When people ask what the *CH*

after his name stands for, Higgs jokes, "It means I'm an honorary Swiss.")[1]
He received the order from the queen at an investiture at Holyroodhouse in
Edinburgh on 1 July 2014.

Above all, he had gone to Stockholm in December 2013 to receive the
Nobel Prize, for which the dress code is de rigueur. Had he not thought of
purchasing a morning suit on that occasion? There had been no need as the
hosts kitted out the recipients in special clothes that are then fitted by a tailor, including elegant shoes adorned with buckles. The formal dressing had
been but one aspect of what became for Higgs a stressful time. The tension
began before he had even left the United Kingdom.

To reach Stockholm, he would have preferred to fly direct from Edinburgh, but instead he travelled with his colleague Alan Walker via London,
because the immediate reaction to the announcement was an invitation to
dine with the Swedish ambassador and a selection of former British Nobel
laureates. They would stay in London overnight and fly to Stockholm the
next day. Pressure began to mount as other engagements were added to their
London transit, culminating in a frantic last-minute rush to the airport.
They reached the check-in only just in time for the plane. Higgs recalled the
two days as "hell".[2]

At least arrival at Stockholm was smooth, as every laureate has a minder
to take care of them and a fast-track entry through immigration. Higgs'
host was an ex-diplomat, who was very informative about what the week
would entail. He learned that one of the first appointments was to visit the
official tailor, to be fitted with the appropriate clothing for the presentation by the king.

The costume turned out to be formal morning dress in the mid-
nineteenth-century style of Alfred Nobel's time. As Higgs recalled, "Getting into the shirt alone takes considerable skill. It was almost a problem in
topology." The demonstration at the tailor's was hopeless. Higgs was tense
and couldn't remember the instructions. On the day of the ceremony, fortunately, "I managed somehow." Then there were the shoes. The first pair were
too small, but when he tried bigger ones, they wouldn't fit comfortably either. He explained, "The problem is that the nineteenth-century dress shoes
do not fit the shape of one's foot; they were rather pointy." On the day of the
ceremony both physics laureates, François Englert and Higgs, had a crisis

with their shoes. "Englert called my room: 'I can't wear these shoes. Can we agree to wear our own?' So we did. We were due to be the first on the stage and it must have been obvious to everyone in the front row—the families and David Willetts, the British minister of science—that we were not wearing the formal shoes."[3]

THE SWEDISH PRIZE

On the afternoon of 10 December nearly two thousand guests filled the Stockholm Concert Hall to see twelve laureates receive their awards from King Gustav of Sweden. They had been guided through the choreography of the occasion earlier, but on the day itself, performing before the throng in the hall, there would be first-night nerves for this once-in-a-lifetime theatre. François Englert and Peter Higgs, winners of the physics prize, would be called to receive their awards first, while the others watched and could see what to expect when their names were called.

The bulk of the audience, back in the body of the auditorium, had to rely on TV monitors to see the detail of the stage. It is carpeted in navy blue, and at its centre is a white circle about a metre in diameter containing a white capital N, insignia of the Nobel Foundation. This would enable the principal actors to "hit the mark" when it was their turn to perform.

The scenery, props, and supporting cast were already in place. These included two rows of empty chairs on stage, covered in red velvet. From the perspective of the audience, those to the right would be for the Swedish academicians of the presentation party, while on the left would sit the twelve laureates. Behind the laureates were two more rows, occupied by former winners dressed in tail suits and proudly wearing the gold button stud that signifies their membership in this unique club. Among them were Carlo Rubbia, discoverer of the W and Z particles, who instigated the experimental quest for the boson and won the prize in 1984; Gerard 't Hooft, who built on Higgs' work to complete the theoretical description of the weak nuclear force and won in 1999; and 2004 winner Frank Wilczek, who had built on his own prize-winning work to identify the two main pathways by which the Higgs boson had been discovered.

Finally, the most conspicuous pieces of furniture were on the right-hand side. Here were four high-backed armchairs in Louis XIV style, upholstered in red velvet and lavishly decorated with gilded sculptures. These were for King Carl Gustav, Queen Silvia, their son Prince Carl Philip, and their son-in-law Prince Daniel.

The pipes of a magnificent organ reach all the way to the high ceiling from a console on a balcony at the stage's rear. On the day of the awards, the organ was but part of the dramatic scenery as an orchestra occupied the gallery. The murmur of conversation suddenly stopped as a drum roll announced arrival of the royal family, the queen resplendent in a maroon gown whose hem trailed on the carpet. All stood as the orchestra played the Swedish royal anthem.

The arrival of the laureates, which was accompanied by the music of Mozart's March in D major, was a performance in its own right. In perfect mirror symmetry, two lines of people entered backstage: the academicians who headed the various selection committees from the right, the laureates from stage left. The male laureates were all adorned in their tail suits, forming a line of aged penguins. Each procession was led by a lone woman, a star student, wearing a white spaghetti strap full-length gown with a sash in the Swedish national colours of yellow and blue draped from her right shoulder to left hip. White gloves to just below her elbows completed a vision reminiscent of a Hollywood musical, except, somewhat incongruously, each young woman also sported a white cap with a shiny black plastic peak that would not have looked out of place on a yacht.

After a ten-minute oration by the chair of the Nobel Foundation and a musical interlude—excerpts from Sibelius' Karelia Suite, to which the king rhythmically tapped his right foot—at last, twenty minutes into a long afternoon, it was time for the first of the awards. Professor Lars Brink, chairman of the Nobel Committee for Physics, stepped forwards to the lectern to explain the background of the award to Higgs and Englert.

Brink, a month past his seventieth birthday, had the physique of an athlete, standing erect with a straight back, his rugged face topped with a bald domed head. He spoke clearly, like an actor making a speech before an audience of nearly two thousand people, the majority of whom understood him as he addressed them in Swedish. An English version of his script was available in the programme, and the laureates—including Higgs—followed it as if to understand what the Higgs boson was all about.

Brink's speech managed to achieve one of the most daunting challenges in science pedagogy, successfully addressing itself to both the general public in the hall and the assembled academics, including laureates from other areas of science. The significance of what we were celebrating was beyond doubt: "With discovery of the Higgs boson in 2012, the Standard Model of physics was complete. It has been proved that nature follows precisely that law that Brout, Englert, and Higgs created. This is a fantastic triumph for science," Brink announced. Then, in an address of some seven minutes, he gave a brief history of modern physics and the singular importance of the Higgs field and of the boson's discovery.

In his oration, Brink not only gave the headline summary of what Higgs and Englert—the two laureates about to be honoured—had done in 1964, but he also introduced a third name, that of Englert's collaborator, Robert Brout. In so doing, he made an explicit acknowledgement that the late Robert Brout in spirit completed a trinity of winners. There were several candidates who might have justifiably been included in the award—another from the Gang of Six, obviously, or perhaps one of the key people who confirmed the boson experimentally. Mention of Brout's name alongside that of Englert by Brink demonstrated that, but for his untimely death, Brout would have been awarded a third share of the prize.

Brink continued with his summary history. He recalled that it was not until seven years after Englert and Higgs' work that "a young Dutch student", Gerard 't Hooft, showed that the theory works, "in a proof of immense complexity leading to the Nobel Prize in 1999". The story had now reached the 1970s when, following 't Hooft, the physics world "very quickly developed a unified theory of the forces that act in microcosm (the strong, electromagnetic, and weak forces)". So was born "the Standard Model of particle physics". This Core Theory demanded new particles, which were speedily discovered, but the new particle that Higgs had predicted, which was now understood to give masses to all massive fundamental particles, was not found. By the 1980s, the entire Standard Model of physics rested on the existence of the Higgs particle: "Thirty years ago we had essentially found everything except this Higgs particle. Was it really there?"

Brink now came to the climax. Seventeen months earlier the experiments at the LHC had confirmed that the boson is real. What had been suspected for decades was now confirmed forever. The final piece in the Standard Model of particle physics had been found. The edifice was robust. Why this particular edifice is the one that forms our material universe is a question for the future. Brink now made the formal invitation for first Englert and then Higgs to step forward to receive their share of the award:

"Professor Higgs, you have together with Professors Englert and Brout found the key to understanding the masses of elementary particles, for which you have been awarded the Nobel Prize. On behalf of the Royal Swedish Academy of Sciences it is my privilege to convey to you my warmest congratulations for your outstanding work. I now ask you to step forwards to receive your Nobel Prize from the hands of His Majesty the King."

Higgs, resplendent in his formal suit, and comfortable in his own shoes, rose from his seat and prepared to walk to centre stage. Forty-eight years since he set out on what would be akin to an ascent of Everest, Higgs had effectively conquered the Hillary step—the final challenge before reaching the peak—on 4 July 2012 when the existence of his boson was confirmed. Now, all that remained while he took nine steps to reach the summit was to remember the choreography: stop at the Nobel Foundation insignia on the carpet; shake the king's hand with your right hand while accepting the Nobel Prize and diploma with the other. Then bow three times, first to the king, then to the bust of Alfred Nobel at the rear of the stage, and finally to the audience in the hall.

Higgs successfully completed the choreography and accepted his award. As a fanfare of trumpets sounded, the audience burst into applause. Higgs returned to his seat. The chairman of the chemistry committee took the lectern to introduce the winners of the chemistry prize. To his relief, Higgs was no longer in the spotlight.

OWNED BY THE WORLD

In April 2014, roughly four months after he received the Nobel Prize, I interviewed Higgs again, this time at the Edinburgh Science Festival. Edinburgh's Queen's Hall usually hosts concerts, but that evening it was full, with some nine hundred people eager to see the city's unlikely celebrity.

Our previous performance, at the Edinburgh Book Festival in August 2012 when he was given a prolonged ovation, had been immediately following discovery of the boson and confirmation of his life's work. This time we were together for Higgs' first public presentation since receiving the Nobel Prize. The applause was again loud and the audience enthusiastic, but the occasion seemed somehow more formal. Previously the Edinburgh crowd had erupted in joy, sharing their pride in an achievement made as if by one of the family. Now in the presence of a Nobel laureate they saw someone whose breakthrough was owned by the world. Winning a Nobel Prize makes changes, if only in how others react to you.

Higgs explained that he had been cursed by the hope of a Nobel Prize since 1980, when a friend in Lund connected to the Royal Swedish Academy of Sciences told him that he had been nominated. At that stage there was no real chance and he took no special notice other than the pleasure of realising that his work had made some impact. As the years passed and the discovery of the boson began to materialize, however, he admitted, "I began to get tense each year at the beginning of October, when the announcement of Nobel Prize winners is made." He added that the actual announcement of the award in 2013 had "come in a way as a relief—at last, it was all over".

Honours continued to accumulate, along with requests for interviews and public appearances, and he became less inhibited about being on show, but he was never truly at ease in the limelight. He would agree to appear so long as he felt secure, such as being interviewed by someone he knew, or in a venue where he felt at home, but the attempt to "get some of his normal life back" would prove difficult. Sometimes he would agree to an engagement, but unexpected problems or changes could disturb his personal equilibrium and the event would have to change format or be abandoned.

In September 2015 we were due to appear at a science festival in Orkney, the small archipelago off the north coast of Scotland. Higgs does not use email and has no mobile phone contact. During the August vacation season this made direct communication almost non-existent, and to check that everything would run smoothly I used local contacts such as Alan Walker. Walker was optimistic about Orkney; Higgs had a long-held respect for the organizer, and the Orkneys offered him the prospect of a peaceful experience.

I was due to give a talk at the festival anyway and so made my travel plans, but the major draw would of course be Higgs. I flew from London to

Kirkwall in Orkney via Edinburgh, where I waited nervously for the connecting flight while wondering if he would show. I breathed a huge sigh of relief to see his rosy face and bald dome among a group of new arrivals on the Edinburgh airport concourse. He walked towards me carrying a small backpack and greeted me saying he was looking forward to escaping to the remoteness of the Orkneys.

The talk was scheduled for the following evening. During the morning, the festival organisers had kindly arranged a visit for Higgs and me to some of the archaeological sites on the islands. One, the Ring of Brodgar, had special resonance. This Neolithic monument consists of individual stone slabs, each some 4 metres high, arranged in a circle of about 100 metres in diameter. They have stood here, on a small treeless hill bordered by the waters of the Loch of Harray and the Loch of Stenness, and encircled by the low hills of the archipelago, for over four thousand years. As the bracing northern winds blow across the bleak moorland, the questions that immediately strike you are: Why this? Why here?

The Ring of Brodgar as metaphor for the ring of magnets at CERN was obvious to us. Were the records of our civilisation to disappear, then four thousand years hence some visitor to the slopes of the Jura Mountains near Lake Geneva might ask the same questions about an underground archaeological relic that we call the Large Hadron Collider.

The forum in Kirkwall was very informal and one of those evenings where entertainers know they have a "lovely audience". The novelty for such a remote outpost of the British Isles of having a Nobel laureate on stage was a huge attraction; the audience was dominated by family groups and many teenage children. We followed the standard format of three short segments interspersed with questions from the audience, but at the end of the presentation we opened to general questions and answers as there were so many wanting to ask about things that we had not thought of ourselves.

After all this time we were asked a question that we hadn't been asked before: what is the Higgs field made of?

That is perhaps the most fundamental question that we now face. All that we know so far is that according to quantum mechanics, when a hot gas of Higgs bosons cools, it condenses to form the universal Higgs field. We do not know how this condensation of bosons happens, or what the nature of the field actually is—does it have structure of its own, forming a dynamic medium whose innards are yet to be revealed, or is it made of featureless bosons fused together like molecules of water, merging first into drops and eventually into entire oceans? For now, all we know is its effect: this field acts on the fundamental particles, giving them mass, enabling atoms to form, stars to shine, and ultimately life to occur.

François Englert and Peter Higgs prepare to receive their Nobel Prizes.

CHAPTER 18

ZIGZAG

THAT EVENING IN Kirkwall in the Orkneys in 2015 was my final interview on stage with Higgs. In our series of conversations, we had covered much of what I have recorded here: the story of how he came to his big idea; how physicists around the world had seized on it, developed it, and confirmed it; and how his later years had become consumed by the demands of being a public figure. We had debated what his big idea means in practice for our understanding of nature and mentioned some of the big unanswered questions that remain.

The audiences had gained insights into Higgs' life and career, but only later did it occur to me that I had never asked how Higgs himself would sum up his life. So, one day on the phone while researching this book, I asked, "If you were to write your autobiography, what would the story be?"

He paused and thought carefully. This was clearly a question he hadn't anticipated, nor apparently been asked before, as he had no ready, prepared answer. Then, after a couple of false starts he crystallised his experience: "I see my career as a sort of zigzag of changes which linked up eventually in ways I had no idea of at the time. There were so many things I learned about on the way that then came together."[1]

One of the abiding memories of that final evening in Kirkwall was of enthusiastic youngsters rapt by hearing about discoveries that have happened in their lifetimes. This was perhaps the first time they had been confronted at first hand by a piece of learning that is not yet in their textbooks, and with that comes excitement: textbooks of the future will contain knowledge they were hearing about from the very source. I pointed out to them that although we had been talking about an idea that was written down more than half a century earlier, many of the scientists in the experiments which discovered the Higgs boson and who would put it into the textbooks were graduate students, as little as four years on from their time at high school. Students listening that evening in 2015, who were in their final year at high school, could by now already have completed an undergraduate degree and be working towards PhDs on experiments at the frontiers of science.

The enthusiasm in Orkney echoed that of the students the laureates had met in Stockholm two years earlier. Their dreams also appeared universal. In Orkney, after a host of enquiries about physics, CERN, and what the discovery of "your boson" means, one eager youngster asked the key question which had first been asked by a student in Stockholm and seems to have been an ambition for many would-be scientists: "Please tell us how to win a Nobel Prize."

"Be lucky!" Higgs replied.[2]

Luck is certainly necessary but is hardly sufficient. Being in the right place at the right time, when the fates align to present you with the possibility of achievement, is nothing if you fail to recognise the opportunity or have the single-mindedness to continue racing to the tape. Thanks to his zigzag of experiences in maths and theoretical physics, Higgs was aware that there was a problem to be solved, but his fortune was that he had read Walter Gilbert's paper on how to evade Goldstone's theorem back in 1964 and immediately realised that Gilbert had failed to complete the course. That Higgs solved the problem within days is the 1 percent of inspiration; he had already invested years of perspiration—of building technical expertise with the intricacies of gauge invariance from his work on general relativity, of studying all the literature on that subject in order to understand its depth, of metaphorically having beaten his head against the wall until the wall gave way so that when presented with Gilbert's oversight, he was able to exploit it.

But he was hardly alone. Of the six who had independently proved a mathematical theorem that later founded much of modern quantum field theory, only Higgs moved the construct towards physically testable theory by making an identikit of the telltale boson. So was conceived the eponymous boson—child of the "only original idea I ever had"—whose half-century gestation would increasingly haunt his life.

Whereas the existence of the boson is now beyond doubt, the question of when and how it became the "Higgs" boson is harder to answer. If there were ever a precise moment, it is now lost in the fog of individual memories. The only certain facts are these: its provenance in Higgs' oeuvre was in an unremarkable set of algebraic symbols written in the form of an equation in the second of his 1964 papers. There is merely a whisper that this equation "describes waves whose quanta have . . . mass", and then there follow some symbolic hieroglyphs from which the amount of the boson's mass could be computed. Or could be if the values of certain quantities, such as how much of the mysterious universal field is needed to minimise energy in the void, were known. Two years later, in his seminal paper of 1966, it was named, literally: it is now a "free scalar boson of mass m_0". Half a century later, Higgs would variously describe it as "the boson that's been named after me", or as informally agreed with Englert, "the massive boson of the electroweak model".[3]

So, how did that name *Higgs boson* come about? Unlike in chemistry, where the names of new elements are officially endorsed by the International Union of Pure and Applied Chemistry (IUPAC), there is no formal body that names new particles. In an utterly democratic way, particles become named by common usage. Certainly, Higgs' cocktail conversation with Ben Lee in 1967 played a part in first publicising his role in discovering the mass mechanism, but the motivation for the excitement in Lee's conference discussion in 1972, which in Higgs' telling had "plastered [Higgs'] name onto everything", was more the remarkable application of the mass mechanism by the young Dutchman Gerard 't Hooft. Within five years, 't Hooft's work had revolutionised our theoretical understanding of nature, seeded the Standard Model, and predicted the existence of novel particles, the capstone of the entire construct being the massive boson.

That this boson was implicitly anticipated in the work of several theorists, and even explicitly already in the case of Jeffrey Goldstone, is largely unknown other than to historians of the field or to those who have worked in it for decades themselves. Physicists today refer to it with Higgs' name because papers written in the past did so.

Two chance circumstances probably led to the boson's association with Higgs, but for which history and hysteria might have been very different. In 1967, Higgs' talk with Lee provided one of these; the other was his conversation that summer with Steven Weinberg.

When later that year Weinberg wrote his seminal paper "Theory of Leptons", in which he conjectured—correctly as it turned out—that this mass mechanism would prove key to the whole structure, he gave Higgs top billing. That others had contemporaneously worked on the mass mechanism only became clear later, and they were inserted into the list of references prior to publication, but below Higgs. Four years later, Weinberg's second influential paper on the topic began to inspire serious interest in the mechanism, but here an inadvertent mistake in the references reinforced an impression that Higgs had an overall priority.[4] When subsequently theorists worldwide began to produce papers on the subject, Weinberg's papers were already physics best-sellers and the term *Higgs boson* was becoming ensconced in theoretical particle physics lore. The 1976 paper by Ellis, Gaillard, and Nanopoulos, with its title "A Phenomenological Profile of the Higgs Boson", next brought the Higgs boson to the attention of the experimental community, even if they read no more than the paper's title.

Brout and Englert were doubly disadvantaged. Their paper made no mention of the boson, as it played no role in the specific question they addressed. As experts in condensed-matter physics, however, they were aware that such a boson should exist—see, for example, figure 6.1c—but did not appreciate its importance for establishing the theory empirically in particle physics. This was their first paper in particle physics, and being condensed-matter theorists, they were largely unknown by the particle physics community.

For the world's particle physicists, their Higgs boson was the light at the end of the tunnel, or it would be if a tunnel large enough to contain the technology to produce the beast could be funded. Campaigns like snappy slogans. The media liked *the God Particle*, invented by Leon Lederman in

1993. Particle physicists, however, promoted *the Higgs boson*, which at the cusp of the twenty-first century had become a brand, the answer to cryptic crosswords, as an anagram within the clue: "Gosh! Big's no way to describe it though it's important in theory."[5] And as it is easier to follow a person than an idea, Higgs was increasingly used to promote the quest. An unassuming man who had one remarkably insightful original idea became a celebrity, a totem for the goals of thousands, and a recluse from the unsocial media that has overtaken his final decades.

The saga of Higgs' boson had begun with a classic image—a lone genius unlocking the secrets of nature through the power of human thought. The fundamental nature of Higgs' breakthrough had been immediately clear to him. However, no one, least of all Higgs, could have anticipated that it would take nearly half a century and several false starts to get from his idea to a machine capable of finding the particle. Nor did anyone envision that that single "good idea" would turn a shy and private man into a reluctant celebrity, accosted by strangers in the supermarket. Some even suggested that the reason why the public became so enamoured with Higgs was the solid ordinariness of his name, one syllable long, unpretentious, a symbol of worthy Anglo-Saxon labour. Had his surname been Kibble, Englert, or any other handle in the Gang of Six, perhaps less attention would have ensued.

Nine years after the discovery we were reminiscing about the occasion when, to my surprise, Higgs suddenly remarked that it had "ruined my life".[6] To know nature through mathematics, to see your theory confirmed, to win the plaudits of your peers and join the exclusive club of Nobel laureates: how could all this equate with ruin? To be sure I had not misunderstood, I asked again the next time we spoke. He explained: "My relatively peaceful existence was ending. I don't enjoy this sort of publicity. My style is to work in isolation, and occasionally have a bright idea."[7]

EPILOGUE

THE VIEW ACROSS THE PLAINS

"When the difficulty of the mountains is once behind
That's when you'll see the difficulty of the plains will start"
(Brecht)

How does discovery of the Higgs boson affect our view of the universe and the future of physics? In the public's mind, the LHC was made to find the Higgs boson. Is this, then, a great success for physics? Higgs was cautious: "The LHC was built to explore many things, not just the boson. There could be a reaction like 'OK, you can close the machine down now. It's expensive and it has done its job.'"[1]

The goal of particle physics for over three decades was to find the source of electroweak symmetry breaking. For anyone who entered the field in the 1970s, the entirety of their career has been spent with the Higgs boson as a beacon: its discovery would be both a final confirmation of the Standard

Model and a gateway to what lies beyond. As soon as the W and Z bosons were discovered in 1983, even the most hardened sceptic had to admit that quantum field theory was alive, that there needed to be a Higgs mechanism, and therefore there should be a boson associated with it. There was brief hope that maybe it was in reach of discovery at CERN's electron-positron collider, LEP—but it wasn't. Then came the need for a higher-energy machine. The Superconducting Super Collider (SSC) in Texas raised expectations but was aborted. Finally: everything was staked on the answer being found at CERN's LHC—and it was.

Higgs now feels CERN needs to devote more publicity to the other things they do there, which in his opinion "are equally important. From my point of view, finding this thing is just the end of a chapter." If so, it is a chapter that took half a century to complete until, on 4 July 2012, a new chapter began, titled "The Post-Higgs Era". In 1966, when he drew attention to the massive boson, the Standard Model had yet to be invented. Higgs had unknowingly identified the peak of a mountain range that no one yet realised existed. Climbing a mountain is hard work but you've got a clear goal: the peak is there and if you keep moving upwards you know you're getting closer to it. With discovery of the Higgs boson, we reached the Standard Model peak in 2012 and established this to be the Core Theory. Then we started down the other side. How should we build on this new understanding of the cosmos during the next fifty years?

The plains extend into the future without any landmarks to guide us, which is in stark contrast to the last forty years when there was a clear and unifying goal for particle physics. In the view of John Womersley, former chief executive of the UK's Science and Technology Facilities Council, "The field feels a little bit listless and without any clear goal at the moment because we can't see anything to hang our aspirations on in the same way that we could when we were climbing this mountain with the Higgs [boson] at the summit."[2]

An advantage of the Higgs quest was that very early on theorists had a good reason to believe that some novel dynamics had to happen at an energy of about 1 TeV. They knew the height of the mountain, in effect, as long ago as the 1970s. Then after the discovery of the W and Z and the precision examination of the Z at LEP and of the W at Fermilab, crowned by discovery of the top quark, thanks to quantum field theory they quickly homed in on the 110-to-130-GeV region for the Higgs boson. In summary: physicists knew where to look.

Today the only certain landmark far away across the plains is the realm of the Planck energy, where the fabric of what we recognize as space and time fragments. It is possible that this faraway land is where the natural laws are revealed. If so, it is a marvel that we have deduced so much about what is out there en route to these extreme conditions of the Big Bang. Powerful though the LHC is, it takes us less than halfway, in energy terms and in powers of ten, from normal ambient conditions to the Planck energy. This ultimate ambition is so far away that the physical principles governing that regime are indiscernible, not just by the most sensitive experiments feasible today but also for the foreseeable future. There may be key landmarks beyond the horizon that are within practical reach, but if so, we don't know how far we must travel in energy to reach them. We are indeed faced with the difficulty of the plains, but the LHC is beginning to map them and create a vision of the new landscape.

The Higgs boson's discovery confirms that the universe is filled with some field that breaks electroweak symmetry through the mass mechanism and gives rise to a range of interesting features essential for the structure of atoms and molecules, the templates of life. If the quarks and leptons, W, Z, and photon, are the actors in nature's play, then the Higgs field is the stage. Without the theatre the play cannot take place. As fish need water, so the particles need the Higgs field to gain their masses and seed structure.

What next then for the LHC? We know the Higgs field is there, we know what it does, and we know how much energy it takes to light it, but what it is made of is still a mystery. This touches on one immediate puzzle that discovery of the Higgs boson has presented: How do these bosons condense to form the universal field? If particle physics were to stop with the discovery of the Higgs boson, it would in effect reduce the last fifty years to little more than collecting an exotic form of postage stamps. The Higgs boson is uniquely important, analogous to the British Guiana One-Cent Magenta in the real world of philately, but interest in it would be limited only to those who collect exotic particles. The more ambitious goal—and the strategy behind half a century of this science—is to identify and understand the nature of electroweak symmetry breaking, the asymmetry that is key to the material universe. The Higgs boson is but its herald.

If the moniker *God Particle* has any relevance, it is as the creator of structure from which all else follows. "Let there be light, and there was light": the hot Big Bang happened. In the first unimaginably small fraction of a second, the Higgs field prepared the fundamental particle seeds. Shape and form emerged afterwards.

Nature's act of discriminating the massless photon from its massive siblings, the W and Z bosons, was midwife to our material universe. The large masses of W and Z enfeebled the "weak" force that transmutes the elements, leaving the electromagnetic force more powerful. The Higgs field having thus provided the elemental ingredients, the passage of time moulded them into more complex systems. As the universe cooled, within minutes quarks had clustered to build protons and neutrons, handfuls of which in turn gripped one another to form compact nuclei of the lightest elements. Nuclei are tightly bunched this way because quarks have mass, and that is due to their interactions with the Higgs field. Later, after nearly four hundred thousand years, things were cool enough for relatively sluggish electrons to be ensnared by those nuclei, forming atoms, at that stage mostly of hydrogen and helium.

After about 150 million years, clouds of gas formed the first stars, the engines that forge the nuclei of heavier elements, such as carbon, oxygen, and iron. About five billion years ago, a whole smorgasbord of elements of the periodic table had been fused, and these formed the huge sphere that became planet Earth. The sun is powered by transmutation of its hydrogen fuel into helium ash, this taking place slowly because of the feebleness of the weak force, which itself is a consequence of the Higgs field. Massless photons, meanwhile, stream across space, warming the Earth. Thanks to these products of electroweak symmetry breaking, the sun has burned long enough that evolution has organised collections of atoms into self-aware human forms, capable of knowing nature.

Confirmation of the Higgs boson has implications far beyond its relevance for the Standard Model of elemental particles and the natural forces that cement them to make complex matter. The Higgs phenomenon may have controlled the birth of the universe itself and may potentially trigger its end.

The *inflationary theory* of Big Bang cosmology emerged around 1980. It posits that the universe began as a hot speck of energy, a tiny seed a hundred billionth of a billionth the size of a proton. This remained the case for an instant—the strength of gravity so strong that space and time as we refer to them had yet to have meaning. The best current theory is that, suddenly, everything ballooned in size, the baby universe exponentially inflating by twenty-six powers of ten in each of the three spatial dimensions in 10^{-32} seconds—that's a hundredth of a thousandth of a millionth of a billionth of a trillionth of a second. This blossoming is nearly as much as it has grown in the slower expansion that has taken place during the subsequent 13.8 billion years.

This theory has explained the structure of the early universe as revealed by measurements of the cosmic microwave background for over three decades and is part of cosmology's Standard Model. There is, however, something missing: what drove the inflation?

What little we know is that the energy field responsible had no sense of direction—the observed large-scale uniformity of the universe testifies to that. In quantum field theory, the associated particle—the *inflaton*—has no spin. This idea had been mulled over by theorists for many years, though no fundamental particle without spin had ever been found. And then early in 2015, after two years of experimental study, the Higgs boson was confirmed to have no spin.

The idea that the Higgs field plays the role of the inflaton is very intriguing. However, this cannot be the case in the framework of the Standard Model. The inflaton must have had a powerful affinity for gravity to weave so dramatically the geometry of space and time. The Higgs boson of the Standard Model has no such coupling to gravity. However, it is possible that something akin to Wilczek's mechanism for giving the Higgs boson an affinity for light particles might be at work. Recall that Wilczek realised that the intermediate role of virtual massive particles—top quarks—could become the portal for linking lightweight quarks and massless gluons to the Higgs boson. A similar mechanism could couple it to gravity, but for this interaction to be strong enough to have driven inflation of the universe would require the transient agents to be very heavy particles, as yet unknown. In other words, inflation would not be driven by the Higgs field alone but by a combination of the Higgs field with other, still uncharted, entities. If this is the way of nature, then very massive particles await discovery out in the plains, but we have no idea how far we must travel to find them.

Although top quarks are not massive enough to elevate the Higgs field into an engine of universal inflation, they are likely to play a profound role in the field's microstructure and dynamics. In quantum field theory, virtual particles bubble in and out of existence on intervals constrained by the uncertainty principle. For example, the electromagnetic field can momentarily convert into an electron and a positron, which then annihilate one another. These *quantum bubbles* modify the simple picture of the field. In the case of quantum electrodynamics, they give rise to subtle effects on the behaviour of electrons in atoms, which have been confirmed by experiment, but the overall large-scale nature of the field is barely disturbed.

Likewise, the Higgs field can generate quantum bubbles, and be affected by them in turn. The situation is very different from the electromagnetic case, however, because the quantum fluctuations grow in proportion to the masses of the virtual particles. The heavier they are, the more radical their effects, which makes the Higgs field a portal into regions beyond our present horizons. The Higgs field can bubble into a top quark and its antiquark, which being the most massive particles yet known have the greatest affinity for it. If exceedingly massive particles exist, their interactions could be so powerful as to distort the fabric of the field itself. When probed at energies higher than accessible at the LHC, the Higgs field is likely to show rich structure, like an apparently placid ocean revealed on closer examination to be frothing with foam. "What is the fine structure of the Higgs field?" is one of the most immediate "known unknowns" of the post-Higgs era.

It turns out that the stability of the Higgs field is very sensitive to the actual strength of the interaction with these particles—in other words, their masses. According to quantum field theory, the observed masses of the top quark and of the Higgs boson—the heaviest known particle after the top quark—imply that these quantum effects might destabilise the Higgs field.

As this field is the engine for everything we are made of, its stability has profound implications for the material universe.

Once again this led Stephen Hawking to intervene in the Higgs saga. When the Higgs boson's discovery had shown that his claims of its invisibility must be wrong, the cosmologist still managed to grab the media headlines. In 2014, almost six years to the day after the LHC had been turned on amid Hawking's pronouncement that the Higgs boson would probably not be found, he made news with a claim that the now-established "God Particle" could destroy the universe. The mass of the Higgs boson of 125 GeV turns out to be the precise amount needed to keep the universe on the brink of instability, a state which Hawking warned could eventually collapse.

Although the media wrote the story with Hawking at its focus, the insight did not originate with him. The possibility that the effects of quantum physics could destabilise the Higgs field has a long history, back to the 1970s. It was the discovery of the Higgs boson, and of the top quark, and the measurements of their masses that had brought the idea into sharp focus—whereupon many theorists began to ponder the implications. The quantum field theory of this is complicated mathematically, but its essence can be illustrated by a familiar analogy with hills and valleys in the landscape.

In the original wine bottle or Mexican hat model of Ginzburg and Landau, and of Goldstone and Higgs, the state of the vacuum—the Higgs field—is like being in a valley between two ranges of hills. Water flows downhill into the valley as nature minimises the gravitational potential energy; the strength of the Higgs field minimises the energy of the vacuum by settling in a metaphorical valley. Now suppose on the far side of the hills there is another valley, whose floor is lower than the present one. That is, in effect, what the properties of the Higgs boson of mass 125 GeV in a universe containing top quarks of mass 176 GeV seem to imply theoretically. If the Higgs field somehow could reach that deeper valley, the quantum vacuum of the universe would tumble into that state much like water finds its lowest level. The resulting cosmic-quake would be apocalyptic.

To get there, however, would require energy to be supplied in order to lift us over the intervening hump. We are safe, or would be but for quantum uncertainty, where the normal conservation of energy can be put on hold for a brief moment, creating in effect a tunnel through the barrier. This quantum fluctuation could happen anywhere in the vacuum of space between the galaxies and create a bubble of more stable form. The vacuum surrounding the bubble would tumble into the more stable form, the more stable state expanding at the speed of light, eventually consuming everything.

Hawking said dramatically that this could happen anytime, and we wouldn't see it coming. Wisely on this occasion he didn't make any bets about the likelihood, because in the event of being proved correct there would be no possibility of collecting the winnings. He did admit that such a disaster is unlikely soon but ominously warned that the danger of the Higgs field becoming destabilised is "too great to be ignored".

The media latched on to Hawking's apocalypse, but the paper that had inspired this vision of the end of days did not actually declare the universe to be under immediate threat. The premonition ignores phenomena that are known to exist, such as gravity and the need for dark matter (more explanation will follow below). If there are yet heavier particles awaiting discovery, their interactions with the Higgs field will be correspondingly strong and further stabilise it. The threat of imminent disaster is theoretical, not real.

Discovery of the Higgs boson confirms that we are immersed in the Higgs field. The biggest disappointment in studying the boson so far is that it has not revealed any anomalous properties that might give clues to the most far-reaching questions to be answered about the source and dynamical nature of the field. Everything about it is consistent with the simplest model constructed to demonstrate the principle six decades ago.

As the Higgs boson is itself massive, two or more can couple to one another like a snake biting its tail. The first step towards understanding the nature of the ubiquitous Higgs field experimentally will be to produce a pair of Higgs bosons and see how they interact with one another. By analogy, it is as if we had confirmed the existence of individual molecules of H_2O when the real goal is to understand the nature of water. A first step would be to study how two molecules coalesce. The coincident production of Higgs bosons in pairs happens so rarely at the LHC that it is probably impractical to learn about it at the machine in its present form, but increasing the intensity and the energy of its proton beams would bring this fundamental process within reach.

Plans for the future have this goal in mind. One active idea is to design an extremely large machine with a circumference of some 150 miles, yielding collisions between protons at up to fifteen times the energy of the LHC. A complementary approach might be to build a precision *Higgs factory*, where beams of electrons and positrons annihilate at an energy of 125 GeV, tuned to create Higgs bosons. This would be analogous to LEP, which was tuned to make Z bosons back in the 1990s. As the Higgs boson couples more strongly to heavy particles, an innovative idea is to use beams of positive and negative muons rather than positrons and electrons, as their extra mass (a muon being some 207 times as massive as an electron) gives a much greater chance of producing a Higgs boson. However, the technology of storing and colliding beams of muons is primitive relative to the well-understood case of electrons and positrons. If any of these developments take place, they are not likely to be producing physics results for several decades, a full century after the idea of the Higgs boson was born. More immediate plans are to increase the luminosity of the beams at the LHC, which will increase the production rate of Higgs bosons (and much else besides). Work on this began in 2018, and the high-luminosity LHC is hoped to be in operation by 2027.

There are clues that out on the plains are perhaps new mountains to be conquered en route to the Planck realm. The most obvious of these is the nature of *dark matter*, stuff that does not shine but whose presence is revealed through its gravitational pull on the visible stars—unless our understanding of the long-range behaviour of the gravitational force is incomplete, which would be even more profound. Stuff made from the elemental particles of the Core Theory, and whose existence is now beginning to be understood thanks to discovery of the boson, constitutes only about 5 percent of the total mass of the universe. We are made of mere flotsam on a sea of dark matter. Cosmologists infer that dark matter consists of electrically neutral particles that are probably even heavier than Higgs bosons. Whatever these dark particles are, they are not on the currently known menu of particles: they are entities beyond the Standard Model. They lurk somewhere out there in the plains and, being very massive, will profoundly affect the dynamics of the Higgs field.

In the 1970s, theorists studying symmetry became enthralled by the possibility of a *supersymmetry* uniting fermions and bosons. *SUSY*, as this is colloquially known, has a strong theoretical pedigree and underpins mathematical developments in superstring theory but is singularly lacking in empirical evidence—unless dark matter is made of SUSY particles.[3] If nature's scheme involves SUSY, the Higgs boson is not an only child but a member of a family containing one or more *Higgsinos*, fermion siblings to the original Higgs boson. The Higgs boson mass being relatively light—125 GeV is far short of the 1 TeV (1,000 GeV) historically identified as the "natural" energy scale for electroweak symmetry breaking—has led some theorists to suspect that supersymmetry and the answer to the puzzle of dark matter lie just over the present horizon. This conclusion comes from quantum field theory calculations of how the Higgs boson itself interacts with the Higgs field. Reminiscent of the calculations in the 1970s that led theorists to anticipate the need for a Higgs boson to maintain logical sense to quantum field theory above 1 TeV, so today analogous analyses of how the Higgs boson mass of 125 GeV is relatively light hint at the need for further massive particles whose properties match with supersymmetry theory.

There are no robust arguments to support the idea that SUSY is within reach of the present LHC or even a future more powerful successor to it, however. Arguments suggesting that SUSY is within reach are certainly not as solid as the computations of the 1970s heralding the 1 TeV energy scale as a guaranteed mountain range on the journey to find the Higgs boson. It is even possible that all interesting physics is at the Planck scale of energy—the extreme where present theories fail pending a marriage of quantum theory and general relativity. If so, we've uncovered the limited varieties of particles and phenomena that froze out within our reach. Whether the mystery of dark particles will be revealed within a few years, or whether we are at the start of another long wait, comparable to that which Higgs endured, we do not know.

With the discovery of the Higgs boson, the picture of particle physics is now internally complete, in the sense that it is mathematically consistent. The moniker *Standard Model* indeed merits elevating, as Frank Wilczek has suggested, to *Core Theory*.[4] However, we know it doesn't fully describe our world. Internal completeness is a mathematical requirement, whereas describing the world around us is the demand of natural philosophy. Even apart from the lack of a quantum theory of gravity, the Core Theory doesn't describe dark matter—which on a cosmic scale far outweighs the stuff that we identified and had begun to explain in the pre-Higgs era. The Higgs mechanism explains how masses arise but gives no clue why they are as they are. The Core Theory has no explanation for the number of fundamental leptons and quarks, nor an answer even to a question as basic as "What makes an electron an electron?"; what, indeed, is *flavour*, the foundation of quantum flavourdynamics?

Leptons appear to be fundamental. The muon couples to the Higgs boson some 207 times as strongly as does an electron, making it correspondingly more massive. If the muon were just a heavy electron, it would be able to shed 206 parts of that mass as energy in the form of photons, tumbling down to stability: an electron. No sign of this transition has ever been seen, however. There appears to be something intrinsic to the muon and to the electron that must be preserved. This is the property we call *flavour*; it has superb empirical provenance, but we have no understanding of what underpins it. Is the Higgs boson alone the source of the mass of leptons (and of quarks or the W and Z bosons), or is there some other contribution, and if so, might identifying the latter explain the nature of flavour? This is an example of a question that requires high-precision data on the decays of Higgs bosons if we are to expose subtle phenomena.

Nor do we know whether the gravitational, electroweak, and strong forces are the totality. It is straightforward to generalise the mathematical structures that underpin these gauge theories leading to the prediction that more forces exist, but there is no evidence that nature makes use of this. Now that the mass mechanism has been established, it is plausible that the gauge bosons of these generalisations are so massive that the resulting forces are too feeble for us yet to discern. If, however, the four established fundamental forces are the totality, we are left with a question: why?[5]

Confirmation of the Higgs boson has emphasised that hidden symmetry—the child of spontaneous symmetry breaking where stability trumps symmetry—is very wide ranging and a key ingredient to describing the natural world. Superconductivity stimulated awareness of the phenomenon in the first place, and when it was taken over to the physics of fundamental particles, it turned out to be key to the whole edifice of the

Standard Model. Or almost all of it, for there is no known fundamental reason why mirror symmetry is overturned in the weak interaction: why is nature left-handed?

This enigma takes us back to the very beginnings of our saga. Glashow's 1961 paper that predicted the massive W and Z bosons was inspired by the violation of mirror symmetry in weak interactions. Even with the discovery of the Higgs boson, however, the reason for this fundamental asymmetry remains an enigma. We suspect the source lies somewhere in the plains but have no certain energy scale by which the answer might be determined, nor any compelling theory to test against experiment.

We need to understand the Higgs boson better, to resolve how the Higgs field is formed and what it consists of. By doing so we hope to open a portal into physics beyond the Standard Model, one that may reveal the true actors and show the Core Theory to be shadow theatre.

More than two thousand years ago, the ancient Greeks started musing about the nature of matter. Today, half a century after Higgs had his singular idea, the discovery of the Higgs boson has brought us to the end of the beginning, not to the beginning of the end. What dark matter is made of, whether there are further "dark Higgs bosons" to be found, and how the Higgs field is formed are questions for the future.

ACKNOWLEDGEMENTS

In researching *Elusive* I had more than thirty hours of interviews with Peter Higgs, many by phone during the extensive lockdown forced by the COVID crisis. Quotations from him in the text come from these interviews unless stated otherwise. In addition, I interviewed many professional colleagues for their memories of the quest, and of their interactions with Higgs and other central characters. My own memories of events were either recorded at the time or cross-checked with others who were present. Where people's memories of details of a shared experience differed—as in the events immediately surrounding the 4 July discovery in 2012—I attempted to find a common version consistent in itself. CERN has extensive video and audio records of that occasion, and of the inauguration of the LHC, which enabled further checks.

I am especially indebted to Richard Kenway and Chris Quigg for comments on my early attempts to describe Higgs' papers, and Tony Hey for reading the first draft; to Lyn Evans for his insights about accelerators; to Charles Seife, Martin Rees, Malcolm Perry, and David Tong for help with decoding Hawking's papers that criticised Higgs' boson; to Alan Walker, Ken Peach, Richard Kenway, and David Wallace for memories of Edinburgh and other events; to medical historian Dr David Boyd for information about Higgs' great-uncle John Coghill and his grandfather James Coghill; to James Gillies, Stephanie Hills, and Jane MacKenzie for their memories and also photographs of 4 July 2012; and of course to Peter Higgs for having spent many hours on the phone from November 2019 to July 2020 when I gathered material to form the plan of the project and again during April to August 2021 as the final version emerged.

I am indebted to many other people for their time in being interviewed and to those who checked the transcription and points of technical detail, in particular Simon Altmann, Sean Carroll, John Ellis, Keith Ellis, Graham Farmelo, Simon Hands, Rolf Heuer, George Kalmus, Peter Kalmus, Gordon Kane, Chris Llewellyn Smith, David Miller, Terry O'Connor, Steve Simon, Frank Wilczek, and John Womersley.

I am indebted to my agent, Patrick Walsh, for his advice on how to present this history; T. J. Kelleher at Basic and Stuart Proffitt at Allen Lane for their editorial insights; Roger Labrie, Madeline Lee, Amy J. Schneider, and Melissa Veronesi for helping bring this edition to press; and my wife for patiently being my audience during our months of lockdown isolation during 2020, when much of the first draft was written. I am deeply thankful to Peter Higgs for his suggestions that helped the final draft emerge. By the time this manuscript was completed, Higgs was ninety-two years old. Having broken his hip and recovered, he generously read sections of the text in the summer of 2021, corrected some misunderstandings, and in one case certainly proved his memory to be razor sharp.

APPENDIX 4.1: GINZBURG AND LANDAU'S MEXICAN HAT

The Mexican hat, which plays a central role in Higgs' and Goldstone's papers, first seems to have appeared in Ginzburg and Landau's model of 1950. The reasons for this iconic structure and its ubiquity in mathematical analysis are quite general. This appendix is for readers interested in knowing more about this history and the associated physical ideas.

Ginzburg and Landau had simply assumed that the probability that a metal contains superconducting stuff is some unknown positive amount. I shall call this number x^2 to guarantee that its value is positive or zero. Their construct contained a piece that was destined to become central to Higgs' breakthrough and has become a pedagogic example of the entire subject of hidden symmetry. This feature is their mathematical model for the energy density in the superconductor below the critical temperature.

In metal, the probability of there being superconducting material is determined by minimising the potential energy of electrically charged particles within. As Ginzburg and Landau had no idea of the dynamics that make the metal superconducting, they could not determine values of properties such as the critical temperature, T_c. However, at temperatures near T_c the potential energy has some general features which enabled the Russian duo to describe broad features of the phenomenon.

Key to their mathematical model was that when the temperature is near T_c, the amount, x^2, of superconducting material is small. The basic question is: how does the magnitude of the potential energy change as x^2 increases?

In general, you don't know, but in the case where x^2 is small—as here—you can write an excellent approximation to the real answer. The key is that if you multiply a small number by itself, you get an even smaller number, for example ½ multiplied by ½ gives you ¼. So, when x^2 is nearly zero, x^2 will be bigger than x^4 and all higher powers such as x^6, x^8, and so on. The answer will therefore be roughly proportional to x^2 and if you want to be more accurate, there will be small corrections in proportion to x^4.

As they had no idea about the dynamics of the superconducting material, they had to allow for the alternatives that as the amount of it grows, the total energy of the metal could either increase or decrease. If the magnitude of this energy is recorded along the vertical axis on a graph, and the amount of superconducting material is along the horizontal, then the former case will be proportional to x^2 while the latter is proportional to $-x^2$. The curve for x^2 is like the cross section of a valley whereas that for $-x^2$ is like a hilltop (figures a and b). In their model, the energy was proportional to x^2 multiplied by $(T - T_c)$. So, when the temperature is above T_c, this quantity is positive—the valley—whereas at lower temperatures $(T - T_c)$ becomes negative and the hilltop ensues.

Even professional physicists like to have mental images of what their equations and algebraic formulae represent, so it is helpful to picture these as the cross-sections of real hollow bowls or hilltops and infer what will happen to a ball positioned on either of these surfaces. In minimising the potential energy, a ball in the bowl will settle at the bottom. In the case of the superconductor, this implies that stability occurs when $x^2 = 0$, which corresponds to there being no superconducting material at all.

So much for temperatures above T_c where, indeed, there is no superconducting material. When the temperature falls below this critical value, so that $T - T_c$ becomes negative, the bowl becomes a hilltop. A ball on the hilltop is precariously balanced, the slightest disturbance tipping it over the edge, causing it to speed away down the slope and be lost. In the case of the superconductor this would suggest that the greater the amount of superconducting material—the larger the magnitude of x^2—the more stable the situation becomes: the superconductor would saturate with an infinite amount of the stuff. In reality, this does not happen because the model is only valid for small values of x^2. If we take account of the next term, proportional to x^4, and if it has a positive sign, the curve will eventually rise again. The shape is now like the cross-section of the base of a wine bottle, or a Mexican hat (figure c), and the ball will settle at one of the hollows: the superconductor will stabilise when some finite amount of the state has formed.

This picture has become a paradigm for mathematical descriptions of hidden symmetry. It is the starting point of Higgs' second paper in 1964 (page 260 and appendix 5.2). Key to the phenomenon in Ginzburg and Landau's model is that at the critical temperature, the shape of the potential suddenly alters, its cross-section changing from a U to a W. In the former case the minimum is at the central point, which is symmetric under reflection, whereas for the W case the minimum is off centre, which breaks the symmetry.

The full power of hidden symmetry comes with the three-dimensional picture of the Mexican hat, which is rotationally symmetric. The only algebraic difference is that in place of x one conventionally uses the Greek symbol φ (phi), which is a binary number, one value, φ_1, being the distance across the page, like the preceding example, and the other value, φ_2, being the distance into or out of the page. The rotational symmetry comes from replacing x^2 and x^4 with $\varphi_1{}^2 + \varphi_2{}^2$ and $\varphi_1{}^4 + \varphi_2{}^4$, respectively.

As they did not know the comparable importance of the φ^2 and φ^4 contributions, they wrote their expression for the energy density with an arbitrary relative size for the two terms. Their insight was that as superconductivity suddenly turns on when the temperature falls below a critical value T_c, the magnitude of the first term will be proportional to the numerical difference $T - T_c$—in other words, it will be positive at warm temperatures and

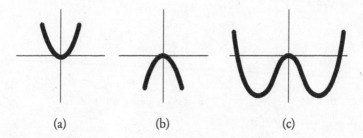

(a)   (b)   (c)

(a and b) Curves for x^2 and $-x^2$ giving a valley and hilltop. (c) Curve for $-x^2 + x^4$.

change sign, becoming negative, when the temperature falls below the critical temperature.

When nature achieves stability by minimising the energy, the result in this model depends dramatically on the temperature. For an energy density controlled by the first (U) shape, the minimum occurs when the value of both φ_1 and φ_2 vanishes—in other words, when there is no superconducting material. When the temperature is less than T_c, however, the sign of the first term becomes negative. The potential energy density has the wine bottle shape, and its minimum is when φ is no longer zero; in other words, there is superconducting material.

APPENDIX 5.1: HIGGS' FIRST PAPER DECODED

The mathematics in Higgs' paper is mostly a review of Gilbert's argument. The two fields φ_1 and φ_2 match the binary field φ introduced by Ginzburg and Landau (appendix 4.1), which was also used by Goldstone. They are gauge invariant, meaning the angle α in equation 1 can have any value and the results of experiments cannot depend on its size. To visualise this, imagine some rotationally symmetric shape φ, with φ_1 and φ_2 referring to the perspective looking respectively north or east. If you rotate your eye-line through some angle, amount α, equation 1 then says what your relative perspectives of north and east will be. Equation 2 is a mathematical way of stating this; the quantity enclosed by the square brackets [ ] is known as a *commutator*. The proof (or refutation) of Goldstone's theorem hangs on the algebraic patterns that emerge when this commutator is analysed.

The key mathematical operation is known as making a *Fourier transform* of this commutator. The result is a *four-vector*—the generalisation in relativity theory of a conventional vector, having projections along both the three dimensions of space and the fourth dimension of time. Goldstone showed that in a relativistic field theory the answer points in the direction of the particle's 4-momentum, denoted $\mathbf{k}_\mu$—that is, its energy and spatial momentum. Six lines below the equation, the term written in algebra as $\delta(k^2)$ which accompanies this $\mathbf{k}_\mu$ physically means *has mass zero*. This is the essence of Goldstone's theorem; there is only one term, and it corresponds to a massless particle: the *Goldstone boson*.

BROKEN SYMMETRIES, MASSLESS PARTICLES AND GAUGE FIELDS

P. W. HIGGS
Tait Institute of Mathematical Physics, University of Edinburgh, Scotland

Received 27 July 1964

Recently a number of people have discussed the Goldstone theorem [1,2]: that any solution of a Lorentz-invariant theory which violates an internal symmetry operation of that theory must contain a massless scalar particle. Klein and Lee [3] showed that this theorem does not necessarily apply in non-relativistic theories and implied that their considerations would apply equally well to Lorentz-invariant field theories. Gilbert [4], how-

ever, gave a proof that the failure of the Goldstone theorem in the nonrelativistic case is of a type which cannot exist when Lorentz invariance is imposed on a theory. The purpose of this note is to show that Gilbert's argument fails for an important class of field theories, that in which the conserved currents are coupled to gauge fields.

Following the procedure used by Gilbert [4], let us consider a theory of two hermitian scalar fields

132

$\varphi_1(x)$, $\varphi_2(x)$ which is invariant under the phase transformation

$$\varphi_1 \to \varphi_1 \cos \alpha + \varphi_2 \sin \alpha ,$$

$$\varphi_2 \to -\varphi_1 \sin \alpha + \varphi_2 \cos \alpha . \tag{1}$$

Then there is a conserved current j_μ such that

$$i[\int d^3x\, j_0(x),\, \varphi_1(y)] = \varphi_2(y). \tag{2}$$

We assume that the Lagrangian is such that symmetry is broken by the nonvanishing of the vacuum expectation value of φ_2. Goldstone's theorem is proved by showing that the Fourier transform of $i\langle[j_\mu(x),\, \varphi_1(y)]\rangle$ contains a term $2\pi\langle\varphi_2\rangle\epsilon(k_0)k_\mu\,\delta(k^2)$, where k_μ is the momentum, as a consequence of Lorentz-covariance, the conservation law and eq. (2).

Klein and Lee [3] avoided this result in the non-relativistic case by showing that the most general form of this Fourier transform is now, in Gilbert's notation,

$$\text{F.T.} = k_\mu\, \rho_1(k^2,\, nk) + n_\mu\, \rho_2(k^2,\, nk) + C_3 n_\mu\, \delta^4(k) , \tag{3}$$

where n_μ, which may be taken as $(1, 0, 0, 0)$, picks out a special Lorentz frame. The conversation law then reduces eq. (3) to the less general form

$$\text{F.T.} = k_\mu\, \delta(k^2)\rho_4(nk) + [k^2 n_\mu - k_\mu(nk)]\rho_5(k^2,\, nk) + C_3 n_\mu\, \delta^4(k) . \tag{4}$$

It turns out, on applying eq. (2), that all three terms in eq. (4) can contribute to $\langle\varphi_2\rangle$. Thus the Goldstone theorem fails if $\rho_4 = 0$, which is possible only if the other terms exist. Gilbert's remark that no special timelike vector n_μ is available in a Lorentz-covariant theory appears to rule out this possibility in such a theory.

There is however a class of relativistic field theories in which a vector n_μ does indeed play a part. This is the class of gauge theories, where an auxiliary unit timelike vector n_μ must be in-

troduced in order to define a radiation gauge in which the vector gauge fields are well defined operators. Such theories are nevertheless Lorentz-covariant, as has been shown by Schwinger [5]. (This has, of course, long been known of the simplest such theory, quantum electrodynamics.) There seems to be no reason why the vector n_μ should not appear in the Fourier transform under consideration.

It is characteristic of gauge theories that the conservation laws hold in the strong sense, as a consequence of field equations of the form

$$j^\mu = \partial_\nu F'^{\,\mu\nu},$$

$$F_{\mu\nu}' = \partial_\mu A_\nu' - \partial_\nu A_\mu' . \tag{5}$$

Except in the case of abelian gauge theories, the fields A_μ', $F_{\mu\nu}'$ are not simply the gauge field variables A_μ, $F_{\mu\nu}$, but contain additional terms with combinations of the structure constants of the group as coefficients. Now the structure of the Fourier transform of $i\langle[A_\mu'(x),\, \varphi_1(y)]\rangle$ must be given by eq. (3). Applying eq. (5) to this commutator gives us as the Fourier transform of $i\langle[j_\mu(x),\, \varphi_1(y)]\rangle$ the single term $[k^2 n_\mu - k_\mu(nk)]\rho(k^2,\, nk)$. We have thus exorcised both Goldstone's zero-mass bosons and the "spurion" state (at $k_\mu = 0$) proposed by Klein and Lee.

In a subsequent note it will be shown, by considering some classical field theories which display broken symmetries, that the introduction of gauge fields may be expected to produce qualitative changes in the nature of the particles described by such theories after quantization.

References
1) J. Goldstone, Nuovo Cimento 19 (1961) 154.
2) J. Goldstone, A. Salam and S. Weinberg, Phys. Rev. 127 (1962) 965.
3) A. Klein and B. W. Lee, Phys. Rev. Letters 12 (1964) 266.
4) W. Gilbert, Phys. Rev. Letters 12 (1964) 713.
5) J. Schwinger, Phys. Rev. 127 (1962) 324.

* * * * *

133

Higgs' first paper

Gilbert had shown that in a theory without relativity the answer does not necessarily point along the direction $\mathbf{k}_m$ but can have a projection along another direction, the vector that in equation 3 he called $\mathbf{n}_m$. The Fourier transform is no longer so tightly restricted. In his paper, Gilbert constructed the most general form, containing three possible quantities, rather than the unique form that emerged in Goldstone's analysis (Higgs displays Gilbert's result in equation 4). The presence of the new terms containing $\mathbf{n}_\mu$ evade Goldstone's theorem, as there is no $\delta(k^2)$—there is no massless particle.

This is all very well mathematically, but in physics you can't simply ignore relativity, and Gilbert had argued that there is no place for any dependence on $\mathbf{n}_\mu$ in a relativistic theory. Higgs had spent some years studying quantum electrodynamics in Coulomb gauge. He knew that in this case there is a vector $\mathbf{n}_\mu$ and that such a construction satisfies all requirements of relativity. One counterexample is sufficient: Gilbert's objection was wrong.

APPENDIX 5.2: HIGGS' SECOND PAPER DECODED

The key feature of V is that it has a shape like a Mexican hat—this is encoded mathematically five lines from the foot of the first column, where Higgs writes, "Let us suppose that . . ." followed by two small equations, one an equality, the second saying that a quantity is positive. This is the mathematical way of saying that the potential has its minimum when the field φ is nonzero, with magnitude φ_0. The shape of a Mexican hat, which Goldstone and the Russians had used, is a particular example of such a potential.

The quantities with the capital F and Greek subscripts and superscripts are the traditional mathematical shorthand for encoding electric and magnetic fields in terms of the electromagnetic potential, A (equation 1). Finally, he allows the phi-fields and the electromagnetic field to interact with one another. The strength of their coupling is proportional to some unknown quantity, which he writes as e; if $e = 0$ this interaction would vanish.

Equations 2a and 2c each involve both φ and A. As written, these equations are hard even for a professional physicist to interpret, but Higgs plays a clever mathematical trick at equation 3 by defining a new quantity, B, which merges the electromagnetic field and phi-field and transforms equations 2a and 2c into equation 4. The physical meaning of this equation is that the unwanted Goldstone particle has miraculously disappeared, absorbed by the electromagnetic field. As a result, the photon has gained a mass proportional to the product of the Goldstone field's strength in the stable vacuum, which Higgs calls φ_0, and the magnitude of electric charge, e—"vector waves with . . . mass $e\varphi_0$".

260

BROKEN SYMMETRIES AND THE MASSES OF GAUGE BOSONS

Peter W. Higgs
Tait Institute of Mathematical Physics, University of Edinburgh, Edinburgh, Scotland
(Received 31 August 1964)

In a recent note[1] it was shown that the Goldstone theorem,[2] that Lorentz-covariant field theories in which spontaneous breakdown of symmetry under an internal Lie group occurs contain zero-mass particles, fails if and only if the conserved currents associated with the internal group are coupled to gauge fields. The purpose of the present note is to report that, as a consequence of this coupling, the spin-one quanta of some of the gauge fields acquire mass; the longitudinal degrees of freedom of these particles (which would be absent if their mass were zero) go over into the Goldstone bosons when the coupling tends to zero. This phenomenon is just the relativistic analog of the plasmon phenomenon to which Anderson[3] has drawn attention: that the scalar zero-mass excitations of a superconducting neutral Fermi gas become longitudinal plasmon modes of finite mass when the gas is charged.

The simplest theory which exhibits this behavior is a gauge-invariant version of a model used by Goldstone[2] himself: Two real[4] scalar fields φ_1, φ_2 and a real vector field A_μ interact through the Lagrangian density

$$L = -\tfrac{1}{2}(\nabla\varphi_1)^2 - \tfrac{1}{2}(\nabla\varphi_2)^2$$
$$-V(\varphi_1^2 + \varphi_2^2) - \tfrac{1}{4}F_{\mu\nu}F^{\mu\nu}, \quad (1)$$

where

$$\nabla_\mu\varphi_1 = \partial_\mu\varphi_1 - eA_\mu\varphi_2,$$

$$\nabla_\mu\varphi_2 = \partial_\mu\varphi_2 + eA_\mu\varphi_1,$$

$$F_{\mu\nu} = \partial_\mu A_\nu - \partial_\nu A_\mu.$$

e is a dimensionless coupling constant, and the metric is taken as $-+++$. L is invariant under simultaneous gauge transformations of the first kind on $\varphi_1 \pm i\varphi_2$ and of the second kind on A_μ. Let us suppose that $V'(\varphi_0^2) = 0$, $V''(\varphi_0^2) > 0$; then spontaneous breakdown of U(1) symmetry occurs. Consider the equations [derived from (1) by treating $\Delta\varphi_1$, $\Delta\varphi_2$, and A_μ as small quantities] governing the propagation of small oscillations

about the "vacuum" solution $\varphi_1(x) = 0$, $\varphi_2(x) = \varphi_0$:

$$\partial^\mu\{\partial_\mu(\Delta\varphi_1) - e\varphi_0 A_\mu\} = 0, \quad (2a)$$

$$\{\partial^2 - 4\varphi_0^2 V''(\varphi_0^2)\}(\Delta\varphi_2) = 0, \quad (2b)$$

$$\partial_\nu F^{\mu\nu} = e\varphi_0\{\partial^\mu(\Delta\varphi_1) - e\varphi_0 A_\mu\}. \quad (2c)$$

Equation (2b) describes waves whose quanta have (bare) mass $2\varphi_0\{V''(\varphi_0^2)\}^{1/2}$; Eqs. (2a) and (2c) may be transformed, by the introduction of new variables

$$B_\mu = A_\mu - (e\varphi_0)^{-1}\partial_\mu(\Delta\varphi_1),$$
$$G_{\mu\nu} = \partial_\mu B_\nu - \partial_\nu B_\mu = F_{\mu\nu}, \quad (3)$$

into the form

$$\partial_\mu B^\mu = 0, \quad \partial_\nu G^{\mu\nu} + e^2\varphi_0^2 B^\mu = 0. \quad (4)$$

Equation (4) describes vector waves whose quanta have (bare) mass $e\varphi_0$. In the absence of the gauge field coupling ($e = 0$) the situation is quite different: Equations (2a) and (2c) describe zero-mass scalar and vector bosons, respectively. In passing, we note that the right-hand side of (2c) is just the linear approximation to the conserved current: It is linear in the vector potential, gauge invariance being maintained by the presence of the gradient term.[5]

When one considers theoretical models in which spontaneous breakdown of symmetry under a semisimple group occurs, one encounters a variety of possible situations corresponding to the various distinct irreducible representations to which the scalar fields may belong; the gauge field always belongs to the adjoint representation.[6] The model of the most immediate interest is that in which the scalar fields form an octet under SU(3): Here one finds the possibility of two nonvanishing vacuum expectation values, which may be chosen to be the two $Y = 0$, $I_3 = 0$ members of the octet.[7] There are two massive scalar bosons with just these quantum numbers; the remaining six components of the scalar octet combine with the corresponding components of the gauge-field octet to describe massive vector bosons. There are two $I = \frac{1}{2}$ vector doublets, degenerate in mass between $Y = \pm 1$ but with an electromagnetic mass splitting between $I_3 = \pm \frac{1}{2}$, and the $I_3 = \pm 1$ components of a $Y = 0$, $I = 1$ triplet whose mass is entirely electromagnetic. The two $Y = 0$, $I = 0$ gauge fields remain massless: This is associated with the residual unbroken symmetry under the Abelian group generated by Y and I_3. It may be expected that when a further mechanism (presumably related to the weak interactions) is introduced in order to break Y conservation, one of these gauge fields will acquire mass, leaving the photon as the only massless vector particle. A detailed discussion of these questions will be presented elsewhere.

It is worth noting that an essential feature of the type of theory which has been described in this note is the prediction of incomplete multiplets of scalar and vector bosons.[8] It is to be expected that this feature will appear also in theories in which the symmetry-breaking scalar fields are not elementary dynamic variables but bilinear combinations of Fermi fields.[9]

[1]P. W. Higgs, to be published.

[2]J. Goldstone, Nuovo Cimento 19, 154 (1961); J. Goldstone, A. Salam, and S. Weinberg, Phys. Rev. 127, 965 (1962).

[3]P. W. Anderson, Phys. Rev. 130, 439 (1963).

[4]In the present note the model is discussed mainly in classical terms; nothing is proved about the quantized theory. It should be understood, therefore, that the conclusions which are presented concerning the masses of particles are conjectures based on the quantization of linearized classical field equations. However, essentially the same conclusions have been reached independently by F. Englert and R. Brout, Phys. Rev. Letters 13, 321 (1964): These authors discuss the same model quantum mechanically in lowest order perturbation theory about the self-consistent vacuum.

[5]In the theory of superconductivity such a term arises from collective excitations of the Fermi gas.

[6]See, for example, S. L. Glashow and M. Gell-Mann, Ann. Phys. (N.Y.) 15, 437 (1961).

[7]These are just the parameters which, if the scalar octet interacts with baryons and mesons, lead to the Gell-Mann–Okubo and electromagnetic mass splittings: See S. Coleman and S. L. Glashow, Phys. Rev. 134, B671 (1964).

[8]Tentative proposals that incomplete SU(3) octets of scalar particles exist have been made by a number of people. Such a rôle, as an isolated $Y = \pm 1$, $I = \frac{1}{2}$ state, was proposed for the κ meson (725 MeV) by Y. Nambu and J. J. Sakurai, Phys. Rev. Letters 11, 42 (1963). More recently the possibility that the σ meson (385 MeV) may be the $Y = I = 0$ member of an incomplete octet has been considered by L. M. Brown, Phys. Rev. Letters 13, 42 (1964).

[9]In the theory of superconductivity the scalar fields are associated with fermion pairs; the doubly charged excitation responsible for the quantization of magnetic flux is then the surviving member of a U(1) doublet.

Higgs' second paper

NOTES

Every effort has been made to contact all copyright holders. The publisher will be pleased to amend in future printings any errors or omissions brought to their attention.

PREFACE

1. Higgs to author, 7 June 2021.

2. Player popularised this aphorism, but it was also used by Arnold Palmer and its origin is disputed.

PRELUDE: THE CASE OF THE DISAPPEARING PROFESSOR

1. Higgs interview, 1 February 2020.

CHAPTER 1: A NAME ON THE BOARD

1. The patronymic Higgs was a local version of *Hicks*, diminutive of *Richard*—the name of their Norman master. *Ware Higgs* originated in 1863 when Peter's great-grandfather, Thomas Higgs, married Anne Ware. The Ware Higgs formula was passed down through eldest sons: Peter's grandfather, Albert George Ware Higgs, and Peter's father, Thomas, known as Tom. (Higgs letter, 29 June 2021.)

2. Unless cited otherwise, quotes of Higgs in this chapter are from interviews on 17 November 2019, 24 November 2019, 9 January 2020, and 19 July 2021.

3. In the 1840s John Coghill lived in Edinburgh at 17 Bank Street, above Deacon Brodie's Tavern on the Royal Mile. He was a spirit merchant, selling the hard stuff to the poor inhabitants of the Old Town—the wealthier people having moved to the New Town. Coghill's business seems to have prospered as by 1844 he was himself in the New Town, running a shop at 10 Rose Street, a short walk from where Peter Higgs himself would settle. (Information on residency from Higgs letter, 29 June 2021, and Edinburgh postal directory 1844, reported in Wikipedia, "John G. S. Coghill," https://en.wikipedia.org/wiki/John_G._S._Coghill.)

4. James Coghill was an assistant surgeon to Scottish militia and cavalry regiments from 1861 to 1865, during which time he married Jane Mills, daughter of an officer in the Royal Scots Greys. He became interested in tropical diseases, and in 1870 he emigrated to the British Crown colony of Ceylon. (D. Boyd email, 28 June 2021.) James and Jane had three children. Jane allegedly enjoyed an extramarital lover, a Mr Loureino, which was cited as cause of the divorce. (National Archives, "Divorce Court File," https://discovery.national archives.gov.uk/details/r/C7971192, and Higgs letter, 13 July 2021.)

5. According to hints dropped to a teenage Peter Higgs by his mother. (Higgs letter, 13 July 2021.)

6. Higgs letter, 13 July 2021.

7. Higgs interview, 24 November 2019, and letter, 13 July 2021.

8. Higgs interview, 9 June 2020.

9. Higgs letter, 13 July 2021.

10. Higgs interview, 24 November 2019, and letter, 13 July 2021.

11. Higgs letter, 13 July 2021.

12. Dirac's biography is told in G. Farmelo, *The Strangest Man* (Faber, 2010).

13. Higgs interview, 17 November 2019, and letter, 13 July 2021.

14. Higgs letter, 13 July 2021.

15. *Western Daily News*, 16 August 1945.

16. Western Daily Press, 16 August announcement of talk by Mott at Bristol Rotary Club, and report of talk in *Western Daily News*, 21 August 1945.

17. The lecture content is reconstructed from Higgs' memories; interviews, 24 November 2019 and 30 August 2021; letter, 13 July 2021; *Western Daily News* report (undated); and my analysis of what would be required to have explained the relevant physics to a general audience at that time.

18. Higgs letter, 13 July 2021.

19. This remark is attributed to American physicist Isidor Isaac Rabi, made possibly at lunch at the University of Columbia, but there is no certain record of when he said this or to whom.

20. Higgs letter, 13 July 2021.

21. Higgs letter, 13 July 2021.

22. The educator, historian, and Anglican Thomas Arnold (1795–1842) called UCL the "Godless institution in Gower Street".

23. Higgs interview, 10 January 2020.

CHAPTER 2: THE SINGLE HELIX

1. Higgs interview, 24 November 2019. "Infinity as the answer" was for data that had finite magnitudes. See the following paragraphs.

2. In 1947 renormalisation of QED was achieved independently by Americans Julian Schwinger and Richard Feynman. Only then did it become known that the technique had already been invented in Japan in 1943 by Sin-Itiro Tomonaga. The three shared the Nobel Prize in 1965. A pedagogic description of renormalisation is in F. Close, *The Infinity Puzzle* (Basic Books, 2011), p. 41ff.

3. Higgs interview, 24 November 2019.

4. Higgs interview, 12 June 2020.

5. J. Watson, *The Double Helix* (Weidenfeld and Watson, 1968).

6. Higgs interviews, 24 November 2019 and 12 July 2021. Higgs' papers are "Perturbation Method for the Calculation of Molecular Vibration Frequencies," published in the *Journal of Chemical Physics* (1955): Part I, vol. 21, p. 1131; Part II, vol. 23, p. 1448; and Part III, vol. 23, p. 1450.

7. Longuet-Higgins was colour blind. Years later, when he and Higgs were both at Edinburgh University, Higgs' wife helped Longuet-Higgins select wallpaper so that it would appeal both to the colour-blind occupant and to visitors.

8. Higgs interview, 24 November 2019.

9. Higgs interviews, 24 November 2019 and 7 June 2021.

10. Higgs interview, 24 November 2019.

11. Higgs interviews, 2 July 2021 and 12 July 2021. Simon Altmann email, 4 July 2021.

12. Higgs interview, 24 November 2019.

13. Higgs' paper is in *Nuovo Cimento*, vol. 4, p. 1262 (1956). INSPIRE, "Peter W. Higgs," https://inspirehep.net/authors/1019617, records only three citations.

14. Higgs interview, 27 November 2019.

15. "Integration of Secondary Constraints in Quantized General Relativity," *Physical Review Letters*, vol. 1, no. 373 (1958); erratum, *Physical Review Letters*, vol. 3, no. 66 (1959).

16. "Quadratic Lagrangians and General Relativity," *Nuovo Cimento*, vol. 11, no. 816 (1959). Higgs himself dismissed this work as "one I don't talk about much, but it earned me an honorary doctorate from UCL in 2010." But why an honorary doctorate so many years later—fifty-one, to be exact? What happened was that Dmitri Vassiliev, professor of maths at University College, discovered that the author of this paper, Peter Higgs, was the same Higgs who had gained fame for the Higgs boson and had actually been a temporary lecturer and published the paper while he was at UCL. Higgs was amused that the maths department proposed him for the doctorate, not the physicists.

17. Higgs interview, 18 January 2020.

18. Higgs interview, 7 December 2019.

19. Higgs interviews, 7 December 2019 and 12 June 2020.

CHAPTER 3: THE PARTICLE EXPLOSION

1. Higgs interview, 27 November 2019.

2. Higgs interview, 4 January 2020.

3. J. Schwinger, "On Quantum-Electrodynamics and the Magnetic Moment of the Electron," *Physical Review*, vol. 73, no. 416 (1948), received by the editor on 30 December 1947.

4. Glashow's remark as quoted in R. Crease and C. Mann, *The Second Creation* (Rutgers University Press, 1988), p. 218.

5. Frank Wilczek makes a powerful case that *Standard Model* should now be elevated to *Core Theory*; see F. Wilczek, *A Beautiful Question* (Allen Lane, 2015), p. 350, and *Lightness of Being* (Basic Books, 2008), p. 164.

6. Quotes here and following paragraphs are from Higgs interview, 27 November 2019.

7. Higgs interview, 19 June 2020.

8. Higgs interview, 19 June 2020.

9. In 1961, the department occupied numbers 1 and 3 Roxburgh Street, which had been internally restructured to make a single building. Higgs' office was in what corresponded to number 3. Today, a blue plaque commemorating Higgs' work erroneously adorns the wall of number 5. By the time the plaque was installed, the institute had moved away, and the whole row of buildings had been adopted by the university for other purposes and the presence of the old Tait Institute was ancient history. The source of the mistake seems to be that the planners failed to take account that Roxburgh Street had odd- and even-numbered properties on opposite sides of the street. In attempting to mount the plaque at the old number 3, they mistakenly selected the third house in the row. The third odd number, however, is 5, hence the wrong location of the plaque. Higgs interview, 19 July 2021.

CHAPTER 4: THE SUPER CONDUCTOR

1. R. Brout to P. Higgs, Higgs interview, 30 August 2020.

2. Y. Nambu, "Quasi-Particles and Gauge Invariance in the Theory of Superconductivity," *Physical Review*, vol. 117, p. 648 (1960). The paper was received by the editors on 23 July 1959. Y. Nambu and G. Jona-Lasinio, "Dynamical Model of Elementary Particles Based on an Analogy with Superconductivity," *Physical Review*, vol. 122, p. 345 (1961).

3. J. Goldstone, "Field Theories with 'Superconductor' Solutions," *Nuovo Cimento*, vol. 19, p. 154 (1961).

CHAPTER 5: HIGGS' EPIPHANY

1. An outline sketch of the jewel was implicit in the model of superconductivity constructed by the two Russian theorists, Ginzburg and Landau, in the 1950s (appendix 4.1). It seems that neither Nambu, Goldstone, nor Higgs was aware of this.

2. Higgs interview, 27 November 2019.

3. Higgs interview, 1 February 2020.

4. Higgs interview, 27 November 2019.

5. Goldstone email to author, 12 July 2010.

6. Glashow as quoted in Crease and Mann, *The Second Creation*, p. 240.

7. J. Schwinger, "Gauge Invariance and Mass," *Physical Review*, vol. 125, p. 397 (1962).

8. Goldstone initially gave examples, such as the Mexican hat described here, but no formal proof. The "proof" was in a later paper: J. Goldstone, A. Salam, and S. Weinberg, "Broken Symmetries," *Physical Review*, vol. 127, p. 965 (1962). In none of these papers was the effect of an electromagnetic field considered.

9. P. Anderson, "Plasmons, Gauge Invariance, and Mass," *Physical Review*, vol. 130, p. 439 (1963).

10. P. Anderson, "A Helping Hand on Elementary Matters," *Nature*, vol. 405, p. 726 (2000).

11. As a teenager, Higgs' father had built a Morse code receiver, and on one occasion picked up a signal from Canada.

12. A. Klein and B. Lee, "Does Spontaneous Breakdown of Symmetry Imply Zero-Mass Particles?," *Physical Review Letters*, vol. 12, p. 266 (1964).

13. Higgs interview, 18 January 2020.

14. Higgs interview, 4 July 2020.

15. W. Gilbert, "Broken Symmetry and Massless Particles," *Physical Review Letters*, vol. 12, p. 713 (1964).

16. Higgs at Cheltenham Festival, 2012, as recalled by Dara Ó Briain, *The Guardian*, 8 December 2013.

17. July 24: date from Higgs' diary and letter to author, 10 September 2010; July 27: date received as recorded on the published paper, P. W. Higgs, "Broken Symmetries, Massless Particles and Gauge Fields," *Physics Letters*, vol. 12, no. 2 (1964).

18. The Greek subscript on the n_μ signifies a trivial relativistic generalisation of the vector **n**.

19. Higgs remarks at seventieth birthday banquet, 1999.

CHAPTER 6: NOW WE ARE SIX

1. Whereas a particle with no energy has no mass, the converse is not true. A massless particle, like a photon, carries energy in proportion to the oscillation frequency of the associated electromagnetic wave. The limit of zero frequency, or infinite wavelength, corresponds to zero energy.

2. They were also aware that this model contains modes with energy—a "massive boson" (figure 6.1c). As they regarded this as "obvious," they made no mention of this Higgs boson. Englert interview, 2 February 2010.

3. R. Brout and F. Englert, "Broken Symmetry and the Mass of Gauge Vector Mesons," *Physical Review Letters*, vol. 13, p. 321 (1964).

4. Schwinger later admitted to Higgs that he "cursed himself for missing the possibility". Nambu's research was interrupted during 1962 by a serious illness in his family, which may be why he too missed this discovery. Higgs interview, 30 November 2019.

5. Higgs letter to the author, 1 September 2010.

6. G. Guralnik, C. Hagen, and T. Kibble, "Global Conservation Laws and Massless Particles," *Physical Review Letters*, vol. 13, p. 585 (1964).

7. Kibble interview, 17 March 2010.

8. Guralnik interview, 1 March 2010.

9. The mathematical extension of the mass mechanism, which can keep the photon massless while allowing particles such as W and Z bosons to become massive, was made by Tom Kibble in "Asymmetry Breakdown in Non-Abelian Gauge Theories," *Physical Review*, vol. 155, p. 1554 (1967). Some of this had been independently developed by Higgs in an uncompleted paper in 1967 (Higgs letter, 15 July 2021). See figure 8.1 on p. 112.

10. Higgs interview, 16 November 2019.

11. Higgs interview, 30 August 2021.

CHAPTER 7: BIRTH OF A BOSON

1. INSPIRE, "Peter W. Higgs," https://inspirehep.net/authors/1019617.

2. Higgs interview, 27 November 2019.

3. Higgs interview, 11 April 2000.

4. B. Zumino, "Gauge Properties of Propagators in Quantum Electrodynamics," *Journal of Mathematical Physics*, vol. 1, p. 1 (1960).

5. Higgs interview, 1 February 2020.

6. Higgs interview, 25 January 2020.

7. Higgs' memories of 1966 come from interviews, 7 December 2019 and 4 July 2020.

8. Three lay claim to this distinction. UNC was the only one to have held classes and graduated students in the eighteenth century.

9. P. W. Higgs, "Spontaneous Symmetry Breakdown Without Massless Bosons," *Physical Review*, vol. 145, p. 1156 (1966).

10. Higgs interview, 30 August 2021.

11. This technically is linear in the quantum amplitude. The chance also depends on other factors known as "phase space", but the overall unusual dependence on mass shows nonetheless.

12. B. Zumino, "Gauge Properties of Propagators in Quantum Electrodynamics," *Journal of Mathematical Physics*, vol. 1, p. 1, 1960; Higgs interview, 30 August 2021.

13. P. W. Higgs, "Spontaneous Symmetry Breakdown Without Massless Bosons," *Physical Review*, vol. 145, p. 1162 (1966).

14. Higgs interview, 30 August 2021. At a conference in Swansea on 12 July 2012, Higgs learned that the four lepton discovery channel proceeded through two Z bosons—one real and one virtual—and the mass of the Z was important in driving this process.

15. Higgs interview, 9 July 2020.

16. Higgs interview, 1 February 2020.

17. Higgs interview, 1 February 2020.

CHAPTER 8: "PETER—YOU'RE FAMOUS!"

1. The pion mass is not exactly zero, but it is lightweight compared to other strongly interacting particles. This deviation from zero is today understood as due to its constituent quarks having small masses, thanks to the Higgs mechanism.

2. Higgs letter, 15 July 2021.

3. Higgs interview, 29 June 2021.

4. S. Weinberg, "A Model of Leptons," *Physical Review Letters*, vol. 19, p. 1264 (1967).

5. This chronologically wrong attribution in S. Weinberg, "Physical Processes in a Convergent Theory of Weak and Electromagnetic Interactions," *Physical Review Letters*, vol. 27, p. 1688 (1971), was further propagated in reference 6 of the major phenomenological study by J. Ellis, M. Gaillard, and D. Nanopoulos, "A Phenomenological Profile of the Higgs Boson," *Nuclear Physics*, vol. 106, p. 292 (1976).

6. S. Coleman, "The 1979 Nobel Prize in Physics," *Science*, vol. 206, p. 1290 (14 December 1979).

7. Wallace email, 20 July 2021.

8. The key breakthroughs in 't Hooft's thesis are in two papers: "The Renormalization of Massless Yang-Mills Fields," *Nuclear Physics*, vol. B33, p. 173 (1971), and "Renormalizable Lagrangians for Massive Yang-Mills Fields," *Nuclear Physics*, vol. B35, p. 167 (1971).

9. Higgs letter, 15 July 2021.

10. Higgs interview, 19 July 2021.

11. Weinberg interview, 6 May 2010.

12. Quotes in this section are from 't Hooft interview, 11 April 2000, and email, 11 September 2010.

13. B. W. Lee, "Development of Unified Gauge Theories: Retrospect," in *Gauge Theories and Neutrino Physics*, ed. M. Jacob (North-Holland, 1978), p. 147.

14. Higgs interview, 16 November 2019.

15. Higgs interview with Decca Aitkenhead, *The Guardian*, 6 December 2013.

16. Higgs letter, 15 July 2021.

17. Higgs interview, 18 January 2020.

18. Higgs interview, 7 December 2019.

19. Higgs interview, 19 June 2020.

20. Higgs interview, 19 June 2020.

21. Higgs letter, 15 July 2021.

22. Higgs interview, 16 November 2019.

CHAPTER 9: THE FIRST DISAPPEARANCE—1976

1. I had given a lecture at that same school but seem not to have overlapped with Higgs' presentations; in any event I have no memory of them.

2. Ellis interview, 21 September 2020.

3. Higgs interview, 9 June 2020.

4. The eV—electron-volt—is the energy an electron gains when accelerated by a potential of 1 volt. A GeV—giga electron-volt—corresponds to a billion eV. Traditionally energies in particle physics are given in these units. Einstein's equivalence of mass and energy is the basis for particle masses also being quoted colloquially in multiples of eV, the rest energy of mc^2 being referred to as *mass* and denoted m or M to save lots of extraneous c^2.

5. Charmonium was discovered in November 1974. The proof of charm came with discovery of charmed particles in spring 1976.

6. The decay of the Higgs boson to muon pairs has now been seen at the LHC.

7. The production of a Z and a Higgs boson in coincidence has been seen at the LHC.

8. J. Ellis, M. Gaillard, and D. Nanopoulos, "A Phenomenological Profile of the Higgs Boson," *Nuclear Physics*, vol. 106, p. 292 (1976).

9. Wilczek email, 28 December 2020, confirms this as 1977. Sean Carroll email, 15 December 2020. See also S. Carroll, *The Particle at the End of the Universe* (Oneworld, 2013).

10. Higgs interview, 15 February 2020.

11. Ellis interview, 21 September 2020.

12. The Tait professorship was awarded to David Wallace, Higgs' PhD student from 1967 to 1970.

13. See reference 6 in their paper "A Phenomenological Profile of the Higgs Boson," *Nuclear Physics*, vol. B106, p. 292 (1976). This also incorrectly cites Brout and Englert as being in *Physics Letters*, vol. 13, not *Physical Review Letters*, vol 13. Guralnik and colleagues' paper, also published in 1964, is given as 1965.

14. For example, see Higgs' admission on p. 103.

15. Ellis interview, 21 September 2020.

CHAPTER 10: EVERY JOURNEY BEGINS WITH A SINGLE STEP

1. This Super Proton-Antiproton Collider operated from 1981 to 1991.

2. Evans interview, 30 November 2020.

3. Evans interview, 30 November 2020.

4. Recall the physics tradition of referring to rest energy of mc^2 as *mass*, denoted m or M to save lots of extraneous c^2.

5. C. H. Llewellyn Smith, "High Energy Behaviour and Gauge Symmetry," *Physics Letters*, vol. 46B, p. 233 (1973); B. W. Lee, C. Quigg, and H. B. Thacker, "Weak Interactions at Very High Energies: The Role of the Higgs-Boson Mass," *Physical Review*, vol. D16, p. 1519 (1977).

6. C. H. Llewellyn Smith email, 22 November 2020.

CHAPTER 11: A MACHINE FOR 1 TEV

1. See pp. 132–134 in chapter 9.

2. Evans interview, 30 November 2020.

3. Evans interview, 30 November 2020.

4. LEP was still under construction and would not be ready for physics until 1989. Signing up to the LHC would be a commitment into the twenty-first century.

5. Higgs interview, 16 November 2019; McKie email, 19 November 2019.

6. Flavour is the property that distinguishes different fundamental particles. For example, the muon is not simply a heavier version of the electron. There appears to be something

intrinsic to the muon and to the electron that must be preserved. We call this property *flavour*; it is a foundation of the equations of quantum flavourdynamics.

7. Higgs interview, 17 November 2019.

8. Statement by Fermilab director Richard Wilson at the 1969 Joint Congressional Committee on Atomic Energy, in response to a question on the value of high-energy physics research to national defence.

9. Llewellyn Smith interview, 11 March 2010.

10. Higgs interview, 16 November 2019.

11. Miller's original is available at "A Quasi-political Explanation of the Higgs Boson; for Mr Waldegrave, UK Science Minister 1993," www.hep.ucl.ac.uk/~djm/higgsa.html.

12. Higgs interview, 16 November 2019.

13. Kenway interview, 22 September 2020.

14. Higgs interview, 16 November 2019.

15. Wilczek in *A Beautiful Question* dated this as 1976. Carroll, *The Particle at the End of the Universe*, has 1977. Wilczek email, 28 December 2020, confirms this as 1977.

16. Higgs interview, 16 November 2019.

17. Kane email, 20 August 2020.

CHAPTER 12: FATHER OF THE GOD PARTICLE

1. L. Lederman, *The God Particle* (Dell, 1993).

2. Higgs interview, 7 December 2019. Higgs' experience mirrors that of Einstein. In 1919 the *New York Times* sent their London correspondent, Henry Crouch, to cover a meeting at the Royal Astronomical Society on the confirmation of Einstein's general relativity theory. Crouch was a sports writer focusing on golf. Crouch did a decent job, nonetheless; his article, "Eclipse Showed Gravity Variation," can be found at Times Machine, https://times machine.nytimes.com/timesmachine/1919/11/09/118179089.pdf.

3. Higgs interview, 7 December 2019.

4. *The Independent*, 3 September 2002.

5. *The Independent*, 3 September 2002.

6. The point Gillies was making is that cosmic rays have been bombarding the upper atmosphere for eons at energies far in excess even of those that the LHC could reach. The fact that we have survived billions of years of such collisions was already some experimental assurance that theorists were right in insisting that experimental particle collisions at the "doomsday machine" would not have apocalyptic consequences. Gillies interview, 5 October 2020.

7. Walker remarks at a King's College London event, 24 November 2010. Jody Higgs died very shortly after Walker's intervention and before the CERN event.

8. Kenway interview, 22 September 2020.

9. Kenway interview, 22 September 2020.

10. Kenway interview, 22 September 2020.

11. Higgs interview, 16 November 2019.

12. Kenway interview, 22 September 2020.

13. Kenway interview, 22 September 2020.

CHAPTER 13: THE "DOOMSDAY MACHINE"

1. Gillies interview, 5 October 2020.

2. Gillies interview, 5 October 2020.

3. Evans interview, 30 November 2020.

4. Gillies conversational remark to author, undated.

5. In addition to ATLAS, CMS, and ALICE, the detector LHCb at the fourth intersection point is designed to be sensitive to the production of hadrons containing bottom quarks.

6. Evans interview, 30 November 2020.

7. Gillies interview, 5 October 2020.

8. Evans interview, 30 November 2020.

9. "Peter Higgs Launches Attack Against Nobel Rival Stephen Hawking," *The Times*, 11 September 2008.

10. "Peter Higgs Launches Attack," *The Times*, 11 September 2008.

11. Higgs as quoted in "Peter Higgs Launches Attack," *The Times*, 11 September 2008.

12. Anonymous email, 23 August 2020.

13. S. Hawking, "Virtual Black Holes," *Physical Review*, vol. D53, p. 3107 (March 1 996).

14. S. Hawking, "Virtual Black Holes," *Physical Review*, vol. D53, p. 3106 (March 1996).

15. About half of the present standard of 6.5 TeV. The LHC is being upgraded and after 2027 will continue to operate at this energy but at much higher luminosity than previously.

CHAPTER 14: "WE SHOULD GO TO CERN"

1. When produced in an experiment at the LHC, a Higgs boson exists for about 10^{-22} seconds.

2. According to the maths underpinning Nambu's original theory that inspired Higgs, the nonzero mass of the pion is a result of its constituent quarks having mass. The pion transmits the strong force between protons and neutrons which form atomic nuclei. The range of the force is inversely proportional to the pion's mass and hence to the mass of its quarks. It is because quarks have mass that atomic nuclei are compact.

3. Farmelo interview, 14 May 2020.

4. Hills interview, 17 December 2020.

5. Gillies interview, 5 October 2020.

6. Walker conversational remark to author, 30 June 2012; Higgs interview, 25 June 2021.

7. Higgs remark to author, 30 June 2012.

CHAPTER 15: THE FOURTH OF JULY

1. Hills interview, 17 December 2020.

2. MacKenzie interview, 18 December 2020.

3. Hills interview, 17 December 2020.

4. Ellis interview, 21 September 2020.

5. Llewellyn Smith interview, 1 April 2020.

6. Ellis interview, 21 September 2020. To the best of Ellis' knowledge, the bottle is now with the Science Museum (Ellis email, 16 September 2021).

7. Higgs remark to author, 11 October 2012.

8. Gillies interview, 5 October 2020.

9. Higgs conversational remark to author, 11 October 2012.

10. Higgs remarks at press conference, 4 July 2012.

11. Gillies interview, 5 October 2020.

12. Womersley interview, 8 December 2020.

13. Womersley interview, 8 December 2020.

14. MacKenzie interview, 18 December 2020.

15. Hills interview, 17 December 2020.

16. Hills interview, 17 December 2020.

CHAPTER 16: "TIME TO PLAN MY ESCAPE"

1. Higgs interview, 16 November 2019.

2. The talk was titled "From QED to the Higgs Boson and Beyond"; see University of Edinburgh, School of Physics and Astronomy, www.ph.ed.ac.uk/events/2016/the-infinity-puzzle-from-qed-to-the-higgs-boson-and-beyond-65427.

3. Higgs conversational remark to author, 11 October 2012.

4. Higgs interview, 9 January 2020.

5. Higgs interviews, 16 November 2019 and 15 February 2020.

6. Kenway interview, 22 September 2020.

7. Kenway interview, 22 September 2020.

8. Higgs interview, 15 February 2020.

9. Nobel Prizes are not awarded posthumously, so Robert Brout, who died in 2011, could not be considered as a third co-winner.

10. In 2015 they were renamed the Princess of Asturias Awards to reflect the new heiress to the Spanish throne, Leonor, Princess of Asturias.

CHAPTER 17: THE GLITTERING PRIZES

1. Quoted in *The Guardian*, 6 December 2013.

2. Higgs interview, 19 July 2021.

3. Higgs interview, 9 January 2020.

CHAPTER 18: ZIGZAG

1. Higgs interview, 12 June 2020.

2. Higgs interview, 9 January 2020.

3. Higgs interview, 16 November 2019.

4. S. Weinberg, "Physical Processes in a Convergent Theory of Weak and Electromagnetic Interactions," *Physical Review Letters*, vol. 27, p. 1688 (1971).

5. *The Guardian*, 13 April 2010.

6. Higgs interview, 17 June 2021.

7. Higgs interview, 26 June 2021.

EPILOGUE: THE VIEW ACROSS THE PLAINS

1. Higgs, Orkney Festival, 8 September 2015.

2. Womersley interview, 8 December 2020.

3. During the 1970s, Higgs had followed research in SUSY theory in hope that it might help in developing a quantum field theory of gravity. He was unsuccessful and never published on the topic.

4. F. Wilczek, *Lightness of Being* (Basic Books, 2008), p. 164, and email, 28 December 2020.

5. In April 2021 the magnetic moment of the muon was measured at Fermilab to an accuracy of ten decimal places. At this level of precision there appears to be a disagreement between theory and data at 4-sigma, which is slightly under the 5-sigma that is traditional for a discovery. This could be a hint of virtual massive particles disturbing the vacuum and/ or further forces, ultra-weak at present energies, affecting the muon's magnetism.

INDEX

ALLEN LANE
an imprint of
PENGUIN BOOKS

Also Published

Andy Clark, *The Experience Machine: How Our Minds Predict and Shape Reality*

Monica Potts, *The Forgotten Girls: An American Story*

Christopher Clark, *Revolutionary Spring: Fighting for a New World 1848-1849*

Daniel Chandler, *Free and Equal: What Would a Fair Society Look Like?*

Jonathan Rosen, *Best Minds: A Story of Friendship, Madness, and the Tragedy of Good Intentions*

Nigel Townson, *The Penguin History of Modern Spain: 1898 to the Present*

Katja Hoyer, *Beyond the Wall: East Germany, 1949-1990*

Quinn Slobodian, *Crack-Up Capitalism: Market Radicals and the Dream of a World Without Democracy*

Clare Carlisle, *The Marriage Question: George Eliot's Double Life*

Matthew Desmond, *Poverty, by America*

Sara Ahmed, *The Feminist Killjoy Handbook*

Bernard Wasserstein, *A Small Town in Ukraine: The place we came from, the place we went back to*

Mariana Mazzucato and Rosie Collington, *The Big Con: How the Consultancy Industry Weakens our Businesses, Infantilizes our Governments and Warps our Economies*

Carlo Rovelli, *Anaximander: And the Nature of Science*

Bernie Sanders, *It's OK To Be Angry About Capitalism*

Martin Wolf, *The Crisis of Democractic Capitalism*

David Graeber, *Pirate Enlightenment, or the Real Libertalia*

Leonard Susskind and Andre Cabannes, *General Relativity: The Theoretical Minimum*